PROFILES AND PLOTLINES

THE NEW AMERICAN CANON

The Iowa Series in
Contemporary Literature and Culture

Samuel Cohen, series editor

PROFILES AND PLOTLINES

DATA SURVEILLANCE IN TWENTY-FIRST-CENTURY LITERATURE

Katherine D. Johnston

UNIVERSITY OF IOWA PRESS | IOWA CITY

University of Iowa Press, Iowa City 52242
Copyright © 2023 by University of Iowa Press
uipress.uiowa.edu

ISBN 978-1-60938-893-5 (pbk)
ISBN 978-1-60938-894-2 (ebk)

Printed in the United States of America

A version of chapter 1 was originally published by Duke University Press as
"Metadata, Metafiction, and the Stakes of Surveillance in Jennifer Egan's A Visit
from the Goon Squad," American Literature, vol. 89, no. 1 (2017): 155–84.

A version of chapter 2 was originally published by Duke University Press
as "Profile Epistemologies, Radicalizing Surveillance, and
Affective Counterstrategies in Claudia Rankine's Citizen,"
Twentieth-Century Literature, vol. 65, no. 4 (2019): 343–68.

Printed on acid-free paper.

Cataloging-in-Publication data is on file with the Library of Congress.

For Justin, Helena, and Finley

CONTENTS

ACKNOWLEDGMENTS

I AM PUBLISHING THIS BOOK with heartfelt gratitude to countless people who have supported me and informed my understanding of the world and this book. Special thanks to the faculty at the University of California, Riverside, for inspiring courage and careful analysis. I am especially grateful to Katherine Kinney and Toby Miller for helping me find my voice and offering invaluable feedback on early drafts of the manuscript. Your continued support has been a gift.

I am deeply thankful for my friends and colleagues at Stony Brook University who have encouraged and enriched my work with their intellectual vibrancy and generosity. I'm particularly thankful for Denise Burhau and Karen Lloyd's supportive friendship and humor. Very special thanks to Michael Tondre for giving graciously of his time in reading and discussing parts of the manuscript along the way. I owe a debt of gratitude to Celia Marshik for affording me the opportunity to write and publish as a research assistant professor in the English Department at just the right time. Roger Thompson, Gene Hammond, Shyam Sharma, and Peter Khost have generously championed my work and given me vital opportunities. I am also grateful to my students at Stony Brook University, especially the graduate students of my Rhetoric of Surveillance seminar for their brilliance and enthusiasm. Especially warm thanks to Abena Asare for our walks, which always leave me focused and inspired. This book could not have been completed without the invaluable support of Stony Brook Child Care Services.

I am especially grateful to the editorial team at the University of Iowa Press, who have been a pleasure to work with. I am particularly grateful to Samuel Cohen and Meredith Stabel for their early confidence in my manuscript and straightforward support. Portions of this book are derived from articles that appeared previously in *American Literature* (2017) and *Twentieth-Century Literature* (2019). My appreciation goes to the editors and editorial staff at Duke University Press for their early assistance in sharpening and publishing this writing.

I wish to thank my dear friends for their sustaining love, humor, and perceptiveness. Ongoing challenging, heartening, and hilarious conversations

Acknowledgments

with Helen Davis, Cristin Deuble, and Lisa Gallegos have improved my life in immeasurable ways. I am deeply grateful to Jordan Lavender-Smith for being not only a cherished friend but also an incisive reader of my work. I am indebted to Evan Lavender-Smith for opening my world to writing and remaining a trusted guide.

I am endlessly grateful for my parents, Reta and David Warren. I thank them for their boundless love and support and for teaching me to think carefully and act with curiosity, empathy, and conviction. Special thanks to Jennifer Bernstein, my magnificent sister, for her humor and for always shining a light on the path ahead. Affectionate appreciation goes to Brandi, Victor, and Mantissa Johnston; I am lucky to call them family and wiser for it.

Thanks to my lovely children, Helena and Finley, I learned to write on a dime and with a full heart. I am profoundly grateful to Helena for her bravery and persistent celebration of life and to Finley for his tenderness and curiosity. There are no words for how much I love and appreciate them both.

Above all, my deepest gratitude goes to Justin Omar Johnston for always celebrating my goals, even before I've met them. Our conversations are the most enthralling parts of my life, and they animate the best pages of this book. I thank him for always seeing the forest when I've gotten lost in the trees. Without his love, commitment, insights, and inspiration, none of this would be possible.

PREFACE

HAUNTING THE ONGOING proliferation of data profiles is the ghostly trace of "profile portraits," otherwise known as "silhouette portraits" or "shades." These backlit images of faces outline the profile contours of the brow, nose, lips, and chin, drawing out the subject's bone structure by overshadowing the flesh and obscuring any indications of the sitter's habits, activities, and experiences that sunburns, flushed cheeks, dark circles, scars, or tattoos, for example, might betray. Allegedly, the single unbroken line exposes and documents the person's underlying constitution or character. From these silhouette portraits, Johann Caspar Lavater's (1741–1801) extrapolated personality types as physiognomy gained popularity inside and outside of academic discourses throughout the eighteenth and into the nineteenth century. The Pocket Lavater (an actual face book) provided portable illustrated guides to help readers decode faces. Portraitists famously "rendered George Washington in profile so as to capitalize on his 'large and well-shap'd nose,' admired by new Americans as evidence of his strength and hawk-like foresight."[1] In literary fiction, Charles Dickens, Thomas Hardy, Charlotte Brontë, Edgar Allan Poe, and Oscar Wilde all made use of physiognomy (however ironically) in their character descriptions, signaling virtues and vices phenotypically. Novels fleshed out these faces, but their use of physiognomy still drew on the notion that the underlying structure of the face could somehow divulge the essential qualities of a person's moral or mental constitution. In other words, writers tapped discourses surrounding facial profiles to merge character and characterization.

As this art form gained scientific standing throughout the nineteenth century, the core or essence of a person's character was classified, epitomized, and simplified by that one unbroken line of the facial profile. These profiles situated a person's individuality in relation to groups of people based on family, race, ethnicity, class, gender, and sexuality. In 1877 Sir Francis Galton, statistician, founder of eugenics, and cousin of Charles Darwin, invented a popular technique for making composite photographs through the consecutive exposure of distinct photographs onto a single plate. Drawing on the popularity of profile portraits and physiognomy, these composites took advantage of the new technology of cameras to create "scientific" categories of faces. According to Galton, these composites were capable of depicting and detecting human types, such as the Jew, the Englishman, the prostitute, and the delinquent. As Anne McClintock explains in *Imperial Leather*, "at this time, evolutionary theory entered an 'unholy alliance' with the allure of numbers, the amassing of measurements and the science of statistics. The alliance gave birth to 'scientific' racism, the most authoritative attempt to place social ranking and social disability on a biological and 'scientific' footing."[2] Ultimately, "in the logic of the racial narratives of the time, the profile of the face [became] the most eloquent sign of the essence of the 'race.'"[3] Photography was quickly exploited to help legitimate the "science" of facial profiling across disciplines, claiming to capture and expose the manifest nature of a person.[4] As this book investigates, profiles—then and now—toggle between populations and individuals: on one hand, they categorize and pathologize entire demographics, while on the other hand they single out individuals as recognizable subjects under this pseudo-scientific gaze. That Galton helped pioneer these racist platforms of "social sorting"[5] and created the first workable fingerprint system—ardently advocating for its use as a reliable identification system—captures the simultaneous drives toward increased standardization and individualization. Ostensibly, profiles (facial and finger) not only reveal a person's character but can supposedly confirm their identity.[6]

Lev Manovich attributes Galton's "desire to externalize the mind" through photographic representations "to the demand of the modern mass society for standardization. . . . The private and individual is translated into the public and becomes regulated."[7] Arguably, this move toward public standardization and regulation is what constructs the private and the individual in the first place. As Michel Foucault explains, "Discipline 'makes' individuals; it is the specific technique of a power that regards individuals both as objects and as instruments of its exercise."[8] In their attempt to rationalize the art form of silhouette portraits, Galton's composite profiles also worked to rationalize racist and misogynistic criteria for appraising and ranking individuals. As "human types," these profiles circulated as markers of more or less value, not unlike the coinage on which they were printed. In the context of contemporary data surveillance, profiles still reflect an individual's relative value—to advertisers, to border patrol, to parole boards, to potential employers, to insurance companies, to loan officers, to admissions committees. For example, when Facebook sold advertisers access to a list of anti-Semitic users,[9] they were entering in the same "unholy alliance" as Galton.[10] When data brokers sold lists of rape survivors and domestic violence survivors to pharmaceutical companies,[11] they were espousing the same objectifying "scientific" gaze as Lavater. When Google and Facebook allowed advertisers to target users for employment, housing, and credit opportunities based on their data profiles,[12] they again attempted to put discrimination and disenfranchisement on supposedly "'scientific' footing."[13]

In the twenty-first century, a "profile picture" most commonly refers to a person's cover photo on social networks. Given that profile portraits have historically sought to classify the supposedly essential qualities of individuals, it is perhaps unsurprising that emergent modes of data profiling retain these residual investments in authenticity and standardization. Setting aside for a moment the invisible data profiles that power social media companies and other surveillance capitalists, a user's outward-facing profile picture remains part of a larger disciplinary architecture that classifies human types. For example, "Natalie Blanchard in Quebec lost her disability insurance benefits (for depression) because she appeared 'too happy' in Facebook photographs that she posted during her sick leave. . . . Much was made, in particular, of a photograph of Blanchard in a bikini, with online discussions of how good she looked in the bikini and of this somehow attesting to her (sound) mental health."[14] Not unlike Galton's composite photographs, Blanchard's profile picture was granted more credibility than her own account, and it was again the contours of her body that gave her away by ostensibly betraying an inner truth about her.

The biometric profiles of the past are even more blatantly alive in the growing field of facial analysis, which "involves predicting individual data using statistical inference from the image itself."[15] Given that 24 billion selfies were uploaded to Google in 2015,[16] and that there are now approximately 85 million surveillance cameras deployed in the United States,[17] companies and researchers are racing to mine this expanding field for data. In their article, "What Personal Information Can a Consumer Facial Image Reveal?," Yegor Tkachenko and Kamel Jedidi of Columbia University acknowledge that "facial analysis can be viewed as a rebranding of the historically notorious practice of physiognomy or 'face reading,'" adding that "researchers in this area have traditionally been interested in isolating predictive power of biological facial features . . . often, in the spirit of biological determinism theories."[18] Tkachenko and Jedidi then claim that, in contrast, their "variety of signals paint a rich consumer portrait" that "could be used to guide ad targeting and online personalization."[19] In a rhetorical shift from profiles to portraits, facial analysis now attempts to make meaning out of every inch and flinch. And still, a person's face presumably speaks for itself. Researchers just need more angles and better models, we are told. Tkachenko and Jedidi renounce biological determinism and aim for a "holistic" approach that combines the "basic demographics extracted from the face," with "image artifacts, basic metrics calculated from facial features, and deep image features extracted by a neural net from the face as well as the rest of the facial image."[20] In other words, maybe it's biological characteristics, maybe it's socioeconomic factors, maybe it's Maybelline—the clients just want "actionable insights." In the end, the solution to racializing surveillance is, purportedly, more surveillance.

While Tkachenko and Jedidi endorse a multifaceted approach to facial analysis to avoid the "spirit of biological determinism," they still concede that, "demographics inferred from facial images could be driving predictions of all other variables" and that "a large part of such predictive power is attributable to basic demographics extracted from the face."[21] They also acknowledge that their results yield "relatively low prediction accuracy," shrewdly framing this as protection against the "potentially grave privacy implications" of facial analysis.[22] Ultimately, consumer-citizens are told they needn't worry because "the confidence in the truthfulness of its predictions for any particular individual would not be very high."[23] Meanwhile, the article also correctly maintains that "companies pay for extremely weak statistical signals."[24] Straddling both sides of the fence, this article finds facial recognition defensible precisely because it is so deficient.

The authors defend the commercial use of "weak statistical signals" by emphasizing that the "value of information is always non-negative."[25] However, this raises the question: "non-negative" for whom? Simone Browne's historical analysis of biometric technologies explains that they are built on a notion of "prototypical whiteness" and therefore result in high "failure to enroll" rates for African Americans and Asians.[26] Browne underscores that a "pseudo-scientific discourse of racial difference forms the theoretical basis" for such attempts "to develop a facial computational model that could qualify (and mathematically quantify) difference."[27] When Tkachenko and Jedidi suggest that—"if a degree of measurement error is acceptable"— companies could reasonably "replace online and offline demographic customer surveys with automated facial analysis," they again raise the question "acceptable" for whom?[28] Would this be "acceptable" for "nonbinary, gender nonconforming, mixed-race, intersexed, or trans people"? How would they "fit into this algorithmic equation"?[29] This suggestion that facial analysis could eliminate the need to hear from people about their own demographic information reveals a deeply troubling "assumption with these technologies that categories of gender identity and race are clear-cut, that a machine can be programmed to assign gender categories or determine what bodies and body parts should signify."[30] This wrong-headed assumption is quite literally codified in algorithms and applications.

So Wayne Booth's reminder that "the author's voice is always present, regardless of how thoroughly it is disguised,"[31] holds true for the authors of algorithms as well. However, in this story, the authors and readers are unknown, and we are the characters. The longer history of profiles illustrates that they are not simply compiled: they are created and then plotted along predictable trajectories. There has long been a cultural imaginary that informs the construction, interpretation, and circulation of profiles. This imaginary has been and continues to be grounded in the notion that representations of the body can reveal essential truths about a subject. Supposedly standing on "'scientific' footing,"[32] this way of seeing and knowing upholds fixed categories of race, gender, sexuality, and ability by marking nonconforming people as "failures to enroll." Certainly, the novels analyzed in this book are also partial. Their stories begin and end and are told from particular points of view. Yet unlike the profiles that preoccupy their pages, they, in the words of Mohsin Hamid, embrace "misfits" and misfittings.[33]

INTRODUCTION

I n an interview with journalist Glen Thrush, former director of the National Security Agency (NSA) General Michael Hayden describes the work of surveillance as a narrative enterprise: as an NSA officer, "You are a storyteller. I mean you can't throw data through the transit and expect a policymaker to digest it and make a decision on it. You actually have to tell the story. And that's what an intelligence officer does."[1] Here, Hayden acknowledges the narrative and compositional dimension of data profiling that is typically obscured to maintain the illusion of its neutrality. Thrush responds, "Therein also lies the danger sometimes, right?," alluding to the potentially grave consequences of constructing a story that has the power to shape military action and target lives. Defensively, Hayden falls back on the theoretical objectivity of data analytics, saying, "Well, okay, so now you are really getting into the science." To be sure, when Hayden evokes some vague notion of "the science" here, he does so as an obfuscation of the realities of data collection and analytics with no intention of "really getting into" it. Instead, he returns to his role as a humanist storyteller:

> There are a lot of things that are true. Let's take the really ugly hideous complex situation in Syria. What's the major plotline? What's the major plot? What's the subplot? By the way, all of the plotlines are true. . . . And now you've got to decide how are you going to organize your data that morning for the President of the United States, because if you look at each of those plotlines carefully, each of those suggest a different course of action.

In other words, which "plotlines" the authors or authorities chose to privilege determines the narrative and its outcomes. Will the plot escalate? Who will perish? It is not the data itself but how it is "organized" and from what point of view that scripts the story.

Glen Thrush follows up by asking Hayden for a specific time, "looking back," when he "chose the wrong plotline." Without hesitation, Hayden names the

Iraq weapons of mass destruction national intelligence estimate, where we chose the plotline that he's got a program and that he's doing this, and rejected alternative views. . . . It wasn't just that we were wrong, which we were, we did not portray to our clients how sure, or in some cases, how unsure we were in our conclusion. . . . When we finally wrote our expository prose, when I read it now, it is far more confident than we were even then; that was the biggest sin.

We are all familiar with the tragic conclusion of this particular plotline that was not only "wrong" but, in Hayden's view, badly authored—even sinfully so. Significantly, Hayden highlights how "expository prose" gives shape and meaning to data, which can then alter the course of reality. Indeed, overly confident stories that "reject alternative views" are mainstays of not only intelligence agencies but also the data surveillance industry on which they often rely.

I begin this book with Michael Hayden's characterization of data profiling as at once scientifically unassailable as well as a form of storytelling because it captures the rhetorical and representational challenges posed by data surveillance as it serves to make lives legible and intelligible to a network of state and commercial actors. As data surveillance has taken up storytelling inside, for instance, boardrooms, banks, presidential briefings, police stations, advertising agencies, and technology companies, contemporary literature has taken up data—not only as an important topic for consideration but as an increasingly dominant technology of narration and characterization in twenty-first-century society. After all, profiling coincides with character development; surveillance reflects points of view; and, as Hayden describes, data points track as plot points in tales of the political economy. *Profiles and Plotlines*, therefore, reveals an energetic reformation of contemporary literature to account for a society and economy of frenetic counting and narrative recounting. Twenty-first-century literature is well suited to address precisely what algorithms cannot or do not account for: the affects of surveillance societies, the ideologies and supposed truth power of data profiles, the gendered and racialized power dynamics of watching and being watched, and the politics of who counts and what gets counted. Literature is adept at this in part because it traffics in subjectivity, bias, defined points of view, unreliable narrators, unreliable author figures, and unisolated variables. To the extent that literature trains readers to peer into people's lived experiences with pleasure and curiosity, it also trains them to understand surveillance as fundamentally partial and subjective. Unlike data profiles, or even the "expository prose" that Hayden references, the books I analyze here eschew single stories and tidy tales by depicting characters who exceed and subvert the commercial and institutional profiles that prefigure—and at times disfigure—them.

I've selected Jennifer Egan's *A Visit from the Goon Squad*, Claudia Rankine's *Citizen*, William Gibson's *Pattern Recognition*, and Mohsin Hamid's *How to Get Filthy Rich in Rising Asia* not because they address data profiling most overtly or directly amid a field of literature interested in this topic, but because each carries a set of literary affordances that constructively re-pace and respace our encounters with data surveillance. By shifting or freezing the frame of focus, these texts apprehend who and what is designed to be overseen as well as overlooked. By slowing the stream of data, they allow moments to simmer and swell so that we might climb inside and occupy those traps. By juxtaposing commercial and state surveillance, they produce critical friction on an allegedly smooth plane of information. By constructing novel chronologies and sequences, they denaturalize the technologies and techniques of data surveillance. One strand of the growing field of digital humanities uses the tools of data science to analyze literature; the literary analysis in this book instead confronts the questions of power and knowledge production raised by these tools. This work combines literary studies, new media studies, affect studies, surveillance studies, critical race studies, and gender studies because ultimately these discourses are inextricably knotted together around the problems of profiling.

Three primary concerns motivate this book, first among them my conviction that we need to rethink—politically, theoretically, and creatively—the dominant discourses of data surveillance and the personal profiles they engender. This requires reckoning with how data profiling is wrongly represented as neutral, inevitable, and omniscient. It also means deconstructing how the pervasive epistemologies of data surveillance, propagated by private and state interests, strategically foreclose resistance by insinuating that any criticism is grounds for suspicion. That is, people are often silenced by such sentiments as "if you have nothing to hide, then you have nothing to fear." The common implicit and explicit rejoinder—*what are you hiding?*—collapses the conversation down to questions of privacy and away from the thornier matters of systemic discrimination and asymmetrical knowledge production. Debating privacy, which can be readily equivocated or bargained away for security and the cunning corporate notion of "personalization," is relatively comfortable terrain for the purveyors of data profiles. This book turns toward contemporary literature for counternarratives that, among other things, contextualize, destabilize, and denaturalize what I call profile epistemology, by which I mean both the typical justifications for data surveillance and the premises that support them. Whereas profiles supposedly pinpoint individuals at the cross sections of data, the novels analyzed here instead conceive of characters at the intersections of historical and ideological forces. This distinction is key to confronting the lived experiences of data profiling, which are neither immaterial nor atemporal. In his book *Slow Violence and the Environmentalism of the Poor*, Rob Nixon reminds us, "In a world permeated by insidious, yet unseen or imperceptible violence, imaginative writing can help make the unapparent appear."[2] Data surveillance depends on its own opacity, even or especially as consumer-citizens are rendered ever more visible, but contemporary novels and poetry "offer us a different kind of witnessing: of sights unseen."[3] They also offer alternative possibilities for understanding what is legible, knowable, and sayable in the data age by re-pacing and re-spacing our experiences of digital surveillance.

This book's second focus concerns how data profiles can calcify norms, exacerbate inequality, and reify "identities of suspicion,"[4] Torin Monahan's term to describe the discriminatory forms of subjectivity that surveillance often produces and reproduces. Scholars have established various terms for this harm, each with their own emphasis. These include "digital discrimination" (David Lyon),[5] "algorithmic oppression" (Safiya Noble),[6] "technologies of discrimination" (Oscar Gandy),[7] "marginalizing surveillance" (Torin Monahan),[8] "racializing surveillance" (Simone Browne),[9] "algorithmic violence" (Mimi Onuoha),[10] "the coded gaze" (Joy Buolamwini),[11] and "the New Jim Code" (Ruja Benjamin)[12] to name a few. Each scholar rightly emphasizes how data surveillance operates in relation to power and privilege to create conditions of risk for already marginalized groups. In a world where every keystroke, click, comment, connection, glance, purchase, query, and movement now "count," pressing questions for contemporary literature are how meaning is made, by whom, and for whom. To be sure, this is not merely a matter of determining who gets to write the historical record. The horizon of data profiling is, as Jasbir Puar states, "prehensive," or a matter of "making the present look exactly the way it needs to in order to guarantee a very specific and singular outcome in the future."[13] In other words, the proliferation of data profiles directly affects the distribution of life chances and one's field of choices. The novels I analyze in the coming chapters expose data profiles as not simply "data doubles" or disinterested shadows of people but as Trojan horses for the very forms of discrimination and characterization they purport to circumvent. These novels and poetry emphatically situate the practices and ramifications of data surveillance in systems of oppression that produce supposedly "risky" subjectivities while obscuring actually risky labor and living conditions.

Finally, this book's third area of concentration is how data profiling inhabits the textual subconscious of contemporary literature, engendering a pervasive mode of critical and aesthetic reflection that addresses the fallacies of data discourse and recharacterizes the lived experiences of data subjects within networks of power. Not only is it true that "many more people read Orwell than read Foucault,"[14] but this book also argues that it is literature's fictionality that makes it especially equipped to grapple with the realities of data profiling. That is, the narrative, creative conceits of novels and poetry afford imaginative recompositions of digital surveillance that expose data's own stories and narrative dimension. Ironically, acknowledging and appreciating this narrative dimension is what grounds data surveillance in reality. Likewise, literary analysis and data analytics are both practiced in "close reading," with a similar conceit that every bit and byte is meaningful and foreshadowing of future behavior. By distinguishing data surveillance as a literary matter, we can ask: who and what are the forces in the political economy that coauthor people's lives and subjectivities and whose interests do they serve?[15] The literature I have selected captures how data surveillance and its supporting stories influence the opportunities, obstacles, confines, and communities that characters encounter. Amid the mandates and maneuverings of data discourse, the novels and poetry herein have found a compelling set of questions to be pursued. Specifically, what adds up to a character or a life, and what is deducted from that equation? Where do we locate credibility and coherence? What does the point of view of data collection necessarily overlook? How might we confront and collectively resist the forces in the political economy that coauthor people's lives and subject formations? What novel engagements with point of view might this confrontation engender? And how is literature itself implicated in systems of surveillance?

The literary analyses in the following chapters illustrate how epistemologies of data profiling might be untethered from claims of omniscience and neutrality, clearing the way to address how data functions rhetorically and materially. To be clear, scientific data is a public good, meaning it can and should be both publicly accessible and good for the public. The critiques of data profiling in this book are not an indictment of data collection and certainly not of science—including computational science. We cannot confront the challenges of our time—from climate change to public health to income inequality to police brutality—without quantitative scientific data, and we have seen how scientific skepticism has been weaponized to aid and abet the far right and maintain the status quo of white supremacist capitalist patriarchy. To be sure, this book is not a condemnation of data collection per se; on the contrary, it is advocating for a more serious and less fanciful understanding of "big data" that considers the context of data collection, what algorithms are optimized for, whose interests they serve, and what remains ignored.

Despite what Eric Schmidt, former CEO and executive chair of Google, maintains, data profiling is not "magical."[16] Richard Maxwell and Toby Miller's book *Greening the Media* provides a relevant analysis of how "cloud computing might as well result from invisible magic from all we can see of it."[17] The invisibility of data server warehouses and their effects, described by Maxwell and Miller, overlaps and intersects with the deliberate invisibility and cloudiness of data surveillance, making it difficult to face them, much less activate opposition. In fact, as Allison Carruth lays bare, we are primed to accept this magical thinking by our "devices [which] seem to open up conduits into impossible-to-apprehend yet wondrous worlds."[18] The literary fiction analyzed herein attempts to bring the discourses around data profiling down from the clouds and back to Earth.[19] In other words, this fiction is, ironically, giving data profiling a much-needed reality check: *Oh, you are storytellers? Okay, then, let's talk about how stories are told. Let's talk about narrative. Let's talk about point of view. Let's talk about audience, authorship, and authority. Let's talk about how you know what you know and how you arrive at meaning.* As Lewis MacLeod writes, "Under the condition of ubiquitous surveillance, the fetishization of data obscures truth and morality because it neglects the narrative dimension that shapes the data itself."[20] This reality check by literature highlights the frictions and fissures that are smoothed over by this supposedly cloudy, magical, friendly ghost that moves at an "overwhelming operational tempo."[21] As literary authors re-pace and respace the narrative, as they slow down and freeze the frames, as they shift the field of focus, we can begin to apprehend this apparition. When we do, we find that profiles are not our shadows after all. Shadows wrongly make data doubles sound like a natural, even inevitable, phenomenon. The supposed "shadows" of data profiles are actually cast by the spotlights of surveillance capitalists—who despite their enormous wealth and influence are not the sun. Importantly, contemporary literature recasts the profiles that prefigure and disfigure characters as mechanisms of control and governance, motivated by corporate and state interests and not by "pure science," an unknowable deity, a messianic profit, or an enchanted spell. To confront how the point of view of surveillance capitalism and data profiling judges and nudges people toward its own profit and control, literature gives this unreliable narrator a face, a name, a profile.

Welcome to Your World

Lest we forget the early techno-utopianism that helped marshal in data discourse, we must only revisit a journalistic profile piece from 2006 when "You" were *Time* magazine's "Person of the Year."[22] The cover features a Macintosh computer and keyboard with the single word "You." typed across what appears to be a YouTube frame on the screen. Alternate covers use a reflective material for the computer screen to quite literally put readers' faces on the cover. The caption reads: "Yes, you. You control the Information Age. Welcome to your world." This greeting echoes the start-up screen of a Mac, which ushers the user into their personal computer, customized with their preferences, desktop, folders, bookmarks, and histories, exemplified by the language choice of that first "welcome." In the case of both the computer start-up screen and the magazine cover, this rhetoric—hailing people as "small s sovereign[s]"[23] of their own digital world—is designed to encourage digital self-expression and participation while, in Wendy Chun's words, "mask[ing] the fact that YOU are 'they.'"[24] Indeed, as Chun elaborates, "networks do not produce an imagined and anonymous 'we' (they are not, to use Benedict Anderson's term, 'imagined communities') but rather, a relentlessly pointed yet empty, singular yet plural YOU," which "is also a demand." The underlying "demand" here for unremitting capture of "YOUR" data and time is disguised as a celebration for "YOUR" supposedly enthusiastic contributions. Yet by boldly declaring this "your world," *Time* raises the question of exactly whose world "you" were living in before. Ultimately, this condescending congratulations for your "control [of] the Information Age" is not unlike a personalized sign on a child's bedroom door in a house that, in fact, belongs to the parents (or, more likely, the bank).

Looking back, the incredulity of that first line—yes, really, you—has aged better than the dubious notion that because a person posted on YouTube they are now in "control." The magazine article professes to tell "a story about community and collaboration on a scale never seen before . . . about the many wresting power from the few," but upon closer reading, it actually tells a story about the many working for the few. This language by *Time* was especially rich given AOL's acquisition of Time Warner in 2000 for a staggering $165 billion, the largest mergers and acquisitions deal in history at the time.[25] Still, the article cites Wikipedia, YouTube, and MySpace as examples of ordinary people coming together "and helping one another for nothing and how that will not only change the world, but also change the way the world changes."[26] What this irrational technological exuberance neglects is that contributing—"for nothing"—does not "wrest" power from "big media"; rather, it provides them with free content and surplus data to sell in the now thriving market of algorithmic profiling. In fact, the article is more correct than it seems willing to admit when it says, "And we didn't just watch, we also worked. Like crazy." Crazily indeed; for decades now consumer-users have "worked" online producing content and data for free. The magazine cheers that, "We made Facebook profiles and Second Life avatars and reviewed books at Amazon and recorded podcasts. We blogged about our candidates losing and wrote songs about getting dumped. We camcordered bombing runs and built open-source software." None of these activities are in and of themselves world-changing, but the article was right to say that "The new Web is a very different thing. It's a tool for bringing together the small contributions of millions of people and making them matter." Surely, these discreet "contributions" online do "matter" to users and society (personally, socially, politically), but they also "matter" greatly for companies such as Alphabet, Meta, and Amazon, as well as for an entire industry of data brokers and advertisers that has capitalized on these free "contributions."

Time boasted that while "Silicon Valley consultants call it Web 2.0 . . . it's really a revolution." This book argues that the profile industrial complex and its dominant epistemology is indeed immensely consequential, but to call it a "revolution" mistakenly suggests that political or economic power has changed hands, when in fact it has consolidated to an alarming degree. Indicative of the early technological utopianism that pits the internet (framed as active and forward-looking) against television (framed as passive and retrograde), the article imagines that energy spent online "wrest[s] power from the few":

> Who are these people? Seriously, who actually sits down after a long day at work and says, I'm not going to watch *Lost* tonight. I'm going to turn on my computer and make a movie starring my pet iguana? I'm going to mash up 50 Cent's vocals with Queen's instrumentals? I'm going to blog about my state of mind or the state of the nation or the *steak-frites* at the new bistro down the street? Who has that time and that energy and that passion?

The astonishment and admiration for people opting to not passively plop down in front of the television "after a long day at work," ignores that even now over half of all adults watch TV shows on the internet daily.[27] In fact, in April 2006, Disney announced that *Lost* could be streamed for free online,[28] and in 2009, *Lost* was named the most-watched show on the internet.[29] In the end, this false competition between the internet and television was actually indicative of the greater utopian fantasy about the promise of Web 2.0 as democratizing and participatory. Most significantly, this article circumvents the fact that when someone reviewed a restaurant, blogged, or remixed 50 Cent's vocals—it was their data and information that was then remixed for profit in the form of metadata.

The article dramatically responds to its own question about who exactly chooses to do all this with, "The answer is, you do. And for seizing the reins of the global media, for founding and framing the new digital democracy, for working for nothing and beating the pros at their own game, TIME's Person of the Year for 2006 is you."[30] First, this grossly overstates the sovereignty of consumer-users and the democratic drive of the internet. Moreover, having just stressed that these "contributions" effectively extend the workday, it is hard to see how "working *for nothing*" is "beating the pros at their own game." In fact, if we accept the article at face value, then the only thing distinguishing "the pros" from "you" is a salary.[31] The article ends with a caveat: "Sure, it's a mistake to romanticize all this any more than is strictly necessary. Web 2.0 harnesses the stupidity of crowds as well as its wisdom. Some of the comments on YouTube make you weep for the future of humanity just for the spelling alone, never mind the obscenity and the naked hatred."[32] Without specifying how much romanticism is "strictly necessary" to preserve, the author tacitly acknowledges that the early utopian fantasy of the internet democratizing communication and information had already lost some of its allure.[33]

Today, the pettiness about spelling and the casual concern over ineffectual content moderation—"never mind the obscenity and naked hatred"—ring tragically inadequate, but even for its time, these quips miss the latent problems of surveillance and the exploitation of what Tiziana Terranova rightly calls, "free labour."[34] Undoubtedly, the internet has provided an important space for the acts of creativity and care that the *Time* article champions, but from the beginning, late capitalism has exploited and exhausted users' participation and labor.[35] Big Data now samples and "remixes" this participation into its own narrative, recasting "you" with your profile. Ultimately, it's fitting that *Time* put "your" face on its reflective cover: after all, the data surveillance industry is fundamentally self-effacing and underwritten by celebrity culture, which often provides it convenient cover, as though profiles are centrally about recognition and connection and not about profits and power.

The Profile Industry

Seventeen years later, it's clear that people were not only producing content "for nothing"; they were also generating troves of personal data. In fact, the World Economic Forum predicts that by 2025, approximately 463 exabytes of data will be generated daily.[36] Meanwhile, people, of course, no longer even need to "turn on the computer" to be a part of this "revolution."[37] With the burgeoning market of "smart" products ("personal assistant" speakers, thermostats, beds, bassinets, toothbrushes, vacuum cleaners, cars, televisions, wine bottles, the list goes on), mobile apps that access and share data including one's location, and ambient forms of public surveillance, "participation" is practically unavoidable.[38] Undoubtedly, for consumers, personal data profiles can be convenient. The expediency of electronic payments is a prime example, but so are email, Google Maps, FasTrak, TSA PreCheck, and the personalization of search engines and online commerce. This convenience comes at the cost of collapsing citizenship into consumerism and exacerbating inequality. Cultural theorists have different names for this phenomenon that emphasize a host of important concerns: Eli Pariser warns against "filter bubbles" that limit access to information and opportunities;[39] Christian Parenti describes "the soft cage" of routine data surveillance;[40] Frank Pasquale critiques the "black boxes" of big data that simultaneously demand the transparency of citizens while hiding behind the convolutions of legalese and the protections of trade secrets;[41] Simone Browne contextualizes algorithmic surveillance in a long history of racializing surveillance that reifies color lines;[42] Marisa Elena Duarte and colleagues demonstrate how "even the most comprehensive data sets cannot represent the complex realities of Indigenous peoples; instead, they represent the questions that researchers ask";[43] Shoshana Zuboff warns of "surveillance capitalism," which ushers in a new economic order based on tapping ever more streams of "behavioral surplus" data to not only predict but actually shape the future.[44] These theorists, among many others, grapple with the proliferation of personal data profiles and algorithmic surveillance by what I call the *profile industry*, composed of advertisers, data brokers, and online "sharing" platforms, and the constellation of national security apparatuses with whom they cooperate.

To be clear, for the profile industry, data does not just help businesses advertise and sell more products—data is the product.[45] Business writers and executives have touted "Big Data" as the "gold rush of the twenty-first century" and the "currency of the twenty-first century enterprise."[46] Accordingly, some companies are focused on how to buy, sell, and trade the unfathomable amount of data being collected, whereas others are invested in transforming "raw data" into so-called actionable insights. Former CEO of Google Eric Schmidt claimed in 2010 that "every two days now we create as much information as we did from the dawn of civilization up until 2003."[47] That is around 5 exabytes of data, or the equivalent of 32,768 gigabytes squared. In 2013, 90 percent of all data in the world at that point had been generated over the previous two years.[48] Now, according to the Pew Research Center, one in four adults in the United States owns a smart speaker that collects ambient data.[49] To be sure, collecting and processing this data is a massively profitable enterprise. For example, Acxiom, the largest processor of consumer data, makes $1.15 billion a year selling companies lists of consumers, such as "potential inheritor," "adult with senior parent," and "diabetic focus."[50] Similarly, retailers pay major US banks roughly $1.7 billion a year to send "targeted discount offers" to their customers, based their "shopping habits gleaned from credit card records."[51] This is apparently a prudent investment given that "data-intensive advertising helps generate over $150 billion a year in economic activity."[52]

For their part, Facebook (not the parent company, Meta) generates four new petabytes of data per day,[53] and as Jay Parikh, the former Facebook vice president and head of engineering and infrastructure, explains, "If you aren't taking advantage of big data, then you don't have big data; you have just a pile of data."[54] In this context, "taking advantage of big data" means parsing it, analyzing it, and selling it. Profiles derived from this information thus reconceive of individuality as the point of intersection between cross sections of data—changeable depending on which variables are selected. They move beyond demography, which designates swaths of the population based on general criteria such as age range, race, and gender, to instead target people based on specific information about their habits, health, opinions, relations, interactions, purchases, movements, and so on.

This is the difference between identifying groups of college-educated, middle-class, middle-aged, married white women and specifically targeting those fitting these criteria who also watch *Severance* on Apple TV in a marathon viewing session, recently began buying prenatal vitamins from Target, walk the perimeter of their neighborhood park on Wednesday mornings, pass a Starbucks on their commute across town, vote in local midterm elections, take a B12 tablet daily, have a clean driving record save one speeding ticket, and worry about climate change most acutely during the late evening. A difference in degree becomes a difference in kind. Moreover, "Big Data, through its integration of second-order habit, offers a form of cognitive mapping that allegedly sees all, by ignoring causes."[55] In other words, while more "fleshed out," this sort of profile still disregards why those particular data points matter and to whom. Instead, the sum of these points is designed to add up to a valuation, a means of sorting the right person from the wrong person as determined by corporate advertisers and institutions of political governance. On the surface, this description might sound not unlike a character sketch, but the meaning of a character comes from context, affects, and interplays. This is not to say that profiles are simply still too thin. In fact, adding connective tissue that further elaborates the context of human action (as fiction so often does) would be to add more data to the profile, not to defeat the logic of the profile. As the literature I analyze in the coming chapters exposes, what is critically missing is the suppressed narrative, arguably literary, dimension that already underwrites and propels the truth-claims of data profiles. Importantly, this includes the authors and readers of data profiles who are structurally elided to maintain the epistemological status of Big Data, to transform the text into logos. Who is the author of this pseudo-character sketch? Who selected these data points, and what story are they implicitly telling? Who will read them, and what is their interpretation and readerly response? How does discrete information get turned into knowledge? Moreover, unlike fictional characters who circulate in the world with more or less artistic effect, the "characters" of data surveillance directly affect the lives of actual people. As Chun plainly pronounces, "YOU are a character in a drama called Big Data,"[56] a drama that demands analysis by a wider audience.

Profile Nation

The unidentified American—
we find him everywhere where trouble is.
—*New York Times*, May 26, 1912

To be sure, companies and corporations are not the only ones in the business of data profiling; nation-states, of course, also have a long and consequential history of surveillance and data collection. Whether targeting consumers, citizens, or potential combatants, profiling often amounts to sorting the "right" person from the "wrong" person. To this point, Christian Parenti excavates IBM's role in the Holocaust to "problematize the political implications of everyday surveillance and information technology" and trouble the public's comfort with the ongoing rise in routine digital surveillance.[57] He reminds readers, for example, that upon taking power in 1933, the Nazis contracted IBM to create a more exacting national census that included eighty variables, allowing them to identify not only Jews but "select subsets of Jews."[58] Relatedly, Simone Browne traces current technologies and techniques of surveillance to their historical antecedents in American slavery and the Jim Crow era. She clarifies that technologies such as the slave pass depended on the illiteracy of slaves, crystallizing the importance of being able to read the documents and data that define our rights and personhood, including currently unintelligible "privacy agreements," opaque algorithms, and national security programs.[59] This is, after all, one reason encryption has been such a crucial site of contestation between the NSA and the technology industry.[60]

After the terrorist attacks on September 11, 2001, the *Philadelphia City Paper* captured a dominant theme with their headline, "Nothing Will Ever Be the Same."[61] In retrospect and with a longer look at history, 9/11 seems "less like a seismic shift from freedom to tyranny and more like an aggressive and opportunistic acceleration" of the nation's surveillance programs.[62] While post-9/11 polls did indicate that more Americans were willing to trade civil liberties for security, this supposed sea change in public opinion is often overstated.[63] Although US digital surveillance has certainly intensified since 9/11, we must resist ahistorical narratives that treat profiling as an entirely emergent phenomenon in a brave new twenty-first-century world.

Without describing every known program, it is worth offering a sense of the scope and scale of national security surveillance and its relationship with the private sector in the United States. The current approach by the NSA, according to one former intelligence officer, remains not to look for a single needle in the haystack but to "'collect the whole haystack . . . Collect it all, tag it, store it . . . and whatever it is you want, you go searching for it.'"[64] While this approach seems to eschew (or at the very least postpone) any selection influenced by preconceptions, how the information gets tagged and indexed (setting aside its eventual analysis) is curatorial. The fact that "whatever it is [national intelligence] want[s]" is presumably there provides opportunity for them to tell "whatever" story they ultimately want to tell, consciously or not. Edward Snowden's legendary leak of classified documents beginning in 2013 exposed some details of this dragnet approach as well as the extraordinary extent of intelligence gathering. Perhaps most notably, the documents disclosed the NSA's PRISM (Planning Tool for Resource Integration, Synchronization, and Management) program, which intercepts internet communications from companies including, Microsoft, Yahoo!, Alphabet, Meta, Paltalk, YouTube, AOL, Skype, and Apple. The PRISM program began in 2007 and is subject to the US Foreign Intelligence Surveillance Court (FISA Court); during its entire thirty-three years, however, the FISA Court has granted 33,942 warrants and denied only 11.[65] Moreover, in 2001 the Obama administration won permission from the FISA Court to reverse the restrictions authorized by Congress in 2008 under the Foreign Intelligence Surveillance Act.[66] With this change, the NSA can now access intercepted phone calls and emails and deliberately search for Americans' communications in its massive databases without a warrant or probable cause to suggest that the people with whom they were communicating were terrorists, spies, or foreign powers. To gather data, the NSA uses a plug-in called GUMFISH to seize control of laptop cameras, CAPTIVATEAUDIENCE to take over computer microphones,[67] and XKEYSCORE software to see "'nearly everything a user does on the internet,' including emails, social media posts, websites you visit, addresses typed into Google Maps, files sent, and more."[68]

In addition to these programs and plug-ins designed to intercept data, the NSA's Sigint Enabling Project works to decrypt data, in part by collaborating with technology companies to "covertly influence" their product designs to build in vulnerabilities. For example, at Microsoft, the NSA "worked with company officials to get pre-encryption access to Microsoft's most popular services, including Outlook e-mail, Skype internet phone calls and chats, and SkyDrive, the company's cloud storage service."[69] It would be a mistake to discuss data profiling by the private and public sectors as simply concurrent or even intersecting trends, when they often work as partners—despite each supposedly standing as the check or balance on the other.[70]

Moreover, as part of the post-9/11 "Information Sharing Environment (ISE)," the government has established eighty "fusion centers" to facilitate "information sharing."[71] The Department of Homeland Security describes fusion centers as "collaborative effort[s] of two or more agencies . . . with the goal of maximizing their ability to detect, prevent, investigate, and respond to criminal and terrorist activity."[72] As Frank Pasquale puts it, "with their generous federal funding, slick conferences, and firm corporate backing, they are beginning to unite the public and private monitoring of individual lives into unified digital dossiers."[73] Although the government is constitutionally constrained, they are, for a price, able to tap into the unregulated collection of data by private industries, leaving "plenty of room for dealing on both sides."[74]

To be clear, the nation-state takes full advantage of the escalating reach of corporate data profiling. For instance, Palantir, a major data analytics company cofounded by Peter Theil, partners with clients including the Department of Homeland Security (DHS), NSA, Federal Bureau of Investigation (FBI), the Centers for Disease Control and Prevention, the Marine Corps, the Air Force, Special Operations Command, West Point, the Joint IED Defeat Organization and Allies, and various police departments, for whom they have created predictive policing programs.[75] Perhaps most controversially, in 2014, US Immigration and Customs Enforcement (ICE) granted Palantir a $41 million contract to track documented and undocumented immigrants.[76] Amazon Web Services (AWS) is also implicated in this deal by hosting Palantir's software. In fact, the formidable grassroots organization Mijente has called AWS "the hidden backbone behind not just immigration enforcement, but many of DHS's nationwide capabilities," drawing attention to the fact that "Amazon has more federal authorizations to handle confidential data than any other company, allowing it to host core data systems for immigration authorities, including the retention of at least 230 million biometric records—irises, facial records, fingerprints, and more."[77] In February 2021, ICE awarded the popular legal research and data analytics firm LexisNexis a $16.8 million contract to provide information from its 283 million distinct individual dossiers.[78] LexisNexis's Risk Solutions division is meanwhile marketed to law enforcement agencies, financial institutions, and insurance companies, claiming to "facilitate cross-jurisdictional collaboration with powerful information sharing and data fusion tools, in support of specific law enforcement and homeland security missions."[79] The novels and lyric poetry under discussion in this book highlight this cooperation between the private and public sectors as they co-construct reality based on their mutual interests in maintaining power and expanding their own reach. When Chun remarks that "surveillance is now a state- and privately funded co-production,"[80] we must ask: what exactly they are producing? This book posits that they are producing not only record profits but surveillance stories with points of view and reoccurring themes.

Profile Society

For the purposes of this book, there are two general types of digital profiles in circulation. First is the profile that consumer-users knowingly create for themselves: for example, on Facebook, Instagram, Twitter, TikTok, Grindr, Tinder, and (with perhaps less awareness) sites like Netflix, YouTube, and Amazon, where users actively curate their recommendations by rating content. This first-order profile is certainly part of what *Time* magazine was celebrating by naming "You" the "Person of the Year."[81] Behind this public-facing profile is a data profile, largely unknown and inaccessible to consumer-users. When recognizable, this second-order profile is often regarded as merely metadata[82]—usually to quell concerns about privacy—but that is somewhat misleading. For instance, while data brokers and online sharing platforms certainly sell access to consumers based on metadata, they also target people based on the content of their searches, emails, posts, purchases, and so on. This personal information is aggregated and recontextualized according to state or corporate interests. Office Max for example, addressed a letter to a grieving father with his name, followed by the epithet "daughter killed in car crash."[83] In addition to its profound insensitivity, one reason this mistake garnered attention is because, unlike user-generated profiles, which are designed to share information, data profiles are thought to remain anonymized. In other words, this mailer inadvertently said the quiet part out loud.

These two types of profiles are interdependent in several ways. First, public-facing profiles provide cover for data profiles by reassuring people that they are "in control" of their own persona and exposure, if not the "reins of global media."[84] Second, public-facing profiles are designed for users to share information about themselves and participate in a social graph that generates troves of personal data. Moreover, I argue that celebrity culture underwrites this phenomenon by promoting the perception that a high public profile amounts to greater individual worth. Accordingly, social media sites (such as Instagram, Facebook, and Twitter) simultaneously sell themselves as public relations firms for the famous and nonfamous alike, even describing "followers" or "friends" as "fans," while simultaneously insisting that users divulge their "authentic selves."

Meta has been especially adept at addressing and reconciling these two kinds of profiles in their public relations. At the 2011 Facebook F8 (pronounced "fate") developer conference, Mark Zuckerberg stressed that the then recent changes to the social networking site would eliminate routine privacy consents to create a "frictionless experience" while the "open graph" system would tally and chart more and more user activity, even offering, for example, monthly and annual reports of a person's eating and exercising habits.[85] Indeed, accelerating routine surveillance enables what Bill Gates called "friction-free capitalism" online in the sense that it allows capital to flow upward more freely.[86] Yet the only way that this experience could seem "frictionless" to users is by its invisibility and the sheer magnitude and frequency of data collection—like driving quickly enough over the ruts in a dirt road to smooth out the ride.

Still, the ubiquity and popularity of social media (along with a suggestion of its fatedness) produce the necessary sense of "anonymity and whatever-ness"[87] in their incredibly individualized data sets. It's worth keeping in mind that in his public relations, Zuckerberg is simultaneously addressing investors and users, smoothing out the friction between them. To accomplish this rhetorical feat, he must seem like an enthusiastic user while still communicating the lucrativeness of these changes to advertisers and market researchers. For example, take Zuckerberg's claim that "Facebook's mission is to make the world more open and connected," a perfectly friendly project that obscures exactly for whom the information is now open. He likewise boasts, "we're helping *you* create a graph of connections," a double-speak that addresses users, investors, and advertisers alike (emphasis added).

Mimetically, David Fincher's 2010 film *The Social Network*, a fictionalized account of Facebook's beginnings, likewise shifts the critical focus away from Facebook's business model and toward the personality or public profile of its founder. The plot begins with Zuckerberg's billion-dollar idea, focusing on the supposed controversy over its originality, and ends with a corporation valued at upward of $80 billion, never once mentioning how Facebook makes its money. Granted, we see Zuckerberg receive a $500,000 angel investment, but the film neglects to illustrate how the popularity of Facebook translates into profits, obscuring or simply ignoring that the wealth of information on users' profiles is repackaged and sold to marketers. Instead, the film focuses on exposing Zuckerberg's motivations and who he really is. The film's existential construction of its protagonist is not unlike Zuckerberg's own approach in his F8 announcement in which he similarly attempts to convince his audience that Facebook exists for users to "express who they really are," repeating variations on this phrase fifteen times. By encouraging "people [to] feel an intense ownership over their profile," he distracts from the immensely profitable data profiles that remain inaccessible to users.

To expose the social striations that are smoothed over by this sort of data discourse, the novels and poetry I engage in *Profiles and Plotlines* generate critical friction between characters and the technologies that surveil them. After all, as Zygmunt Bauman rightly puts it, "Power can move with the speed of the electronic signal."[88] From a narrative perspective, the frenetic counting of profile culture produces a lightning fast, blurry, ever-expanding force that makes data surveillance seem both inevitable and inescapable. The novels I analyze confront this force by re-pacing and respacing experiences with data surveillance to depict alternative ways of seeing and knowing. In her book *Blog Theory*, Jodi Dean "wager[s] . . . that critical media theory is possible in book form. The wager is inspired by a time-honored tactic in workers' struggle: the slow-down."[89] I wager that the same tactic is not only possible in literary books, but artfully executed. Claudia Rankine's *Citizen*, for example, demonstrates how freezing the visual frame and drawing out the moment can create space for reflective and affective responses to breath. Crucially, in her lyric poetry, re-pacing and respacing encounters with surveillance allows readers to better perceive how surveillance is foundational to white supremacy and other systems of oppression. As David Lyon reminds us, "surveillance streamlines the process of doing things at a distance, of separating a person from the consequences of an action." For example, "border controls can appear automated, dispassionate, even as they deny entry to the asylum seeker from the 'wrong' ethnic background, fearful for her life if she is sent back home."[90] Literature can puncture this illusion of detachment,[91] in part, by collapsing that distance and drawing out the affects that it's meant to produce and those it's meant to quash. The novels analyzed here reveal the atmospheric pressures and configurations that permit some truths to rise and others to fall.

Nevertheless, recognizing that participation and visibility in profile culture are "both a gift and a trap,"[92] this book carefully distinguishes between how subjectivity is produced and how it is occupied, lived, and resisted. Social media, for example, is undoubtedly a useful tool for organizing movements and connecting with others. The organizers of Ejercito Zapatista de Liberacion Nacional, Black Lives Matter, Idle No More, the Standing Rock protests, and any political campaign will tell you as much.[93] Still, by providing this tool, data mining social platforms also invigorate white supremacy and expose their users to the vulnerabilities of hypervisibility. For instance, when the international private security firm TigerSwan launched a militaristic surveillance campaign against the water protectors who were protesting the Dakota Access Pipeline on the Standing Rock Reservation, TigerSwan closely monitored protesters' social media accounts.[94] Likewise, Tesla paid a consultancy firm, MWW PR, to surveil a Facebook group to thwart employees' efforts to unionize in 2017–2018.[95] It's clear that beyond opening up their users to online surveillance, tech platforms also help mark individuals for systemic discrimination by deeming them either "risky investments" or just plain "risky."

Partial Profiles

In this book, I seek to address how personal data profiles constitute a form of knowledge production and a material force in the world that can be better grasped through their fraught relationship with fiction. It is worth first recalling the multiple interconnected instantiations of "profiles" that have proliferated throughout life and literature, from facial silhouettes, to brief written bios, to user-generated online profiles, and finally to "data doubles" or personal data dossiers. In each case, profiles are, by definition, partial. They sketch the contours of a person's face or the contours of a person's life from ideological and spatial vantage points: profile portraits are taken or drawn from the side; celebrity profiles in magazines offer limited access to their subjects, negotiated by editors and agents; social media profiles are carefully curated depictions of users' lives. To be sure, the data profiles that now circulate unseen are also partial, in both senses of the word. In other words, despite their omnipresence, they are neither omniscient nor neutral.[96] To make use of them ethically and constructively, we must acknowledge their points of view as well as their significant (often deliberate) blind spots.

Like the profiles that precede them, data profiles too often map onto preexisting hierarchies of human "types" and exacerbate systemic discrimination. Using habits as "proxies, the 'coarse' and 'outdated' categories of race, class, sexuality, and gender are accounted for in unaccounted ways."[97] When Google, for example, deems a teenager to be "college bound," based on data that includes socioeconomic and demographic information, that person is more likely to receive information about SAT prep classes, scholarship opportunities, and application materials. On the other hand, teenagers who do not fit this profile for success are far less likely to encounter these resources. According to the Department of Justice, when Meta Platforms "enabled and encouraged advertisers to target their housing ads by relying on race, color, religion, sex, disability, familial status, and national origin to decide which Facebook users will be eligible, and ineligible, to receive housing ads,"[98] they committed algorithmic violations of the Fair Housing Act. Examples of algorithmic social sorting that exploit and exacerbate inequality are endless. Rather than using data profiles to draw foregone conclusions based on old, often discriminatory narratives, we should heed Wendy Chun's advice and use data modeling as the "grounds for creating new and different [futures]."[99] Otherwise, as Chun writes, using habits to generate source code "reduces the living world to dead writing" and "presumes no difference between source code and execution, instruction and result. It perversely renders code, because of machinic, dead repetition, into logos."[100] Steeped in the manifold discourses and preoccupations of their times, the novels and poetry analyzed in the following chapters rupture these stagnant stories by exposing their partiality and impossible simplicity. To begin, this moves the conversation from "it was written" to "it's being written," which raises the questions by whom, from what worldview, and to what ends?

Data Discourse and Surveillance Stories

> The intellectual's role is dialectically, oppositionally . . . to challenge
> and defeat both an imposed silence and the normalized quiet of unseen
> power . . . and the discourse used to justify, disguise, or mystify its
> workings while also preventing objections or challenges to it.
> —EDWARD SAID, "The Public Role of Writers and Intellectuals" (31)

A 2008 article in *Wired* magazine confidently maintained that "with enough data, the numbers speak for themselves."[101] In other words, Michael Hayden's statement notwithstanding, one should be able to simply "throw data through the transit"[102]—undigested and without qualification. With a similar stance, an economist at MIT Sloan School of Management, Erik

Brynjolfsson, compared the "potential impact of Big Data" to that of the microscope, which "allowed people to see and measure things as never before," suggesting that data surveillance is a "revolution in measurement."[103] Yet the questions remain: who exactly is "allowed" access to this data? Who decides what "things" are deemed measurable? What comes to pass when the "things" are people? While data certainly provides novel ways of seeing, it neither speaks for itself nor merely magnifies reality. Whether targeting combatants or consumers, data profiling instead sorts the right person from the wrong person, inscribing value and values.

Nevertheless, the tale we are told is that algorithmic profiles provide consumers-citizens with customization, convenience, and efficiency and liberate us from harmful human biases and shortcomings. No matter that humans wrote the opaque, seemingly automagical algorithms or that they use biased training data; the information, we are told, is neutral and objective. The alibi that algorithms, unlike humans, are impartial has become a rhetorical commonplace, yet there is ample evidence to the contrary. For instance, in January 2020, Robert Julian-Borchak Williams, a Black man, was wrongfully arrested for shoplifting in Detroit when a facial recognition algorithm misidentified him as matching a blurry image from a surveillance video.[104] This error is unsurprising given that facial recognition systems are ten to one hundred times more likely to misidentify African American and Asian faces than white faces.[105] When the police arrested Williams at his home, they refused to say why, "only showing him a piece of paper with his photo and the words 'felony warrant' and 'larceny,'" evidently confident that the conclusion of the DataWorks software would speak for itself. When his wife asked the police where they were taking him, they told her to "Google it," practically parodying their own capitulation to algorithmic governance. When it became clear that Williams was innocent (after collecting his DNA, mugshot, and fingerprints), "One detective, seeming chagrined, said to his partner: 'I guess the computer got it wrong.'"[106] Not unlike Hayden's deflection toward "the science," the officers conveniently ceded responsibility and chalked this one up to an algorithmic error. In conversation with Glen Thrush, Hayden seemed to take pride in his role as a "storyteller," but in moments like these, "the science" resurfaces as a convenient scapegoat. In truth, the stereotypes that inflect and inform every story told about and through data surveillance are also written into its codes.

Not only does the dominant rhetoric of data discourse wrongly insist on the neutrality of algorithmic surveillance, it also strategically deems any suggestions to the contrary as outright suspicious. For instance, contradicting Hayden's characterization of intelligence work as subjective and sometimes "wrong," the commonplace that "If you have nothing to hide, you have nothing to fear" persists. The implication is clear: if one does express "fear" or concern, then they must be hiding something. This adage of surveillance societies also wrongly imagines a universal "you," who is surveilled impartially and harmlessly. This is demonstrably mistaken. Cast as risky, dangerous, deviant, or expendable, racialized and otherwise marginalized communities are far more likely to be harmed and even killed because of surveillance stories and their cumulative effects. The surveillance strategies that "effected indigenous disappearance in order to establish the settler state itself";[107] the tens of thousands of civilians killed by unmanned aerial vehicles since about 2012;[108] the trauma routinely inflicted on trans people at airport security;[109] the recent manufacturing of drones armed with rubber bullets, tasers, and tear gas to use against peaceful protesters; and the wildly disproportionate conviction rates and sentencing terms for African Americans in the United States demonstrate how blatantly manipulative this axiom really is.[110]

The tech industry actively propagates this tenet of profile epistemology, which Lev Grossman describes as "a popular attitude among Silicon Valley elites."[111] When former Google CEO Eric Schmidt quipped, "If you have something that you don't want anyone to know, maybe you shouldn't be doing it in the first place,"[112] the uproar (to the extent that there was one) mostly admonished the company for privacy invasions. However worthwhile, this focus on privacy overlooks how state and private institutions strategically frame any condemnation of data surveillance as grounds for suspicion, thereby foreclosing critical response. Of course, Schmidt's glib retort could be leveled right back at Google. As Shoshana Zuboff reminds us, secrecy is baked into their business model and has come to be "institutionalized in the policies and practices that govern every aspect of Google's behavior onstage and offstage."[113] Here, it's worth recalling Foucault's formulation that disciplinary power is "exercised through its invisibility," while imposing a "compulsory visibility" on its targets.[114]

In his profile piece on Mark Zuckerberg, Grossman writes, "Sometimes Zuckerberg can sound like a wheedling spokesman for the secret police of some future totalitarian state. Why wouldn't you want to share? Why wouldn't you want to be open—unless you've got *something to hide?* 'Having two identities for yourself is an example of a lack of integrity,' Zuckerberg said in a 2009 interview."[115] In other words, Zuckerberg's response to users' reservations about sharing the same information with coworkers as with family members or close friends is to suggest that these people lack character. His choice of the word "integrity," meaning both moral uprightness and the state of being whole, is noteworthy. Evidently, to have integrity is to conform to oneself and to behave as a reliable consumer who can then be targeted reliably by advertisers. For an industry based on targeting users with advertisements and influencing their future behavior, unpredictability is not merely a social liability; it's also an economic liability. However, the notion of one essential self that can and should be presented to the world in all the same pictures, posts, and "likes," again collapses the self into a single unbroken line that cuts across the realities of how people live. In other words, Zuckerberg strategically frames difference as deception, a vice that should be overcome through the therapeutic practice of "sharing," which will then, of course, generate more data used "to preempt disruptions and make users more predictable."[116] Last, the irony of Zuckerberg's statement is that data profiling itself has "two identities": the public-facing profiles on platforms that captivate users and the obscured data profiles that capitalize on their habits and information. Indeed, these "two identities" are integral to their business model, which depends on the notion that algorithmic surveillance is interested in us "for all the right reasons" (to quote the parlance of reality television) while also entirely disinterested in us personally.

Still, the partiality of data profiles belies the pseudo-omniscient metanarrative they project. We are told that Big Data resolves the predicaments posed by postmodernism with new ways of mapping and navigating our "increasingly confused and confusing globalized world," and yet consumer-users are left "always searching, rarely finding." While the "conversion of the world into nodes and edges—agents and connections—is imagined as dissolving postmodern confusion,"[117] this supposed advancement "has not enabled individual subjects to understand and change the system; rather it has been used to preempt disruption and make users more predictable."[118] Confronting this world view, twenty-first-century fiction widens the cracks between the "nodes and edges" to make room for minoritarian movements and new ways of being and seeing to seep through. Chun describes networks and data analytics "moving away from subjects and narratives, towards actors and captured actions that they knit into a monstrously connected chimera."[119] However, it's important to understand that even as networks ostensibly replace stories with data, "they [still] *imagine* connections"[120] that they compose or "knit" into a narrative that inscribes people as "monstrously" patchworked profiles. At times adopting characteristics of literary postmodernism, the works analyzed in *Profiles and Plotlines* accentuate the seams where actions are knit together in the new master narratives of neoliberalism and algorithmic governance. They show the constructedness of Big Data's patchwork, in part, by reminding us of their own partiality and composition. After all, as Rosi Braidotti warns, "attempting to reconcile the pieces would be madness."[121] In other words, we are better off recognizing that the discontents of neoliberalism cannot be solved by more neoliberalism. We are better off recognizing that the persistent "confusion" is not just our own. As data surveillance repackages and expedites familiar systems of oppression, postmodernist tactics reopen supposedly closed circuits and create space for elaboration, creation. In the words of Luce Irigaray, "It's our good fortune that your language isn't formed of a single thread, a single strand or pattern. . . . You touch me all over at the same time. In all senses."[122]

Metadata and Metanarratives

> What sort of world is it that obliges us to take into account,
> at the same time and in the same breath, the nature of things,
> technologies, sciences, fictional beings, religions large and small,
> politics, jurisdictions, economies, and unconsciousnesses?
> Our own, of course.
> —BRUNO LATOUR, *We Have Never Been Modern* (129)

One clear strategy of data surveillance is to project "an unchangeable perspective, a way of situating without ever being situated."[123] This assumes the authority to pinpoint consumer-citizens within sociopolitical and commercial culture while evading supervision, much less regulation. In part, state and corporate surveillance manage this through what Pasquale calls "black boxes" that shelter indecipherable privacy "agreements" and proprietary algorithms.[124] In contrast, the literature I write about situates digital surveillance within the social and political economy to destabilize its supposed omniscience and truth-power. In other words, it watches the watchers. Still, to avoid reproducing the logics of surveillance, the novels and poetry invite readers to reflect on literature's own ways of seeing and knowing.

Too often "the data" is evoked as an obfuscation or excuse—a rhetorical retreat that positions data analytics as somehow observing from outside the world, above and beyond the social (perhaps from the cloud; it's unclear). This abstract stance suggests that data science is about the world without being of the world. Marsha Kinder insists that every "database or archive is designed for a particular kind of knowledge production with specific goals, and the decision of what items to include or exclude, and what categories to use as structuring principles, and what metadata to collect for later retrieval—all of these decisions serve master narratives with ideological implications."[125] Well-meaning fear over "politicizing" "the data" misunderstands not only how data is already and unavoidably political and social, it also presumes that such attempts to stand on firm ground won't themselves be politicized. I argue that if the data scientists working for the public good were more transparent about how data analytics really function as a process involving people, politics, objects, institutions, and so on, they would be in a stronger position to convince people of their claims. To be sure, the fact that Big Data has a narrative dimension is a strength and not a vulnerability. Suppressing it (and implicitly framing it as a weakness) is disingenuous; it is also a lost opportunity to situate scientific data in the social world—indeed, to be scientific about it. Otherwise, data science itself becomes a "master narrative," incapable of self-reflection. Here we might bring to bear the insights of literary and rhetorical theory. Literature more broadly and metafiction in particular make explicit that omniscience is always a fictional conceit and should not be taken literally.

Characteristically explicit about its own constructedness, cognizant of the Heisenberg uncertainty principle, and skeptical of totalizing perspectives, postmodern literature emphasizes (explicitly or implicitly) that selves are co-constituted through multiple other points of view, including the surveillant and now algorithmic gaze. Rather than misrepresenting characters as coherent and fully knowable, the twenty-first-century literature discussed in this volume represents the lapses and leaps in computational thinking, breaking open the machines to show their inner workings, their recycled bits, their shiny new seductive pieces, their fragile gears, their inflexible codes, and their human "administrators."[126] By sometimes adopting the surveillant point of view, these novels illustrate the narrative structure and discursivity of this machinery, which often produces an unreliable narrator. By demonstrating that this world is constructed from familiar materials and systems, none of which are magical, they indicate that other worlds are possible. They also expose the cracks and crevices that this "liquid surveillance" seeps into, altering the terrain as it goes.[127] In their pages, we see that digital surveillance does not just operate from atop a tall watch tower but oozes and flows into politics, economics, and the inner lives of consumer-citizens. We also see that literature, even more nimbly, can expose the effects, affects, and permutations of this profiling.

Although certainly not a new narrative technique, metafiction emerged in the 1960s as an influential tactic among postmodern writers for theorizing representational modes and the construction of knowledge. As Patricia Waugh puts it, metafiction arises from "a more general cultural interest in the problem of how human beings reflect, construct and mediate their experience in the world."[128] Given its self-reflexive interest in representation and mediation, contemporary metafiction is now especially well suited to grapple with digital surveillance and the proliferation of metadata. While not all the texts I analyze are overtly metafictional, they do reflect on their construction to contend with how data surveillance mediates consumer-citizens' experiences and subjectivities. Characters become self-conscious of how their digital identities and subjectivities in profile culture are not just texts but indexes. We become overdetermined, searchable selves. Behavior, experiences, and characteristics are distilled and cross-referenced to create terms such as "future inheritor," or "likely Democratic midterm voter."

Whereas the protagonists in works by Kathy Acker and John Barth come to recognize themselves as characters, the protagonists of the novels and lyric poetry in *Profiles and Plotlines* come to see themselves—however fleetingly—as traceable, fungible data sets. Like their postmodern forebears, these characters are often struck by their own fragmentation and intertextuality. At times they glimpse the surveillant assemblage and recognize themselves as moving targets. Jodi Dean writes that "A critical theory of communicative capitalism requires occupying (rather than disavowing) the trap in which it enthralls and configures contemporary subjects," and the literature herein inhabits this trap.[129] Characters are not necessarily aware that an author has written them into existence in the likes of John Fowles's *Mantissa*, but they do recognize that their existence is prefigured by their data doubles and shaped by the material and rhetorical forces of surveillance. Of course, metafiction has long been interested in surveillance, but while Thomas Pynchon's early fiction, for example, is steeped in Cold War paranoia and the possibility of some intrigue to be untangled, contemporary fiction theorizes not only the ubiquity but also the disturbing banality of being watched.

Specifically, the literature reclaims and reinvigorates the increasingly toothless notion of "self-expression" within the political economy of consumer surveillance.[130] David Foster Wallace laid bare how television and consumer culture robbed irony of its bite in the 1990s;[131] now profile culture is hollowing out the notion of self-expression. Wallace's remedy was for fiction to embrace a new sincerity, to become less bloodless. However, it is precisely the bloodless engagement with consumer-users that makes profiling seem palatable and noninvasive to the public. Profiles are personalized but not personal. Profilers also depend on our sincerity and openness to garner as many "actionable insights" as possible. Yet as a result, self-expression has become a trite capitalist commonplace—itself regarded with ironic detachment. How do contemporary novelists respond? Rather than making simplistic appeals to privacy, they question how both "the self" and "expression" have been reconfigured as data streams; they contextualize "selves" and "self-expression" to account for the forces and discourses that shape them.

Wallace writes, "If the postmodern church fathers found pop images valid *referents* and *symbols* in fiction, and if in the seventies and early '80s this appeal to the features of mass culture shifted from *use* to *mention* . . the new Fiction of Image uses the transient received myths of popular culture as a *world* in which to imagine fictions about 'real,' albeit pop-mediated, public characters."[132] Now the "mediated public characters" that prefigure many contemporary literary characters are dividual data doubles. In other words, while Robert Coover reimagined Richard Nixon and Max Apple fictionalized Walt Disney,[133] many contemporary authors are writing characters haunted by their pattern of life profiles. These profiles begin as the "transient received myths" of who people really are. In "fictionalizing" data profiles, the authors highlight how they were already fictions or myths to begin with. As literary postmodernism long maintained, there is no stable, essential subject; today we might say that there are just interplays between the profile and the person. Both are socially and economically constructed. Both are born at the intersections of social, ideological, economic, and political forces. Both are fragmentary and mediated. Neither is natural, objective, or whole. The pressing questions become not about identity per se but about risk, power, credibility, embodiment, and epistemology.

Finally, the following chapters explore the critical self-reflection that our culture of nearly ubiquitous data profiling demands of contemporary literature and literary studies. Given its penchant for "metawatching"—or watching itself watch the watchers—contemporary literature is especially well suited to not only challenge the aesthetics, thematics, and ideologies of digital surveillance but also to enact a form of "oppositional looking" or countersurveillance. We see this, for example, with the recent interest in "documentary poetics" that would certainly include Claudia Rankine's Citizen.[134] Meanwhile, the forces of the data age put pressure on writers to reckon with the ways literature too can reproduce the regressive logics of surveillance. Wallace characterized fiction writers as "born watchers,"[135] but this affinity for observing and writing the lives of others must contend with a literary tradition that too often equates authorship with hegemonic authority and the white male gaze. The fiction I engage with in this book, therefore, reflects on its own positionality and ways of knowing and seeing in a world where profiles prefigure characters and underwrite their identities.

Specifically, the literature discussed here considers how the writer's perspective, while not totalizing, may nevertheless reflect privilege; how observation or surveillance is always political, contextual, and embodied; and how identity is both an "artistic construct" and a commercial or economic construct.[136] The history of the postmodern literary canon makes clear how the presumed authority of being both a white man and a writer are entangled, and this conflation of authorship and authority can reproduce the dominant logics of surveillance. In other words, it not just that literature has an explanatory power to address data surveillance and its speculative economics, but that literature has also been affected by this reality, which must prompt further self-reflection on the politics and ethics of literature and literary studies. In a sense, the rise of Big Data makes urgent the need for fiction that is self-conscious of its own gaze and methods of meaning-making. It calls for

Introduction

a self-reflexivity that does not equate authorship with authority even as it considers the power relations of watching and being watched. Importantly, the realities of data profiling provide literature and literary studies with new perspective on their own limitations and blind spots. As D. A. Miller and Mark Seltzer have both famously argued,[137] literature can all too easily reproduce the disciplinary power structures that it critiques. Indeed, the novels and poetry in *Profiles and Plotlines* are grounded in societies of control, occupying that territory to reveal its fragility and limitations, which are also their own. Although fiction certainly does not sit outside history and structures of power, it can smuggle in that which data cannot see.

Structurally dependent on point of view and perception, literature can't help but engage surveillance. Books invite readers into new perspectives, spaces, thought processes, and experiences. Yet unlike data discourse, literature also trains readers to see this insight as subjective, partial. The literature I have selected here is not just incidentally entangled with systems of surveillance; it activates these systems to highlight their dependencies and externalities. After all, the blind spots of surveillance are by design. It's the excess that defines the field of focus and reveals the underlying ideologies. In response, the novels and poetry in *Profiles and Plotlines* enact a countersurveillance, insisting on the subjectivity and narrative dimension of algorithmic governance that is strategically held just out of sight.

Of course, a novel might reinforce the harmful truth-claims of Big Data, such as "if you have nothing to hide, you have nothing to fear," but the very structure of literature and literary analysis challenge those sort of decontextualized claims. We can only understand characters' habits, locations, and behaviors in contexts that are irreducible. Drawing correlations won't suffice. Literature demands analysis and even so the interpretations are open to new readings depending, in part, on the audience's context and perspective. The very role of readers stipulates that literature never "speaks for itself." That authors channel—as both mediums and canals—the discourses, views, affects, worries, and wonders of culture means that the author figure can never speak for itself. Novels and poetry can, of course, reproduce the same troubling ideologies that uphold algorithmic governance, but their literariness always belies the underlying supposition that with enough discrete data, people are fundamentally and objectively knowable.

The first chapter, "Watching the Watchers: Metadata and Feminist

Introduction

Metafiction in Jennifer Egan's *A Visit from the Goon Squad*," considers how metafiction in particular is capable of contending with the significance of metadata and data surveillance, given its preoccupation with watching itself watch. Making a critical intervention in the historically male-centered canon of US metafiction, the novel conscientiously engages the power relations of watching. Comprising thirteen interrelated short stories set between 1973 and 2024, *Goon Squad* centers around changes in the music industry due to digitization. In the background of the novel and at its chronological center are the attacks on September 11 and, incidentally, the launch of the iPod. In a sense, these two events structure the novel's investments in data surveillance. Moreover, to the extent that the novel's form mirrors a musical album, it also forms a network of characters, speaking to a more complicated set of forces that convert analog recordings into digital data but also translate relationships, habits, and subjectivity into metadata. Finally, my reading of *Goon Squad* suggests that the profile industry's relatively new mandate that consumer-users be both "irresistible and invisible" has long been demanded of women,[138] thereby contextualizing the epistemology of the profile industry and consumer surveillance within patriarchy and celebrity culture.

The second chapter, "Out of Line: Affective Counterstrategies to Racializing Surveillance and Profile Epistemology in Claudia Rankine's *Citizen*," contextualizes contemporary data profiling and social sorting in the history of racial discrimination, surveillance, and biometrics. I argue that engaging surveillance entails not only reckoning with the legacies of slavery and white supremacy but also learning from the history of Black resistance. In an extended passage, Rankine portrays the treatment of tennis player Serena Williams by the media and referees, highlighting the development of "hawkeye" technology to officiate the games. Ultimately, *Citizen* illustrates how, in the face of racial discrimination, this sort of technological solutionism adds insult on top of injury. In this chapter, I argue that the common defense of surveillance that "if you have nothing to hide, then you have nothing to fear" is entangled with racialized respectability politics, which insist on a "proper" response to racism. After all, in the overlapping systems of white supremacy and ubiquitous surveillance, outrage is mistaken for guilt. Finally, I address how critical race theory and affect theory can open up forms of oppositional looking and countersurveillance to undermine the ostensible objectivity of data.

The third chapter, "'Both a Gift and a Trap': Speculative Surveillance and Labor in William Gibson's *Pattern Recognition*," analyzes the novel's passage from the simulacra of brand culture and consumption to the sites of hidden labor in the profile economy. The elaborate plot of *Pattern Recognition* stages an arms race between the protagonist, Cayce Pollard, and an advertising executive, Hubertus Bigend, to find the "maker" of a series of online viral videos. As a devoted fan, Cayce hopes to protect the footage from corporate co-optation, while Bigend's interest lies in "the numbers." I argue that regardless of whether the footage is ever monetized, the fans already have been. That is, in the speculative economy of data profiling, the "numbers" are the product. With a twist on the traditional Marxist narrative, the novel offers a rich surveillance-scape that systematically underexposes labor and production by overexposing brands and consumer-citizens themselves.

The final chapter, "Data Fictions, Neoliberal Narratives, and the Military-Industrial Gaze in Mohsin Hamid's *How to Get Filthy Rich in Rising Asia*," figures data surveillance and profiling as both the "carrot and the stick" in neoliberalism.[139] On the one hand, security surveillance is presented as aspirational, a privilege of the wealthy and powerful. On the other hand, profiling is a means of targeting "risky" subjects and actively producing them by exacerbating the unequal distribution of life chances. The protagonist of the novel, simply called "You," is born impoverished and jaundiced in the countryside of Pakistan and dies having amassed and then lost a great deal of wealth as a water industrialist. As a parody of the self-help genre, Hamid humorously and tragically represents the "cruel optimism" of neoliberal appeals to personal responsibility and how they intersect with profile culture.[140] Ultimately, Hamid produces what I call "surveillance storytelling" or "data fiction." In effect, the novel hacks into the structures and infrastructures of surveillance to create "your" profile and tell the story of "you" differently. Specifically, the novel takes on surveillance by the "world's military apparatuses" in the era of drone warfare, portraying the discursivity of this machine, which actually characterizes as it profiles. Like Rankine's *Citizen*, *Filthy Rich* is written in the second person, speaking to the shift within profile culture from a "we" or "they" to "a series of interconnecting and connected 'YOUs.'"[141] In distinct ways, each text engages point of view to reckon with and resist efforts to transfigure subjectivity into moving targets through data surveillance and analytics.

Introduction

The conclusion, "Amazon, Authorship, and Algorithmic Governance," turns toward Amazon as exemplary of how surveillance capitalism attempts to algorithmically author the future. While Mark McGurl rightly argues that Amazon has reshaped the literary landscape in part by contributing to its genre-fication, I argue that this is best understood alongside the proliferation of data profiles, which have effectively constructed ever more exacting genres of consumer-citizens. In other words, I maintain that the company's impact on contemporary literature and society derives largely from its tight embrace of data surveillance and profile epistemology. Jeff Bezos credits Amazon's success to its self-proclaimed obsession with customer service, but the conclusion makes clear that customer service can no longer be understood outside of data discourse. Finally, *Profiles and Plotlines* ends by highlighting data's potential to become a public good that does good for the public.

CHAPTER ONE

Watching the Watchers

Metadata and Feminist Metafiction in
Jennifer Egan's A Visit from the Goon Squad

N eoliberalism demands that consumer-citizens dutifully manage their personal profiles like investment accounts. As it happens, individuals have about as much control over their data profiles as they do over financial markets. Sure, we can post only the most prudent pictures under the most restrictive security settings or pick only the most prudent investments, but ultimately, the algorithms and systems that govern both are largely opaque.[1] Moreover, some people have a greater interest in sustaining this opacity while others are more vulnerable to faulty profiling and predatory marketing. Data from shopping records, credit reports, and computer clicks are aggregated in profiles attempting to appraise and represent a person's riskiness and human capital. Personal data is collected, interpreted, repackaged, and auctioned off. In other words, profiles presume to make human capital visible and rateable in an economy of speculation.[2] For this reason, a study of profiles is inextricable from the politics of surveillance and metawatching.[3]

As a form of surveillance, often preoccupied with watching itself watch, metafiction can help contextualize the proliferation of personal data profiles within a longer history of surveillance that links nineteenth-century imperialism to twenty-first-century security apparatuses and the state's growing cooperation with the consumer surveillance industry. At its best, metafiction models open-book transparency by the watchers, while simultaneously allowing for individuals (or characters) to remain complex and irreducible. Even as this book, in part, critiques contemporary profile society, metafiction—as a technology of surveillance—clarifies that watching in and of itself is not the problem. After all, as Upton Sinclair and Edward Snowden have illustrated, society needs watchers. Nevertheless, whether reading metafiction or metadata, we must conscientiously consider the power relations between the target and the watcher.

Of Jennifer Egan's *A Visit from the Goon Squad*, a *Washington Post* book reviewer cheered, "If Jennifer Egan is our reward for living through the self-conscious gimmicks and ironic claptrap of postmodernism, then it was all worthwhile."[4] Egan's Pulitzer Prize–winning novel comprises thirteen interrelated short stories, reflexively written in various literary styles, yet it avoids the stigma of gimmicky metafiction. I argue that this is partly because, in addition to being self-reflexive and formally experimental, *Goon Squad* engages the ideologies underpinning postmodern metafiction. Pivoting on Patricia Waugh's definition of metafiction as "fictional writing which self-consciously and systematically draws attention to its status as an artifact in order to pose questions about the relationship between fiction and reality," I suggest that Egan's data-fiction also interrogates the modes of ambient surveillance sitting at the intersection of "fiction and reality."[5] In other words, *Goon Squad* keenly depicts the politics of positionality with regard to surveillance, metadata, and metafiction.

Since at least the 1960s, metafiction has critically engaged perspective and reflexivity, so it is now well positioned to contend with the meaning and consequences of metadata. Egan's work draws on the critical contributions of metafiction while still acknowledging that it can assume asymmetrical power relations. Feminist critics, for example, have pointed out that as feminism, postcolonialism, and critical race theory worked to recover lost histories and narratives, writers of metafiction (and postmodernism more broadly) conveniently pronounced the end of historical metanarratives. Sabina Lovibond asks, "How can anyone ask me to say goodbye to 'emancipatory metanarratives' when my own emancipation is still such a patchy, hit-and-miss affair?"[6] Now metadata provides an emerging model of history that can be either "cached" or "cleared" but, most importantly, sold.[7] This is the new history of *homo economicus*—told through profiles that affect consumer-users unevenly. To be sure, this neoliberal version of history written in metadata reinforces and widens existing inequalities. Egan's work suggests that as long as writers elide their own subject positions and privileges, metafiction and metadata emerge as mirror images in a neoliberal funhouse.

Of course, metafiction has long been interested in surveillance, but while Pynchon's early fiction, for example, is steeped in Cold War paranoia and the possibility of some intrigue to be untangled, Egan's novel theorizes not only the ubiquity but also the disturbing banality of being watched. It's not conspiracy—it's capitalism. *Goon Squad* not only "draws attention to its status as an artifact," it also highlights the consumer-user's status as an object or renewable resource to be mined by portraying the narrative and regulatory power of profiles to police people as divisible and searchable code.

Egan's work brings the lessons of metafiction to bear on our understanding of profile society: the fallacy of grand narratives or totalizing perspectives, the Heisenberg uncertainty principle that observing something necessarily affects it, and the recognition that identity is always already an "artistic construct."[8] Meanwhile, her work illustrates crucial lessons of profile society that must likewise inform our understanding of metafiction: that the writer's perspective, though not totalizing, may nevertheless reflect privilege; that observation or surveillance is political, contextual, and embodied; and that while identity is an "artistic construct," it is also a commercial construct. *Goon Squad* speaks to both sets of concerns, at once critiquing postmodern metafiction and drawing on the characteristics or tactics of literary postmodernism to confront the preoccupations of the data age. Specifically, Egan's novel emphasizes the need for feminist metafiction that critically addresses the power relations of writing, watching, and surveillance.

Profiling consumer-users is a growing industry that demands ever more sophisticated and ubiquitous forms of data collection. The profiles represent neither individuals nor populations but the endlessly divisible subject, encoded and dispersed in data. As such, the profile industry positions subjects schizophrenically straddling the individual/mass divide. It insists that people feel simultaneously newsworthy and relatively insignificant. These contradictory states of mind encourage consumer-users to casually "share" their habits, purchases, "likes," photographs, and whereabouts. Celebrity culture underwrites this comprehensive surveillance by promoting the perception that a high public profile reflects high human capital and self-worth. Accordingly, social media, such as Facebook, Instagram, and Twitter position themselves as public relations firms for the famous and nonfamous alike, tracking and treating "followers" or "friends" as a fan base. For instance, a Facebook ad depicts a woman holding a microphone alongside the copy "If you've got friends, you've got fans," dangerously conflating the two. Of course, as Jodi Dean acknowledges, "most people in technoculture know full well that they aren't *really* celebrities"; still, "even if one knows that she isn't a celebrity, she acts as if she believes she were" because "the technologies believe for her."[9]

Through the lens of celebrity culture, what might be considered an invasion of privacy is dismissed as the price of publicity. Conversely, the more the culture focuses on "celebrities who try to perform our publicness for us," the more anonymity and relative privacy the public feels in contrast.[10] Relatedly, social media's emphasis on user-generated profiles distracts from the industry's far more extensive practices of data-based profiling that are concealed and pardoned by cursory privacy agreements. Supported by celebrity culture, the profile industry cultivates complete disclosure and self-promotion as well as the delusion of anonymity. As Egan summarizes in her story "Black Box," first released on Twitter 120 characters at a time: "The goal is to be both irresistible and invisible."[11] Finally, Egan's fiction acknowledges that the profile industry's relatively new mandate that consumer-users be both "irresistible and invisible" has long been demanded of women, and her work steadfastly contextualizes surveillance and the profile industry within patriarchal power.

By setting *Goon Squad* around the music industry's transition from analog to digital media, Egan teases out the symbiotic relationship between the profile industry and celebrity culture. While the character Bennie Salazar, a disillusioned music producer, blames the music "industry's decline" on digitization,[12] the novel critiques a more complicated set of forces that do not simply convert analog recordings into digital data but, more disturbingly, translate consumer behavior into metadata. In other words, Egan sets her characters' anxieties about "selling out" in the larger context of neoliberalism and widespread data profiling. As Bennie puts it, "It's not about music. It's about reach" (312). Accordingly, the novel not only structurally and stylistically resembles a concept album, it also approximates a database of networked characters. Rather than simply denouncing digital technology, Egan's account of the recent history of the music industry scrutinizes the "reach" of the profile industry.

Overseeing and Overlooking

Chronologically, the novel begins with the chapter "Safari," which sets Lou, a music executive, his girlfriend Mindy, his two children, and his bandmates on a safari in Kenya. The story is especially thick with themes of watching. It also carries the baggage of the great white male explorer made so familiar by Ernest Hemingway, who is credited with first introducing the Swahili word *safari* into English. In fact, this chapter specifically recalls Hemingway's contentious short story "The Short Happy Life of Francis Macomber": both stories are about safaris in Kenya, and they share an implied affair between the central female character and the tour guide. In Egan's story, the "surly" guide, Albert—"with his longish brown hair and mustache" (64)—"looks like a real explorer" (74) to Lou's son, evoking the histories of how a "real explorer" appears and sees. The chapter depicts what could be called safari surveillance, which combines the imperial tourist gaze, rooted in naturalizing and trivializing "the Other," with a form of violent masculinity. Lou's band-mates, for example, are "locked in a visceral animal-sighting competition," indicating that visual mastery and the threat of danger are integral to the experience (66). Even when one of the men is attacked by a lioness, who is then shot and killed in an entirely preventable encounter, the characters gleefully regard the event as a "story they'll tell for the rest of their lives" (71). This is reminiscent of Hemingway's characters approaching Africa as a testing ground for violent masculinity.

Crucially, this power (like tourism and surveillance) depends on overlooking as much as it oversees. Egan projects this history into the future when one of the "Samburu warriors" will have a grandson, Joe, who "will go to college at Columbia and study engineering, becoming an expert in visual robotic technology that detects the slightest hint of irregular movement (the legacy of a childhood spent scanning the grass for lions). He'll marry an American named Lulu and remain in New York, where he'll invent a scanning device that becomes standard issue for crowd security" (62). We see Joe and his "visual robotic technology" briefly in the novel's final chapter, "Pure Language," set in 2024.[13] This genealogy between "scanning the grass for lions" and "a scanning device . . . for crowd security" connects the lookout for dangerous animals with the security state's investment in detecting "irregular movement." Egan draws out the racist legacy of this colonial gaze when Lou sees his daughter, Charlie, dancing "alone, by the fire" and "wants to grab [her] skinny arm and yank her away from these black men, but does no such thing, of course. That would be letting her win" (61). His response to Charlie dancing near "these black men" as well his concern over "letting her win" epitomizes the patriarchal and sexual economy of colonial white masculinity.

While ostensibly an opportunity to see parts of Africa, the safari—which centers white Western men—deliberately conceals and makes unintelligible the experience of the African people, represented as a dangerous "black, muttering expanse of the bush, where they've been cautioned never to go" (62). Although interaction with African men is unavoidable during the safari, Egan's prose—consciously or otherwise—signals the complete invisibility and incomprehensibility of African women. For example, even as we learn that one of the warriors dancing next to Charlie eventually has a grandson who will marry a white American woman, the novel never mentions the black African grandmother or mother. Indeed, whether "scanning" Africa or "scanning" a crowd, surveillance is always a matter of whom and what is overlooked as well as overseen.

By tracing future technology used for security back to the safari and imperial alibis of protecting white women, Egan situates "crowd control" and the proliferation of surveillance technologies in a longer history of imperialism. After all, surveillance technologies are not developed in a vacuum outside the context of social injustice. On the contrary, they are often the vanguard of violence against gendered and racialized others. Not unlike the optics of safaris, state surveillance—represented by Joe's "robotic eye" and the "whirring" helicopters—is designed to expose and expunge "dangerous" subjects, which is itself a political category.

Not only do "Safari" and "Pure Language" (the first and last chapters, chronologically) draw out the connections between imperialism and security apparatuses through the warrior and his grandson, they also represent the link between state surveillance and rampant consumer surveillance, pointing toward this real and troubling cooperation. Like these other forms of watching, consumer surveillance is designed to conceal both its "reach" and biases (formalized in algorithms). In Goon Squad, we move from the edges of the "the bush," which has long been misrepresented as "pure nature," to glimpsing backstage at the distilled and ostensibly "pure language" of profiling and marketing, for which Joe's wife, Lulu, is the poster child. Working for Bennie Salazar to orchestrate a word-of-mouth marketing campaign for Scotty Hausmann's upcoming concert, Lulu uses marketing jargon from her graduate classes to recruit Alex. Despite his ethical reservations about working in secret, Alex accepts Bennie's offer that "each team member would deal individually with Lulu, with Alex orchestrating in secret from above" (319).

That is, the "blind team" is unaware that there is a third level of oversight. While much is made of the novel's lateral structure that obviously invokes the internet and social media, *Goon Squad* also draws attention to the hierarchies of communication, visibility, and capital that are most often concealed. For example, most consumer-users are well aware that Facebook, Google, or any given internet platform is overseeing their communications and usage, but they might be unaware of the extent to which their data is visible to third parties, including paramilitary and law enforcement agencies.[14] The marriage of Lulu and Joe dramatizes the marriage of security and consumer surveillance, both of which depend on overseeing the consumer-citizens who are overlooking this troubling partnership.

"A graduate student at Barnard *and* Bennie's full-time assistant," Lulu is "a living embodiment of the new 'handset employee': paperless, deskless, commuteless, and theoretically omnipresent" (317). Like the term *blind team*, which strategically evokes the friendly rhetoric of sports, "full-time" takes on new meaning here. Following current trends, the fact that Lulu's work is "paperless, deskless, and commuteless" actually means that there is more of it, even (or especially) as it is rendered less visible. This has surely become a familiar reality for many during the COVID-19 pandemic. In this regard, Egan evokes the feminization of "handset employees" like Lulu, whose invisible labor emulates that of mothers. Moreover, Egan draws out how the uncounted (and therefore deeply discounted) feminized labor of postindustrial society directly depends on the technologies and techniques of ubiquitous surveillance. Mark Fisher's book *Capitalist Realism* situates this "new 'handset employee'" in the societies of control identified by Gilles Deleuze, which "operate using indefinite postponement: Education as a lifelong process . . . Training that persists for as long as your working life continues . . . Work you take home with you . . . Working from home, homing from work."[15] Given the new popularity of Zoom, for instance, we might think about how this platform, as convenient as it has been, participates in modes of surveillance while extending the work day and users' supposed availability. Ironically, this has meant that as people perform more discounted or free labor,[16] the tech companies have yielded what Zuboff aptly called "stratospheric profits" during the pandemic, largely through algorithmic surveillance.[17] Moreover, an important "consequence of this 'indefinite' mode of power is that external surveillance is succeeded by internal policing."[18] Lulu exemplifies this exhausting work of self-control in postindustrial societies—along with the bodily symptoms it produces.

Lulu is aware of the metaphors we live by and argues to Alex that "those metaphors" for critiquing new forms of marketing—"'up front' and 'out in the open'—are part of a system we call atavistic purism. AP implies the existence of an ethically perfect state, which not only doesn't exist and never existed, but it's usually used to shore up the prejudices of whoever's making the judgments" (319). On one hand, Lulu acknowledges that there is no "pure language," but on the other hand, she seeks solace in "capitalist realism" and the rationalizations of neoliberalism, which purport to operate outside ideology as simple facts of nature. Egan mockingly portrays Lulu as a disciple of this thinking the same way that she portrays the book's other graduate student, Mindy, as a disciple of structural anthropology. Yet by linking neoliberal capitalism to structuralism, imperialism to law enforcement, and state surveillance to consumer surveillance, Egan underscores the naïveté and cost of accepting these systems as "pure."

When Alex deconstructs Lulu's reasoning, she is overcome with exhaustion and the physical symptoms of maintaining this capitalist realism:

> Lulu underwent the most extreme blush Alex had ever witnessed: a vermilion heat encompassed her face so abruptly that the effect was of something violent taking place, as if she were choking or about to hemorrhage. . . .
> "You're right," Lulu said, taking a rickety breath. "I apologize."
> "No sweat," Alex said. The blush had unsettled him more than Lulu's confidence. He watched it drain from her face, leaving her skin a jarring white. "You okay?" he asked.
> "I'm fine. I just get tired of talking."
> "Ditto," Alex said. He felt exhausted.
> "There are so many ways to go wrong," Lulu said. "All we've got are metaphors, and they're never exactly right. You can't ever just Say. The. Thing" (312).

By emphasizing Lulu's physical symptoms ("the most extreme blush . . . a vermilion heat . . . as if she were choking or about to hemorrhage . . . rickety breath . . . her skin a jarring white"), Egan turns questions of linguistics back toward the body, materialism, and affect. As Fisher points out, "Without delirium and confidence, capital could not function,"[19] and Lulu embodies this struggle. This is labor, and it is exhausting precisely because the body is never exhausted by language. However, neither is the body simply "*The. Thing.*" that exists outside language. Rather, the body stands at the threshold between binaries—public and private, internal and external, natural and social—and is thus a powerful place to consider and begin deconstructing the conflict that Lulu experiences.

As an exemplary "handset employee," Lulu relies on the "pure language" of marketing and attempts to repress the body by, for example, forswearing the language of epidemiology in favor of physics: "'no one says "viral" anymore,' Lulu said. 'I mean, maybe thoughtlessly . . . now we study particle physics'" (317). By emphasizing Lulu's physical response to the constraints of language, Egan stages the return of the repressed, not just for Lulu but also for postmodern metafiction, which, like modernism, still perpetuates a mind/body dualism that charges women with "being the body for men while men are left free to soar to the heights of theoretical reflection and cultural production."[20] This is also the problem that feminist studies of surveillance and metadata must confront. By tracing the genealogy from safari surveillance to security surveillance to consumer surveillance, we see that surveillance is designed to conceal certain externalities.

Metafiction, on the other hand, ostensibly reveals externalities and demonstrates how they were always already internal to the text. Egan presses on these connections to illustrate how metafiction has also produced its own outsiders through what amounts to a similar set of biases. Throughout *Goon Squad*, Egan embeds minor characters into the margins to observe the action. Most notably, two "elderly bird-watching ladies" occupy a readerly position of overhearing or overseeing the safari from the periphery (60). Analogously, the chapter's title recalls the Apple Safari web browser, which casts users as explorers, while layers of hidden "trackers" inconspicuously monitor their movements across the web. After a private conversation between Lou's girlfriend, Mindy, and the safari guide with whom she has a quiet affair, "it occurs to Mindy, vaguely, that the elderly bird-watcher was inside the jeep the whole time that she and Albert were talking" (70). To continue the analogy, it is not that people are entirely unaware that their seemingly private actions and interactions are monitored; it is just that this awareness remains "vague" and unthreatening. Lou's daughter also notes, "The bird-watchers are watching us," and in the final sentence of the chapter, her brother says, "I don't think those ladies were ever watching birds" (83). Egan repeatedly highlights the bird-watchers' inconspicuousness, explaining that "being old and female, they're easily missed" (72). If the bird-watchers symbolize the seemingly innocuous "friendly" power of surveillance, I argue that metafictionally they also represent undervalued and "easily [dis]missed" female readers and writers. For example, after declining Oprah Winfrey's invitation to be included in the Oprah Book Club, Jonathan Franzen expressed dissatisfaction with the idea of writing for a predominantly female readership:

> So much of reading is sustained in this country, I think, by the fact that women read while men are off golfing or watching football on TV or playing with their flight simulator or whatever. I worry—I'm sorry that it's, uh—I had some hope of actually reaching a male audience and I've heard more than one reader in signing lines now at bookstores say "If I hadn't heard you, I would have been put off by the fact that it is an Oprah pick. I figure those books are for women. I would never touch it."[21]

Franzen feebly distances himself from the implicit disparagement of books that are seemingly "for women," by adding, "those are male readers speaking."[22] Nevertheless, the clear implication is that capital-L literature is not only meant for men, but it is, by definition, the literature that men read.

Incidentally, as Laura Helmuth explains in her article, "Jonathan Franzen Is the World's Most Annoying Bird-Watcher," Franzen is also "probably the most famous [bird-watcher], thanks to his novels and the essays he's written for *The New Yorker* about his birding exploits."[23] Franzen frequently frets about his image (he has to wear a birding-bra!) and fears that bird watching makes him too conspicuous in New York City, all while rejoicing in the power of watching a feminized view of nature. In all of his celebrations of bird-watching, he is decidedly the subject, while the birds—often conflated with his past lovers—are clearly the objects.[24] Moreover, he carefully establishes that his "affair with birds" makes him a better lover and not more feminine as he worries people might think, exclaiming, "How different my marriage might have been if I'd been able to go birding!"[25] Parroting this sort of sexism, the women in Egan's chapter are either dangerously visible (Mindy and Charlie stand out like wild animals) or virtually invisible (Fiona and Mildred blend into the scenery like plants). By foiling Franzen's persona as a bird-watcher, "the elderly bird-watching ladies" call attention to alternative subject positions for women as readers/writers/watchers, which don't rely on overidentifying with the object or assuming the male gaze. Egan emphasizes that the bird-watchers are practically invisible to the other characters, but the narration repeatedly highlights their presence and the fact that they are watching. By evoking Franzen, his take on "watching," and his standing in the literary community, Egan's work productively addresses the politics and privilege of watching or metawatching, which too often includes the surveillance of women as nature.

Overseeing and Overhearing

Critics have noted that September 11, 2001, is at the chronological center of *Goon Squad*, but so is the launch of the (now retired) iPod, which occurred on October 23, 2001. New methods of consumer surveillance engendered by the iPod and the success of iTunes coincide with the surge in state surveillance and profiling post-9/11. In *Security, Territory, Population*, Foucault outlines that "sovereignty is exercised within the borders of a territory, discipline is exercised on the bodies of individuals, and security is exercised over a whole population."[26] The iPod operated on all three of these registers, especially as it intersected with the War on Terror. First, earbuds created the illusion of "sovereignty" over what artist and theorist Brandon LaBelle calls "acoustic territories."[27] In the face of increased state surveillance, the iPod represented a personal retreat or sonic barrier. Picture passengers tolerating long lines at airport security within the acoustic territory of their own playlists. Next, the iPod exercised discipline "on the bodies of individuals" by materially and affectively altering work, waiting, moving, and commuting. In fact, the iPod's most iconic advertising campaign highlighted its effect on users' bodies. Silhouettes surrounded by different colored backdrops, dancing to a beat only they can hear, became emblematic of freedom—freedom of movement and expression. As Foucault clarifies, freedom is "no longer the exemptions and privileges attached to a person, but the possibility of movement, change of place, and processes of circulation of both people and things."[28] The iPod, affectively and commercially, embodied this ethos. However, Foucault also warns that "More precisely and particularly, freedom is nothing else but the correlative of the deployment of apparatuses of security."[29] Last, as much as the iPod brand emphasized personal expression, Apple, and specifically the iPhone, participate in the security "exercised over a whole population"—most obviously through their utility to the National Security Agency (NSA),[30] but also through consumer profiling. To be sure, Apple is the most self-restrained of the big four tech companies, but iTunes and the iPod undoubtedly helped usher in surveillance capitalism and new forms of data profiling. Perhaps ironically, the brand's emphasis on personal expression is what facilitates its surveillance functions.

Egan captures the complications and implications of this when Lou first exposes Mindy to a personal cassette player: "Occasionally he'll hand the device to Mindy, wanting her opinion, and each time, the experience of music pouring directly against her eardrums—hers alone—is a shock that makes her eyes well up; the privacy of it, the way it transforms her surroundings into a golden montage, as if she were looking back on this lark in Africa with Lou from some distant future" (65). This gesture of handing the earphones to Mindy and sharing the music with her is communal and social, yet the experience of listening remains "hers alone." She is overcome by the "privacy of it," and, at the same time, the event "transforms her surroundings into a golden montage," indicating a cinemafication of her reality. For Mindy, the "music pouring directly against her eardrums" is both physically intimate— a "shock that makes her eyes well up"—and also an out-of-body experience, "as if she were looking back . . . from some distant future." Egan echoes this sentiment later when she suggests that "years from now" the characters on the safari will "search for each other on Google and Facebook, unable to resist the wish-fulfillment fantasy these portals offer" (71). This first encounter with personal portable music players anticipates the experience of music in the digital age, which confers anonymity and individuality, privacy and publicity.

Novelist William Gibson argued that the Sony Walkman did "more to change human perception than any virtual reality gadget,"[31] and according to sociologist Michael Bull, "the iPod, even more than the Walkman, privatizes one's space . . . giving the user the unprecedented ability to weave the disparate threads of the day into one uniform soundtrack."[32] Even as earphones provide a sense of "aloneness" or "sonic space,"[33] there are still two distinct types of visibility at play here: the shift to a cinematic perspective of the self with an accompanying "soundtrack" and the newfound sharing of these personal "narratives" on a mass scale via the profile industry. In describing the early days of the iPod, Steven Levy writes that "because the ubiquity of the iPod amplifies such concerns in the media and in websites like Myspace (where musical choice is as much a badge of identity as is gender or geography), we seem to be immersed in an age of musical voyeurism. Not to mention musical exhibitionism."[34] He claims that "simply handing over your iPod to a friend, your blind date, or the total stranger sitting next to you on the plane opens you up like a book. . . . It's not just what you like— it's *who you are*."[35] Arguably, the same could have been said about displaying your record collection; the significant difference is that we are all "handing over" this information to multinational corporations (and carrying the entirety of it in our hands). Not only are users effectively advertising their musical choices to other potential consumers, they are also providing social media with valuable surplus data.[36] In other words, users are both the promoters and the raw materials for predictive products.

Egan again raises critical questions of surveillance and profiling when Bennie plays music for Sasha in the car, piecing together a tacit argument about the decline of the music industry through his selection of songs: "He began weighing each musical choice, drawing out his argument through the songs themselves—Patti Smith's ragged poetry (but why did she quit?), the jock hardcore of Black Flag and the Circle Jerks giving way to alternative, that great compromise, down, down, down to the singles he'd just today been petitioning radio stations to add, husks of music, lifeless and cold as the squares of office neon cutting the blue twilight" (36). Sasha remarks, "It's incredible . . . how there's just nothing there," and Bennie momentarily thinks she is responding to his argument before realizing that she is actually referring to the space where the World Trade Center had once stood (36). Pankaj Mishra's review of *Goon Squad* points out that this scene, which connects the "lifeless and cold" music with "squares of office neon" and finally the attacks on 9/11, "commemorates not only the fading of a cultural glory but also of the economic and political supremacy that underpinned it."[37] Furthermore, Bennie's reference to the "squares of office neon" undermines any sentimentality in Sasha's statement, even as both characters long for something less "lifeless." Bennie suggests that the music industry has degraded from politically engaged "ragged poetry" to commercially responsive "husks of music." Relatedly, Sasha's remark that there is "just nothing there" evokes the Bush administration's neoliberal response to 9/11, which urged the public to "go shopping more." Both characters' critiques speak to neoliberalism's "great compromise" of substituting shopping for political engagement and marrying consumer data-mining with state surveillance. At the end of the novel, Scotty's concert at Ground Zero brings together Bennie's and Sasha's concerns and exposes their complicated connections.

The novel's final chapter, "Pure Language," projects current trends in marketing and music into the future to envision a society of comprehensive consumer and state surveillance. Around the year 2024, Bennie is working to produce and promote his longtime friend Scotty Hausmann's first live concert, to be held in Lower Manhattan. Bennie hires Alex, who "promised Bennie fifty parrots to create 'authentic' word of mouth" for the show. Alex determines that effective "parrots" are those unique individuals with the right combination of "need," "reach," and "corruptibility" (315). Initially Alex concludes that none of his contacts have more than two of these three traits, which causes him to question why he himself has agreed to be a parrot: he certainly needs the money and has the reach, but he had previously thought of himself as a "purist." He wonders if it is "because he never could quite forget that every byte of information he'd posted online (favorite color, vegetable, sexual position) was stored in the databases of multinationals who swore they would never, ever use it—that he was *owned*, in other words, having sold himself unthinkingly at the very point in his life when he'd felt most subversive?" (316). Egan's tone captures the mass naïveté of providing personal information online to multinationals that simply swear to "never, ever use it." Alex decides that "what he needed was to find fifty more people like him, who had stopped being themselves without realizing it" (317). As Zara Dinnen writes, "Being connected is rarely disclosed for the mediational condition that it is: . . . that our digital connections are produced along with our subjectivity, as subjects and citizens of the algorithmic social sphere of automated governance."[38] Alex recognizes here that people "stopped being themselves" (317) by unwittingly becoming profiles of themselves, shifting from individuals to "dividuals" through technologies and economies of consumer surveillance.

Taking entertainment industries and advertising as its primary examples, the book ostensibly questions the ethics of "selling out" for fame or money. However, Egan ultimately and, more seriously, deconstructs the notion of any such outside by undermining the meaning of personal ownership in a profile society. For example,

> Bennie had never used the word "parrot"; since the Bloggescandals, the term had become an obscenity. Even the financial disclosure statements that political bloggers were required to post hadn't stemmed the suspicion that people's opinions weren't really their own. "Who's paying you?" was a retort that might follow any bout of enthusiasm, along with laughter—who would let themselves be bought? But Alex had promised Bennie fifty parrots to create "authentic" word of mouth for Scotty Hausmann's first live concert. (315)

The very idea of creating "'authentic' word of mouth" becomes doubly ironic. Not only is advertising already popularly regarded as inauthentic, everybody, to the extent that their profile precedes them, is already a parrot. The "suspicion that people's opinions weren't really their own" proves to be true, but not in the sense that people are simply insincere; rather, "people's opinions" are already sold in the marketplace of consumer surveillance. In this sense, we have all "let [ourselves] be bought." What Egan first presents as a scandalous exception she smartly illustrates to be the new rule. Moreover, for the vast majority, the answer to the quip "Who's paying you?" is "nobody." The real joke is that, by and large, consumer-citizens are not paid for their highly valuable opinions and profiles—but the joke is on us. Like Lulu, whose labor is mobile, constant, and therefore largely unpaid, consumers are working for free. This is again the point made and missed by Time magazine's 2006 cover story, as discussed in the introduction to this book.

In a dystopian technofuture affected by climate change and characterized by rampant consumerism and state surveillance, Scotty's concert at Ground Zero, or "The Footprint," hit a nerve "when he began singing the songs he'd been writing for years underground, songs no one had ever heard, or anything like them—'Eyes in My Head,' 'X's and O's,' 'Who's Watching Hardest'—ballads of paranoia and disconnection ripped from the chest of a man you knew just by looking had never had a page or a profile or a handle or a handset, who was part of no one's data, a guy who had lived in the cracks all these years, forgotten and full of rage, in a way that now registered as pure. Untouched" (336). As Egan explains, "two generations of war and surveillance had left people craving the embodiment of their own unease in the form of a lone, unsteady man on a slide guitar" (336). On one hand, Scotty "registers as pure" because he has managed to avoid the reach of the profile industry. On the other hand, this chapter exposes Alex's ethical compromises and efforts to promote Scotty's show, the waves of "preverbal" (313) toddlers or "pointers" (335) who shore up Scotty's success, and the "whirring," and "low, deep thrum" (331) of police choppers overhead that in effect provide musical accompaniment to this ostensibly "lone, unsteady man." Altogether, Egan provides a complicated portrait of a new authenticity engendered in profile culture. In fact, Scotty's purity is heavily produced, promoted, and protected, so that living off the grid becomes a fashion statement or publicity stunt that is itself advertised through the grid and authenticated in profile society.[39]

Scotty's song "Eyes in My Head" sounds revelatory and rebellious to the adults in crowd, given that in the age of panoptical reproduction so many "eyes" exist out there, "the density of police and security agents (identifiable by their government handsets) suddenly palpable, along with visual scanning devices affixed to cornices, lampposts, and trees" (331). Of course, the panopticon also internalizes the gaze so that the "eyes in [one's] head" are not solely one's own. Alex's conflicted feelings about managing the "blind team" and using social marketing to promote the concert represent both experiences of surveillance—the "eyes" he strategically places around the venue and the internalized surveillance producing his paranoia. Indeed, the question becomes "Who's Watching Hardest?" in an arms race between manufacturers of metadata, the metawatchers who endeavor to "watch the watchers," and arguably the metafictionalists who meaningfully engage profile society.[40]

Moreover, the interdependence of government surveillance, social marketing, and techno-consumer surveillance in Egan's near future speak to a troubling profile-military-industrial complex. Egan writes, "Traffic had stopped, and choppers were converging overhead, flogging the air with a sound Alex hadn't been able to bear in the early years—too loud, too loud—but over time he'd gotten used to it: the price of safety. Today their military cackle felt weirdly appropriate, Alex thought, glancing around him at the sea of slings and sacs and baby backpacks, older children carrying younger ones, because wasn't this a kind of army? An army of children" (330). If the emerging consumer demographic of toddlers, or "pointers," driving the music industry appears as an "army" in this distinctly post-9/11 security state, then handsets are their weapons, again suggesting a trajectory toward more amalgamation between paramilitary security and the profile industry through the ubiquity of mobile technology. In other words, part of what converges in this scene is the "price of safety," the "price of publicity," and the "cost of doing business"—disturbances that "Alex hadn't been able to bear in the early years . . . but over time he'd gotten used to." As Egan writes it, the sounds of the military "flogging the air" create a "cackle" that reverberates the sounds of 9/11, which are now "just of out of earshot, the vibration of an old disturbance." The shockwaves of 9/11 "seemed more insistent than ever: a low, deep thrum that felt primally familiar, as if it had been whirring inside all the sounds that Alex had made and collected over the years: their hidden pulse" (331). It is impossible to hear Scotty's music without the accompanying "cackle," "vibration," "deep thrum," "whirring," and "pulse" of September 11, the "war on terror," and military-industrial surveillance. In fact, Scotty's concert—"orchestrated" through the very practices that his fans celebrate him for denouncing—makes this noise seem "more insistent than ever." In this regard, as much as the security protects the crowd, the concert provides an occasion or platform for security. Finally, it's significant that the sounds of security surveillance seem to have been "whirring inside all the sounds that Alex had made and collected over the years." Ultimately, the data he has "made and collected" is a reasonable definition of a profile, and Egan insightfully posits "security" as the "hidden pulse" of the profile industry.

Next we are told that "it's hard to know anymore who was really at that first Scotty Hausmann concert—more people claim it than could possibly have fit into the space, capacious and mobbed though it was. Now that Scotty has entered the realm of myth, everyone wants to own him. And maybe they should. Doesn't a myth belong to everyone?" (336). It is first ironic that Scotty should "belong to everyone," considering that it was his ability to remain unowned that moves the crowd. Next, the crowd's ownership over Scotty evokes another pervasive "myth" that the systems of surveillance, which effectively coproduce his concert, somehow "belong to everyone"—that social media, metadata, and security surveillance are public goods.

Finally, Scotty's concert conjures the insidious myth that something isn't real unless it is visible. This myth is connected to the notion that visibility is the highest marker of achievement or value, an "exceptional fantasy" I discussed previously with regard to celebrity culture buttressing the profile industry. Egan captures the wrongheadedness of this myth by placing Scotty's concert at the Footprint—the future memorial for the World Trade Center. By calling it the Footprint, she points to both the geopolitical and ecological imprints of 9/11, invoking the physical impact of the attack and its related carbon footprint through negative space. It might seem like "there is just nothing there," as Sasha previously remarked, but through her depiction of the Footprint, Egan connects the surge in state surveillance hovering overhead and the crisis of climate change heating the Earth from below. The penultimate chapter, "Great Rock and Roll Pauses," which is written in PowerPoint, describes the effects of climate change most vividly: "Cool air, but you feel the heat coming up from the earth like from behind a person's skin. I think I feel it through my shoes, but do I? I was right: the ground is warm" (238). Paralleling the noisy "choppers . . . converging overhead" is a heat "coming up from" below. This framing encourages an ecological critique of consumer and state surveillance that moves beyond the more common discourses of privacy and access. Specifically, *Goon Squad* suggests that responses to the surge in surveillance after 9/11 and the proliferation of consumer profiling must acknowledge the environmental effects of surveillance.[41]

By emphasizing the various sounds synchronizing into music during the concert, Egan calls attention to the more or less invisible systems of surveillance, effects of 9/11, and effects of climate change. The following passage written in text-speak from the novel's final scene functions similarly by emphasizing the sounds of the words over their obscured visual representation:

> And the hum, always that hum, which maybe wasn't an echo after all, but the sound of time passing.
> th blu nyt
> th stRs u cant c
> th hum tht nevr gOs awy. (340)

First, "u cant c" the stars because of the light and air pollution, again connecting climate change to the invisible systems of surveillance—"the devices affixed to cornices, lampposts, and trees" (331). Still, however invisible, these technologies create a "hum tht nevr gOs awy." As a sort of constant white noise, this hum could easily go unnoticed, could simply become naturalized as part of the environment, like the trees. However, in a novel so much about sound and music, Egan tunes our ears into this common frequency that cuts across the personalized soundscape of the iPod.

From Celebrity Profiles to Data Profiles

Celebrity culture, surveillance, metadata, and metafiction converge most literally in the chapter "Forty-Minute Lunch: Kitty Jackson Opens Up About Love, Fame, and Nixon." This chapter thoroughly embodies and embeds this set of practices in the asymmetrical power relations of gender and race. Formally, it is a celebrity profile that ends with a pointed description of data profiles. It most overtly parodies a type of masculinist metafiction that neglects how gender is central to understanding the embodied experience of watching and being watched, writing and being written about, surveilling and being surveilled. In Egan's words, the chapter is "a send-up of the celebrity profile,"[42] but it might also be understood as a send-up of the self-conscious ogler/writer that David Foster Wallace describes in his essay, "E Unibus Pluram: Television and U.S. Fiction."[43] Wallace begins by declaring that "fiction writers as a species tend to be oglers. They tend to lurk and to stare. They are born watchers. They are viewers. They are the ones on the subway about whose nonchalant stare there is something creepy,[44] somehow. Almost predatory. This is because human situations are writers' food."[45] From its outset, Wallace's essay is interested in identifying and classifying writers. He not only describes their tendencies and demeanors, he defines fiction writers as a species of "born watchers." The ways this classification draws on the topoi of aggressive masculine sexuality has thus far been undertheorized.

Immediately, the image of "writers as a species" hunting down "human situations" as "food" evokes the all-too-familiar and violent image of women as meat. Even when Wallace makes a seemingly concerted effort to provide an example of both a male and a female writer worrying nervously about "how they appear, how they seem, whether their shirttail might be hanging out of their fly, whether there's maybe lipstick on their teeth, whether the people they're ogling can maybe size them up as somehow creepy, as lurkers and starers,"[46] the words *creepy, lurkers, starers,* and especially *predatory* connote a familiar form of sexual violence against women. Furthermore, the joint images of a man's shirttail hanging out of his fly and a woman with lipstick on her teeth are sexually suggestive and hardly neutralize the importance of gender. On the contrary, by ostensibly balancing his examples, Wallace instead presents a false equivalency that neglects the significance of gender, as well as race and class, in the act of staring at another person. The writerly gaze that he describes is, indeed, also the male gaze—the male gaze watching itself watch and feeling creepy about it. The repetition of "somehow creepy" elides the implicit gender dynamic and signifies Wallace's refusal to acknowledge it. He imagines that this behavior and shame is unique to fiction writers, as part of some exceptional "subspecies."[47] In reality, what underpins the "almost predatory" quality of this scenario is the terrible commonness of men lurking and staring at women in public.

Wallace's essay goes on to explore how television resolves the discomfort of people watching to account for its addictive appeal. Yet he argues that as TV viewers become accustomed to self-consciously "watching [themselves] watching" and "yearn[ing] to experience 'experiences,'" a certain subset of US literature (best exemplified by Don DeLillo) begins writing more and more about writing, taking metawatching as a significant subject for fiction.[48] However, to take seriously Wallace's argument about the impact of metawatching on US fiction, a feminist genealogy of metafiction and contemporary fiction must consider the embodied politics of watching and being watched as a type of surveillance, which, I argue, increasingly takes the form of a digital profile. By connecting the gender politics of surveillance to Wallace's well-known essay on the state of metafiction, "Forty-Minute Lunch" makes just this intervention.

By writing in the genre of celebrity profiles, Egan is able to merge the high-art aspirations of highly self-conscious writing with the low-art obsessions of celebrity culture—while taking into account how women are excluded in the first instance and overexposed in the second. This ultimately problematizes Wallace's classification of fiction writers as a "human subspecies that loves to watch people but hates to be watched itself" by contextualizing this penchant for watching within a world where women are so often valued for their "watchableness" and where staring at someone on a subway can seem not only "creepy" but threatening.[49]

The humor and horror of Jules's profile comes from his self-absorption and self-pity, which bear an uncanny resemblance to Wallace's descriptions of "terribly self-conscious" fiction writers who are debilitated by the pretty people who populate television.[50] Jules shares Wallace's wonder at the ability of celebrities to "act natural"; he, like Wallace, laments celebrity culture's "deep thesis that the most significant quality of truly alive persons is watchableness."[51] Although Wallace's point is well taken, he neglects to see how this imperative to be "watchable" affects "persons" unevenly based on other "significant qualit[ies]"—such as gender, race, and sexuality. Kitty's watchableness, for instance, is both an imperative and a risk. Whether engaging celebrity profiles, which promise "access" to celebrities, or data profiles, which promise access to celebrity itself, Egan's portrayals bring to bear the effect of gender in profiling. As long as publicity is itself scandalous for women and other oppressed groups, profiling—whether by the profile industry, the entertainment industry, or the NSA—is risky business.

"In the footnote-ish fashion that injects a whiff of cracked leather bindings into pop-cultural observation," the narrator, Jules Jones, focuses his profile on the nineteen-year-old actress's effect on him, his ego, and his writing (168). Importantly, he writes this profile piece from prison after attempting to rape Kitty in Central Park, thereby connecting his status as a sexual predator with his "predatory" view of writing. In contrast to Jules's style of metafiction, which is superseding and self-centered, Egan's novel jumps through time and between characters with a glance. In fact, the digital quality and reference point in *Goon Squad* makes Jules's article in *Details* magazine seem all the more analog and constricting. Much has been said about the unique structure of *Goon Squad*, but to be sure, it is not simply the formal features that distinguish Egan's writing from the class of contemporary writers she parodies. After all, once you escape the "tyranny of the line," you must confront the oppressive social reality that it cuts across.[52]

From prison, Jules determines that his encounter with Kitty hinged on the moment when she dipped her finger into the salad dressing and licked it off. He explains that women "normally stifle behavior that might be construed as overly encouraging, or possibly incendiary." He tells himself that she does not stifle this behavior "because you do not register as a 'man' to Kitty Jackson, and so being around you makes her no more self-conscious than would the presence of a dachshund" (173). On the one hand, this reading recalls Wallace's claim that "the most colorful, attractive, animated, *alive* people in our daily experience—are also people who are oblivious to the fact that they are watched," a realization that according to Wallace leaves writers feeling all the more self-conscious and insecure.[53] On the other hand, Kitty represents the pressure on women to police their every gesture for fear of being either "overly encouraging" to men, or in this case overly discouraging—both of which are potentially "incendiary." Egan's work clarifies that the demand to seem unselfconscious and also completely watchable while still obliging and performing for every onlooker is not simply a pressure of media culture that propels the profile industry and spurred a new wave of self-conscious metafiction. Rather, like so many symptoms of postmodernism (fragmentation, schizophrenia, and indeterminacy, for example) this is precisely the type of bind that women and racial minorities have long faced. In sum, Egan's brief interview by a hideous man exposes the gendered politics, which seem so conspicuously repressed in Wallace's otherwise astute essay.

In an interview, Egan addresses the limitations of "trying to render up an authentic experience having no access to the star, really" to satisfy readers who "want a sense of having really touched some heretofore unseen aspect of the star."[54] By characterizing contact with celebrities as a matter of touch, Egan connects the shortcomings of celebrity profiles to Jules's vexation at not having physical and sexual access to Kitty. In this sense, she draws out the sexual aggression intrinsic to Wallace's conception of postmodern fiction writers. Wallace warns, for example, that watching celebrities "leads us to confuse actual fiction-research with a weird kind of fiction-*consumption*"—as opposed to relying on "human situations" for "food."[55] Yet for Wallace, both approaches position writing as consumption. Egan parodies this model of the writer-predator when Jules, unable to "wrest readable material" from Kitty, repeatedly resorts to reducing her from a "lofty" star to a lowly animal that he can imagine actually devouring (174). For Jules, Kitty is either larger than life or bare life, but never exactly human. For example, directly after admitting to the "volatile stew of anger, fear, and lust" he feels toward her, he compares her shoulders to squabs and imagines "pulling apart all those little bones and sucking the meat off of them one by one" (176). By linking Jules's misogynistic fantasies of consuming Kitty to his frustrated attempts at "wrest[ing] readable material" from her, Egan critiques the rapacious method of metafiction that Wallace's descriptions take for granted.

If we accept Wallace's claim that metafiction—"this high-cultural genre"[56]—was profoundly influenced by television and the popularity of self-conscious watching, then analysis of the gendered politics of metawatching might help account for the masculinization of US postmodernism and metafiction. Kathleen Fitzpatrick's work *The Anxiety of Obsolescence* considers the canonization of Don DeLillo, John Barth, Don Barthelme, William S. Burroughs, Robert Coover, Jonathan Franzen, William Gass, John Hawkes, Norman Mailer, Thomas Pynchon, Kurt Vonnegut, and David Foster Wallace to question "not whether print culture is dying at the hands of the media, but rather what purposes announcements of the death of print culture serve, and thus what all this talk about the end of the book tells us about those doing the talking."[57] Overwhelmingly, of course, "those doing the talking" about the death of the novel are white men. Underlying this vilification of visual media is a conservative defense of the status quo, including the white male privilege enjoyed by so many postmodern novelists bemoaning the death of the novel.

Egan dramatizes Fitzpatrick's argument that postmodern writers' hand-wringing over the state of "print culture" actually masks their anxiety about preserving white male privilege—a privilege dependent on remaining unmarked. Recounting his attack, Jules, in his typically self-referential fashion, asks, "How is all this affecting me?" He answers, "Well, we're lying on a hill in Central Park, a somewhat secluded spot that is still, technically speaking, in plain sight. So I feel anxious, dully aware that I'm placing my career and reputation at some risk" (182). By redirecting attention back to his own career and reputation, Jules embodies a rape culture in which violence toward women matters only insofar as it threatens men's reputations and well-being. It is important that the source of his anxiety is being in "plain sight." Here, Jules's alignment of authorship and authority with seeing while remaining unseen echoes the protagonist from Don DeLillo's metafictional novel *Mao II*: the reclusive writer Bill Gray reluctantly decides to finally be photographed and then laments, "'I've become someone's material.'" As the photographer, Brita, takes his picture, Bill wonders, "'What am I giving up to you? And what are you investing me with, or stealing from me? How are you changing me? . . . And when did women start photographing men in the first place?'"[58] Again, the power or authority of writers is aligned with an unmarked white masculinity that watches but is not watched. Like Jules's fear of Kitty "reversing the beam of scrutiny," DeLillo's protagonist expresses the dominant thinking that "*men act and women appear.*"[59] Ultimately, Egan's work illustrates how the power and authority of being both a white man and a writer are entangled—repositioning metafiction as itself a form of surveillance.

Although postmodern literature has been credited with representing identity as artistry, literature in the data age must also reckon with how identity
is constructed and constricted by the marketplace. Even so, this includes
calling into question the supposed newness of identity as a commercial construct and reminding readers that women and racial minorities have long
been valued or devalued as commodities in white-supremacist patriarchal
capitalism. By writing through narrative and data profiles, Egan embeds her
critiques of both traditional metafiction and the rise of metadata in the irreducible and messy contexts of asymmetrical power relations. Jules considers
it a vulgar affront to his own middle-class masculinity that "the promotion
of said movie is the sole reason [Kitty] is in [his] company," bemoaning that
she, a woman, is the more public figure (180). Kitty's profile is indeed a commodity, and this interview is represented as an investment of her time, time
that is carefully monitored throughout their meeting and supposedly kept
by her manager off site—another nod toward the neoliberal imperative that
individuals take personal responsibility for managing their own profile or
preventing their own rape. Yet Egan makes clear that there is a difference
between having a public profile (or being high-profile) and having agency and
access to publicness. Even as it critiques familiar, often abstracted voices of
postmodernism, Goon Squad clarifies that postmodernism is not the threat to
feminism—neoliberal techno-capitalism is. After all, a postfeminist neoliberal capitalist perspective would claim that a woman's earning potential is the
sole indicator of her status in society, a position that Kitty's character patently
undercuts.

Notably, both celebrity profiles and data profiles are a matter of access.
On the one hand, celebrity profiles promise access to the celebrity's inner
life. I agree with Egan that the celebrity profile is a "bankrupt genre"—not
only because it places writers in the impossible position of "trying wildly to
infuse some kind of meaning into the exchange . . . trying to render up an
authentic experience having no access to the star, really"—but also because
it clings to the pretense of any such authentic or coherent identity in the first
place.[60] Hence, the mocking tone and "mystical appearance of a rainbow"
when Jules ostensibly discovers the "real Kitty." Data profiles, on the other
hand, are uninterested in fixed subject positions and identities; rather, they
encode a person's dividuality to regulate access across various platforms.
While sites like Facebook pitch themselves as platforms for users to express

their "authentic selves," no matter how much personal information users provide or how many updates they post, the profiles are perpetually incomplete and outdated. Celebrity profiles, as a genre, model and underwrite this cultural compulsion to "share" ever more information by promoting fame and visibility as the ultimate signifiers of success and significance. Only then is one's privacy even worth protecting. In this sense, profile culture banks on celebrity profiles: through our profiles we are all "reality stars." Yet "this sense of being more, better, a star, shifts immediately into a sense of utter banality . . . the celebrity mode of subjectivization is thus weak and uncertain" and in constant need of an update.[61]

By ending this "send-up of the celebrity profile" with a paradigmatic description of data profiles, Egan elaborates the multiple dimensions of profile society. In a lengthy footnote, Jules responds to a "recent editorial ('Vulnerability in Our Public Spaces')" by suggesting that the city "simply erect checkpoints at the entrances to Central Park and demand identification from those who wish to enter" (185). Emblematic of the security apparatus in profile society, Jules explains,

> Then you will be able to call up their records and evaluate the relative success or failure of their lives—marriage or lack thereof, children or lack thereof, professional success or lack thereof, healthy bank account or lack thereof, contact with childhood friends or lack thereof, ability to sleep peacefully at night or lack thereof, fulfillment of sprawling, loopy youthful ambitions or lack thereof, ability to fight off bouts of terror and despair or lack thereof—and using these facts, you can assign each person a ranking based on the likelihood that their personal failures will occasion jealous explosions directed at those more accomplished. (185)

The strategy is to subdivide the population to control it, safeguard it, and manage its riskiness. The personal "facts" needed for the profile and ranking move from the quantitative to the qualitative, from data to narrative, and as Jules explains, "The rest is easy: simply encode each person's ranking into an electronic bracelet and affix it to their wrist as they enter the park, and then monitor those encoded points of light on a radar screen, with personnel at the ready to intervene" (185). As "encoded points of light," the public achieves stardom: their private lives are made public and flashed across a "screen" as their status or "ranking" rises and falls. As Jodi Dean encapsulates, criminality is no longer "the paradigmatic form of subjectivity in contemporary surveillance. Celebrity is."[62]

However snarky or sarcastic, Jules's solution to crime in Central Park echoes the "Society of Control" that Deleuze diagnoses: "The numerical language of control is made of codes that mark access to information, or reject it."[63] In our profile society, identity is dispersed across and through multiple databases, undermining notions of coherent identity and linear and totalizing life narratives. *Goon Squad* is often praised for its open-endedness and webbed structure, yet Egan makes clear that openness should not be mistaken for freedom. Profiles are no more open than the "open graph"; they are no freer than the "free market." They are governed by algorithms and therefore by ideology and politics. Profiles depend on ubiquitous surveillance, yet their very vastness is paradoxically reassuring. The public is meant to be seduced by their newfound significance and simultaneously relieved by their utter insignificance. Granted, people increasingly see through these rhetorical screens, but as D. A. Miller writes: "Of course, I know, but still. . . ."[64] In other words, while abstractly knowing that ceaseless bids for their information and data are neither personally rewarding nor necessarily innocuous, they disavow it—regularly, on social media.

Egan's story also critiques how protecting women in public is often an alibi for protecting the public from women. That is, public spaces are deemed risky once they are occupied by women. The vulnerability of women in public thus authorizes increased security and police intervention, while also reinforcing the idea that sexual violence is inevitable. The easy solution is not to address the structural problem of misogyny and violent masculinity but to accommodate, control, monitor, and ultimately exploit this as a supposed fact of life. Frightfully, Jules's over-the-top suggestion resonates with many post-9/11 profiling practices, from provisions in the USA PATRIOT Act to the NSA's PRISM program, which highlights the expanding role of mobile technology in state surveillance. Furthermore, Egan's chapter recalls the 1989 Central Park jogger case, which made terribly clear how crimes against women are exploited as an alibi for racist reactions that bolster public support for the prison-industrial complex—which disproportionately incarcerates minorities. Along these same lines, feminist surveillance scholar Andrea Smith describes her experience at an antiviolence conference when "the participants supported the war in Afghanistan because they believed it would liberate women from the violence of the Taliban; their reliance on state-driven surveillance strategies for addressing violence through the military and criminal-justice systems prevented them from seeing that militarism itself perpetuates violence against women."[65] Furthermore, the "protection" of one marginalized group is too often used to oppress another, and those who claim that surveillance is a nonissue "if you don't have anything to hide" often enjoy white cis-heterosexual male privilege. Instead, Wendy Chun asks the important and constructive question: "how can we understand publicity not in terms of a need for safety and protection, which is neither safe nor protecting, but rather the fight for a space in which one can be vulnerable and not attacked?" Both offline and online, the answer includes "develop[ing] new habits of connecting that disrupt the reduction of our interactions into network diagrams that can be tracked and traced."[66] By occupying the trap of network diagrams, Goon Squad exposes all that they ensnare, all that buoys them. Yet it also smuggles in "new habits of connecting," new ways of seeing and knowing.

Goon Squad contextualizes the practices of metawatching within gender politics and histories of surveillance, advancing a form of metafiction that considers both the rising prevalence of profiling and its own surveillant gaze. Egan's fiction keenly engages the ways profiles govern access and regulate risk across platforms through the policing of people as divisible, searchable, social code. Unlike the notion of character, which misinterprets information about an individual as complete or totalizing, profiles are inherently incomplete and changeable. Egan's novel embraces the gaps and resists the mythology of coherent, knowable identities. Nevertheless, Goon Squad also acknowledges that the algorithms that make data legible are never neutral or divorced from lived experiences. This critical lesson must inform our understanding of metafiction as it is likewise embedded and embodied in our data-surveillance society.

CHAPTER TWO

Out of Line

Affective Counterstrategies to Racializing Surveillance and Profile Epistemology in Claudia Rankine's Citizen

I n the neoliberal age of data surveillance, discrimination is regarded as not only permissible but prudent. Credited with taking personal responsibility, consumer-citizens are praised as discriminating shoppers, fans, viewers, voters, patients, and so on. Meanwhile, people's misfortune, debt, incarceration, and poor health care, for example, are blamed on their indiscriminate choices. This neoliberal ethos offers yet another rubric for naturalizing and rationalizing widespread "social sorting" as well as the massive routine surveillance it demands.[1] While social sorting sounds more innocuous than racial profiling, David Theo Goldberg reminds us that "classification, as [Zygmunt] Bauman argues, is at basis about setting apart, about cutting things off from each other into discrete containers, about *segregation*. Classification thus involves those acts of inclusion and exclusion so central to the experience of racism."[2] Increasingly, these "discrete containers" take the form of databases, spreadsheets, and data centers filled through routine methods of mass surveillance. In fact, scholars such as Safiya Umoja Noble, Simone Browne, Christian Parenti, David Lyon, and Craig Robertson all contextualize contemporary surveillance technologies in a long history of racialization and racial subjugation that moves, for example, from slave passes to passports.[3]

Algorithmic surveillance demands consumer-citizens be ever-more visible even as the technologies and techniques of data collection are sheltered under technical and organizational opacity. Put differently, surveillance depends on the illiteracy of its targets. Parenti explains that "the [slave] pass and the racially defined contours of (white) literacy and (Black) illiteracy upon which it relied, acted as the slaveocracy's information technology and infrastructure of routine surveillance."[4] With this realization in mind, we can better understand our current infrastructure of surveillance and the possibilities for thwarting it. This includes not only reckoning with legacies of slavery and white supremacy but also learning from the history of Black resistance: "First and foremost we see the openings provided by literacy: the slave who could read and write became the antebellum hacker, the information outlaw, who could crack the code of the planters' security system. Literate African Americans could resist with the very tools of white oppression; they could in effect bend the political technology of literacy back upon itself."[5] This history suggests that any call for technological literacy must include an analysis of hegemonic power. Furthermore, this description of the literate "hacker" and "information outlaw" uses the language of informatics to characterize abolitionists, drawing together the work of poets, novelists, activists, and the likes of Edward Snowden into the "openings provided by literacy."[6] At stake in the demand for digital literacy, then, is the importance of decoding systems of racializing surveillance, especially as they circumscribe who and what is legible and intelligible.

Meanwhile, the standard defense of surveillance and profiling—"If you have nothing to hide, then you have nothing to fear"—has become a neoliberal commonplace, masquerading as common sense and masking white supremacist capitalist patriarchy. Given how many innocent Black people have been murdered by the police, the claim that Black Americans with nothing to hide actually have nothing to fear is blatantly absurd and painfully insulting. Past and present practices of racial profiling have made a mockery of this disingenuous platitude. Yet perversely, in the overlapping systems of white supremacy and ubiquitous surveillance, outrage is used to reaffirm guilt and justify abuses of power. Lauren Berlant suggests that "a relation of cruel optimism exists when something you desire is actually an obstacle to your flourishing,"[7] and I argue that as systemic racism and anti-Blackness depend on this cruel optimism, they produce a politics of respectability, one that insists that a response to racism remains proper and properly powerless.

Following the insights of Lauren Berlant, Sara Ahmed, and Claudia Rankine,[8] I contend that disrupting the commonplace that only guilty people object to surveillance demands an affective epistemology to counter algorithmic epistemologies and the truth-claims they sponsor. This also involves valuing the "uses of anger," as elaborated by Audre Lorde and others,[9] to help sever the ties between and thus destabilize algorithmic profile societies and patriarchal white supremacy. Berlant reminds us that the "seeming detachment of rationality" that characterizes profile epistemology "is not a detachment at all, but an emotional style associated normatively with a rhetorical practice."[10] In contrast, the affective epistemology I read in Rankine's lyric opens up what Berlant calls a "place where we rehabituate our sensorium" through "an encounter with the historical present via the intensities of [her poetry's] tone, whether emergent, chaotic, or waning."[11] Focusing on Rankine's book *Citizen: An American Lyric*, I tease out the relationship between anti-Blackness and the US data-surveillance society and elaborate what literature and critical race theory can teach data studies about forms of oppositional looking and countersurveillance. After considering how neoliberal surveillance marshals and polices affect along racial lines, which are "always imagined as already transgressed,"[12] I turn to Rankine's counterstrategies, which mobilize affect to different ends and specifically undermine the supposed detached rationality of profile epistemology.

Line Judges

By incorporating images and essay into the poetry, Rankine's *American Lyric* recounts and reflects on racially charged encounters in a supposedly "postracial" era. Repeatedly, she returns to a narrator watching tennis matches on television, providing a relatively long analysis of Serena Williams at the intersections of anti-Blackness and sexism. While the following pages will connect the microaggressions faced by Williams to overpolicing and racializing surveillance, I am not suggesting an equivalence between police brutality and the acts of racism directed at her. Nor do I wish to ignore the relative privilege afforded to Williams by her wealth. Rankine has been quick to acknowledge that *Citizen* largely inhabits a world of middle-class professionals. Nevertheless, "when one reacts, one is not reacting to any one of those moments" of microaggression,[13] and importantly, Rankine connects the racism directed at Williams with various and varying forms of racializing surveillance and violence.

Shortly after the publication of *Citizen*, Williams completed her second "Serena Slam" by winning all four major tournaments in a row. Notably, the *New York Times* published two articles relating to her 2015 win at Wimbledon, the first titled "Tennis's Top Women Balance Body Image with Ambition" and the other "It's Time to Appreciate Serena Williams's Greatness."[14] Disappointingly, these articles recall the "bankrupt genre" of celebrity profiling that Jennifer Egan laments and that I discuss in chapter 1. Even after a significant backlash to the offensive sexism and racism of the first article, the second article still feigned a naïve disbelief about the lack of appreciation for Williams's "greatness," suggesting vaguely that "it will indeed be intriguing to see whether Williams, still winning big at age 33, will connect with her public on a deeper level after some of the ambivalence and controversies of the past." Aside from a brief mention of the "racist taunts" hurled at Serena Williams and her sister, Venus, at Indian Wells in 2001, in the course of wondering about why she doesn't "connect with the public on a deeper level," the article never once addresses race, nor does it attempt to clarify what is actually meant by "the ambivalence and controversies of the past." Conspicuously, the *Times* fails to confront the racism Williams faces, opting instead to imply, in a stunning reversal, that the public must adopt the "bias" of her supporters if they are to "come around." "I'm biased," Andy Roddick explains: "I know Serena behind the curtain. I've seen the sweet side, and I know what kind of person she is. I wish other people got to see more of her. It's pretty impressive. The story goes that if you win long enough, people come around. She's won plenty long enough."[15]

It is here, in the space between these two *New York Times* articles—in the cruel optimism that more exposure is the solution—that Claudia Rankine intervenes and asks, "What does a victorious or defeated black woman's body in a historically white space look like?"[16] What's at stake isn't to see more of Williams but to "know Serena behind the curtain" of anti-Blackness, to see not just her sweet side but to appreciate "the anger built up through experience and the quotidian struggles against dehumanization every brown or black person lives simply because of skin color" (24). *Citizen* thus offers not a celebrity profile, a peek "behind the curtain" of fame to reveal the real and sweeter Serena; instead, Rankine provides a study of racial profiling and the resistance it provokes, as well as the affects these produce.

Rankine frames her analysis of how the public, the mass media, and the umpires treat Williams with Zora Neale Hurston's insight: "I feel most colored when I am thrown against a sharp white background" (25). A "sharp white background" might refer to tennis itself, often called the lily-white sport, but in *Citizen* it also comes to represent myriad instantiations of the color line, Williams's position reflecting the systemic and everyday discrimination against Black people in America. Even as the tennis court represents a supposedly level playing field, it offers a suggestive site for considering "surveillance and the work it does to zone spaces, draw lines, and shape looking relations."[17] Rankine highlights how Williams's body is deemed always already at fault and out of place. After introducing Hurston's frank statement, the lyric shifts focus to how, in Glenn Ligon's installation, Hurston's quote appears on canvas with "plastic letter stencils, smudging oil sticks, and graphite to transform the words into abstractions" (25). Rankine comments that "this appropriated line . . . seemed to be ad copy for some aspect of life for all black bodies" (25), pointing at the commodification of Black people in the abstraction from their lived experiences. Against the "sharp white background" of the page, Rankine's lines of lyric poetry and prose insist on the embodied and affective experience of the color line that the treatment of Williams, for example, overtly produces and then disavows.

To understand the relationship between sports officiating and surveillance in Rankine's work, I draw on Browne's term "racializing surveillance" to signal "those moments when enactments of surveillance reify boundaries and borders along racial lines, and where the outcome is often discriminatory treatment."[18] But to begin, consider John Fiske's formulation that "surveillance is a technology of whiteness that racially zones city spaces by drawing lines that Blacks cannot cross and whites cannot see."[19] Of course, the bright white lines of the tennis court demarcating the boundaries, boxes, and alleys of the game are spectacularly visible, as are the line judges and officials minding them. The rules of racializing surveillance, however, superimpose another set of lines "that Blacks cannot cross and whites cannot see." Trapped in what Parenti calls a "soft cage," Serena Williams is always at risk of stepping out of bounds or crossing a line that her overwhelmingly white opponents, officials, and spectators naturalize to the point of invisibility. In Rankine's analysis, the power of the "even playing field" as a spectacle overshadows color lines and institutes a rationale for surveillance and discrimination.

Rankine's description of a game officiated by Mariana Alves, "the most notorious of Serena's detractors," immediately highlights a conventional deference to the white gaze by identifying Alves as "the *distinguished* tennis chair umpire" who was merely "*excused* from officiating any more matches on the final day of the US Open after she made five bad calls against Serena in her semifinal matchup against fellow American Jennifer Capriati" (26–27, emphasis added). Sardonically, she extends to Alves the benefit of the doubt, even as "the serves and returns Alves called out were landing, stunningly unreturned by Capriati, inside the lines, no discerning eyesight needed. Commentators, spectators, television viewers, line judges, everyone could see the balls were good, everyone, apparently, except Alves" (27). Although Rankine feigns ignorance about what could possibly explain the bad calls—"No one could understand what was happening"—many viewers, including Rankine herself, understood this as racial discrimination. As Rankine recalls, however, although they "define what is in or out of place," color lines are maintained by the presumption that "whites cannot see" them. To point out these lines would be to betray the color-blindness of neoliberal and neoracist politics. The default option is thus, as with the *New York Times*, to maintain an apparently color-blind stance of bewilderment.

In the face of this color-blind bewilderment, Rankine emphatically calls out "what was happening": "Though no one was saying anything explicitly about Serena's black body, you are not the only viewer who thought it was getting in the way of Alves's sight line" (27). That is, Williams's "black body" is simultaneously hypervisible, overwhelming the entire field of focus, and "explicitly" ignored. Insisting on Williams's physicality and blackness, Rankine lingers on physical details, describing "Serena, in her denim skirt, black sneaker boots, and dark mascara . . . wagging her finger and saying 'no, no, no,' as if by negating the moment she could propel us back into a legible world" (27). To the extent that Williams's styling recalls street clothes, it "negates" or threatens the exaggerated white decorum of tennis and "propel[s] us back into a legible world" beyond the strict white gentility of the sport (27). Her finger-wagging and protest—"no, no, no"—rebukes Alves for violating the rules. Of course, herein lies the question of who has the power to define and then suddenly change the rules: to define what is "legible." Just as Serena attempts to "negate the moment," Rankine inscribes a counternarrative that foregrounds the power relations in determining what is "legible," knowable, and sayable.

In the name of technological solutionism and "democratic" surveillance, the match between Serena Williams and Capriati "would be credited for demonstrating the need for the speedy installation of Hawk-Eye, the line-calling technology that took the seeing away from the beholder" (27). Here we see the enthusiasm for surveillance technologies to solve the problem of personal bias or perception, as though technology is designed, operated, and understood outside prejudicial social and political systems. This echoes Jules's call in A Visit from the Goon Squad for digital checkpoints around the perimeter of Central Park to prevent people like himself from attempting rape. Though less obviously offensive, Hawk-Eye in this context is a prime example of a technological response to discrimination that fails to address the underlying bias or the ways in which "rules" are enforced unevenly:

> [Serena] is in the second set at the critical moment of 5–6 in Clijsters's favor, serving to stay in the match, at match point. The line judge employed by the US Open to watch Serena's body, its every move, says Serena stepped on the line while serving. What? (The Hawk-Eye cameras don't cover the feet, only the ball, apparently.) What! Are you serious? She is serious; she has seen a foot fault, one no one else is able to locate despite the numerous replays. "No foot fault, you definitely do not see a foot fault there," says McEnroe. "That's over-officiating for certain," says another commentator. . . . Yes, and even if there had been a foot fault, despite the rule, they are rarely ever called at critical moments in a Grand Slam match because "You don't make a call," tennis official Carol Cox says, "that can decide a match unless it's flagrant." (28–29)

Before Hawk-Eye, Alves called Williams's serves out of bounds despite landing within the lines; a year later, the line judge called Serena herself out of bounds. The commentators were again left in disbelief, but Rankine cuts through the confusion. Specifying that the "line judge [was] employed by the US Open to watch Serena's body, its every move," she represents Williams as a target of surveillance and scrutiny. Perhaps most revealing is Carol Cox's explanation that a foot fault is rarely called at a critical moment in the game, "unless it's flagrant." How and when rules apply—on and off tennis courts, in and out of legal courts—is a matter of discretion and discrimination. Hawk-Eye didn't "take the seeing away from the beholder," it merely redirected the sightline to the real problem: Williams's body, already coded as "flagrant" and at "fault."

We then see how "over-officiating" encloses and restricts modes of opposition and resistance. After the bad call, "Serena turns to the lineswoman and says, 'I swear to God I'm fucking going to take this fucking ball and shove it down your fucking throat, you hear that? I swear to God!'" (29). While Rankine acknowledges the outburst "as offensive," she finds it "difficult not to applaud her for reacting immediately to being thrown against a sharp white background. It is difficult not to applaud her for existing in the moment, for fighting crazily against the so-called wrongness of her body's positioning at the service line" (29). Williams is routinely told to contain herself in the face of racism, lest she confirm the racist assumption that she must be an "angry black woman"—though, of course, no record of so-called respectability would ever undo this assumption, much less address the racism underlying it. It is because her right to react and even exist is routinely challenged, that Rankine applauds Williams for "fighting crazily against the so-called wrongness of her body's positioning." Audre Lorde writes, "Women responding to racism means women responding to anger; the anger of exclusion, of unquestioned privilege, of racial distortions, of silence, ill-use, stereotyping, defensiveness, misnaming, betrayal, and co-optation."[20] As a Black woman, Williams's personhood and position is routinely subject to "racial distortion," a distortion literalized by the line judges calling out the "so-called wrongness of her body's positioning." It is not surprising that "Serena's reaction is read as insane" (30)—yet another distortion, a "misnaming" of the sort so frequently used against women, especially women of color.

In writing that Williams's "punishment for this moment of manumission . . . result[ed] in the loss of the match, an $82,500 fine, plus a two-year probationary period by the Grand Slam Committee," Rankine's use of "manumission" evokes the emancipation of slaves, clarifying that Williams's real offense is self-possession and rebellion against racism (30). To be sure, this is not to suggest an equivalence between the racial discrimination that Williams faces and slavery but to recognize the historical antecedents to current forms of oppression and racialized surveillance. Focusing on her breach of decorum functions to distract from and perhaps even excuse the racism and discrimination she is reacting to in the first place. If only Serena could act "properly"; if only Serena could comport herself like Arthur Ashe, whom "the sports writer Bruce Jenkins felt was 'dignified' and 'courageous' in his ability to confront injustice without making a scene" (35). Never mind that Ashe once corrected a reporter who "suggested that having AIDS must be the greatest burden [he] ever had to bear" with "No, it isn't. . . . Being Black is the greatest burden I've had to bear. . . . Having to live as a minority in America. Even now it continues to feel like an extra weight tied around me."[21] Moreover, to praise Ashe's "calm and measured logic," his "dignified" and "courageous" ability to avoid "making a scene," is to privilege white comfort and blame Black people for the uneasiness of confronting injustice. As Ahmed aptly argues, "feelings become fetishes . . . through the erasure of the history of their production and circulation."[22] In the obsession with appraising either Williams's former "stubbornness" or her "new comportment," the media obscures the racist history of these affects and their circulation.

To be sure, when Williams falls in line, proceeding "without any reaction to a number of questionable calls," the reaction to this, too, eclipses the racist context: "She is a woman in love, one suggests. She has grown up, another decides, as if responding to the injustice of racism is childish and her previous demonstration of emotion was free-floating and detached from any external actions by others" (35). In addition to the sexist assumption that love would cure Serena of her "childish" emotions, such a response typifies a disregard for "the injustice of racism" and subsequent pathologizing of Black people's anger. Respectability politics, that is, provides no protection and in fact advances white supremacy. When "Caroline Wozniacki, a former number-one player, imitates Williams by stuffing towels in her top and shorts, all in good fun, at an exhibition match," Rankine mocks CNN for glibly asking, "Racist? CNN wants to know if outrage is the proper response" (36). Again, this type of stunt reinforces respectability politics by presuming that CNN viewers should be invited to weigh in on the proper response to racism.

Citizen thus clarifies how the conservative appeal to respectability amounts to a call to obedience, and sponsors a cruel optimism:

In any case, it is difficult not to think that if Serena lost context by abandoning all rules of civility, it could be because her body, trapped in a racial imaginary, trapped in disbelief—code for being black in America—is being governed not by the tennis match she is participating in but by a collapsed relationship that had promised to play by the rules. Perhaps this is how racism feels no matter the context—randomly the rules everyone else gets to play by no longer apply to you, and to call this out by calling out "I swear to God!" is to be called insane, crass, crazy. Bad sportsmanship. (30)

Racial discrimination in sports so perfectly captures how neoliberalism is entwined with white supremacy; like neoliberalism, sports are predicated on an "imaginary" in which ostensibly neutral rules are established and the game is played out fairly—even as the players are subject to strict surveillance. In accordance with this premise, complaints about injustice or bad calls are derided as bad sportsmanship. This is precisely the trap of white supremacist profile culture, which "promise[s] to play by the rules" and then calls you crazy when "the rules everyone else gets to play by no longer apply to you"—when you appear on the no-fly list, when you are denied a loan based on your neighbor's bad credit, when you are stopped and frisked, when your peaceful protests are met with military force, or when you are arrested and killed. Meanwhile, the public is assured that if they have nothing to hide, they have nothing to fear—until they do. Throughout *Citizen*, Rankine represents these connections among racialized surveillance, respectability politics, and the neoliberal profile culture at large. Highlighting how anger and opposition are classified as transgressions in and of themselves, she attends to affective lines that bar people from "fighting back crazily" to suppress dissent and make routine surveillance and profiling seem reasonable and warranted. For instance, US politicians went out of their way to frame the Black Lives Matter uprisings against the murder of George Floyd by police officers as violent and "inappropriate" (what could be more violent and inappropriate than suffocating a man to death for over eight minutes?), and then used this false representation of the protests as an excuse to fly a predator drone over the protesters in Minneapolis and spy planes over the protesters in Washington, D.C., to collect cell phone location data.[23] Again and again, anger and resistance to white supremacy and state violence is exploited as an excuse to perpetuate more state violence.

Resisting explanatory frameworks that rely on questions of decontextualized, individual insanity or merely personal violations of propriety, Rankine resituates Serena Williams's "disappointments and frustrations" in an aggressive system of anti-Blackness. Expanding the analysis beyond the "sharp white background" of the tennis court, she writes against Black erasure and the neoliberal rationales of fairness and decorum:

Again, Serena's frustrations, her disappointments, exist within a system you understand not to try to understand in any fair-minded way because to do so is to understand the erasure of the self as systemic, as ordinary. For Serena, the daily diminishment is a low flame, a constant drip. Every look, every comment, every bad call blossoms out of history, through her, onto you. To understand is to see Serena as hemmed in as any other black body thrown against our American background. (32)

Rankine warns against the con of fair-mindedness that serves to naturalize the erasure of Black people as ordinary and rational. Indeed, the very term "*fair-minded*" suggests how what counts as reasonable is defined by white supremacy—how light is coded as right. In contrast to Williams's so-called insanity, the "daily diminishment" that torments like a "low flame, a constant drip" is not so easily visible as a media spectacle. It is through Rankine's slow writing that "every look, every comment, every bad call" can "blossom out of history, through her, onto you." Indeed, *Citizen* steadfastly faces microaggressions and over-officiating with close-ups and paused frames, enacting a countersurveillance that "understands" differently. In this way she works to expose the practices and affects of racialized surveillance that are meant to be unseen and undetectable as such.

It has been my contention that, rendered invisible by technical and bureaucratic black boxes and foreclosing resistance by treating criticism as grounds for suspicion, contemporary profile society also solicits our complicity by promising convenience and human capital in exchange for our privacy and data. In responding to a bad call by repeating, "Don't look at me. Really, don't even look at me. Don't look my way. Don't look my way," because, as Rankine says, "it is that simple" (32), we might see Williams as resisting this bad bargain. While as a player with media endorsements, Williams clearly courts some degree of celebrity,[24] the politics of surveillance concern more than the violation of privacy, as the moment when she responds to the umpire's bad calls by repeating, "Don't look at me. Really, don't even look at me. Don't look my way. Don't look my way" makes clear (32). Williams is standing before an audience and umpires expressly there to watch her, yet her insistence that the umpire not "even look at [her]" is perfectly understandable. It is not her privacy that she demands but her freedom from an unaccountable racializing surveillance. Rankine thus asks surveillance studies to think beyond privacy and contemplate how "those processing personal data do so responsibly, fairly, and accountably."[25] It misses the point to say that if Williams doesn't want the officials looking at her she can simply leave the court, just as it begs the question to suggest that the public simply turn off their devices or opt out of privacy agreements.

Indeed, more and more contemporary practices of surveillance ask that we not only look the other way but that we also say "please." Rankine recalls hearing "someone ask the philosopher Judith Butler what makes language hurtful," to which she responded, "We suffer from the condition of being addressable" (49). Reflecting on Butler's answer, Rankine writes, "You begin to understand yourself as rendered hypervisible in the face of such language acts. Language that feels hurtful is intended to exploit all the ways that you are present. Your alertness, your openness, and your desire to engage actually demand your presence, your looking up, your talking back, and, as insane as it is, saying please" (49). Although the condition of addressability leaves people vulnerable, it also allows for some possibility of speaking back, of actively engaging. As a Black woman, Williams is especially "rendered hypervisible," but her "detractors" routinely "exploit all the ways that [she is] present" and her "desire to engage"; meanwhile, surveillance not only "demand[s] your presence" but also insists on passive engagement, so when Serena loudly denounces the gaze of white supremacist surveillance—adamantly refusing to say "please"—she forcefully invokes and refuses a history of policing and punishing African Americans for merely looking at white people.[26] As bell hooks reminds us, "an effective strategy of white supremacists, terror and dehumanization during slavery centered around white control of the black gaze."[27] This history of racialized violence emerges when Williams indecorously resists the entitled and hostile gaze of the umpires.

Concurrent with the racism of respectability politics is the cultural supposition that information about a person's body defines who they really are beneath it all. This can take the form of biometric authentication (fingerprint technology, facial recognition software, and retinal scans, for example), transphobic gender identification, genetic essentialism, and even the soft biometrics that sort and assess people's worth, riskiness, and so on based on their physical appearance. While Black people are pressured to dutifully perform respectability, the power to transcend race (and racism) here is assumed to rest within one's power. Yet no matter how people act or what they say, their bodies can ultimately reveal the "truth." These seemingly contradictory assumptions are unified in the epistemology of profile society, which both demands visibility and controls perception. According to the logic of this racializing surveillance, even as it's up to Serena Williams to act respectably, it is her musculature, her gestures, and her speech that provide the supposed evidence about who she really is.

While much is made of Williams's so-called aggression, nowhere is this logic more obvious than in the criticisms of her celebrations. After winning two gold medals at the 2012 Olympics, Rankine reminds us, Williams's "three-second celebratory dance on the center court at the All American Club" was reported by the US media as her "Crip-Walking all over the most-lily-white place in the world" (33). When she is reprimanded by reporters—"You couldn't help but shake your head. . . . What Serena did was akin to cracking a tasteless, X-rated joke inside a church. . . . What she did was immature and classless" (33)—the coded "color-blind" rhetoric of decorum again excludes any explicit reference to Williams's race, freeing the media to equate Blackness with the pornographic and the unholy. This hypersexualization of Williams's "X-rated" footwork typifies the characterization of Black women as Jezebels, the counterpoint to the other common critique that Williams is too masculine. Either way, as a Black woman she is "unladylike." To say, "You couldn't help but shake your head" is to address an implicitly white audience, or line judge, in the position to denounce Williams while naturalizing "your" racist response.

In a later interview with Piers Morgan, "Serena responds [to his reporting that the American press was calling her celebratory dancing a Crip Walk or gangster dance] incredulously by asking if she looks like a gangster to him. Yes, he answers" (34). As absurd as his answer might sound, Morgan's uncritical racial profiling does suggest the power of tropes to shape common sense and define what counts as reasonable. Furthermore, as much as technologies such as Hawk-Eye profess to revolutionize the gaze by capturing some objective truth, they function in a long history of maintaining that the racialized "body would reveal a 'truth' about the subject, despite the subject's claim."[28] Based on her three-second dance, we are asked to believe that Williams's body exposed the truth about her—a truth entirely constructed by the delusional perceptions of racial profiling.

Speaking Affect to Power

In 2008, an article in *Wired* enthused that "with enough data, the numbers speak for themselves."[29] If, in the wake of postmodernism, this promise of transparency comes as a relief, we should bear in mind the underlying question of whether individuals can also "speak for themselves" and, if so, whether they speak with as much authority as "numbers"—given that the truths that data or biometric profiles reveal about people often contradict the accounts offered by people themselves. In "The Data Don't Speak for Themselves," Robert Behn argues that "when the data speak, they do so only through some framework, some theory, some causal model, some logical construct, some perception of the world and how it works. After all, any set of data is just a collection of abstract numbers. The data acquire meaning only when they are connected to some version of reality."[30] With the surge in data profiling, however, we see a rise in "notions that these technologies are infallible, that they are objective, and that they are based on mathematical precision without error or bias on the part of the computer programmers who calibrate the search parameters of these machines or on the part of those who read these templates to make decisions."[31] Such confidence in technology has helped data profiling gain traction across the private and public sectors, grounded in a theology of absolutes and absolution apparent, for example, in George W. Bush's repeated derision of nuance as "something between pedantic nuisance and genuine treason."[32] Promising to transcend nuance and human prejudice, data profiling thereby frees its users to disproportionately harm underprivileged populations under the auspices of merely letting "the numbers speak for themselves."

This specious realism can be countered by an epistemology of unabashed affect that can help disrupt the exploitive truth power of the now pervasive profile epistemology, which claims to know better. Speaking with Berlant, Rankine clarifies that she is "not interested in narrative, or truth, or truth to power, on a certain level" but is "fascinated by affect, by positioning, and by intimacy. . . . What happens when I stand close to you? What's your body going to do? What's my body going to do?"[33] For her, poetry offers a way to explore such questions, a way of juxtaposing elements to allow for "what happens." Commensurately, she refuses narrative, instead positioning photography and news clippings alongside the personal accounts in her poetry to produce new affects, and these affects, not "truth" per se, are what drive her writing: "On myriad levels, we are . . . going to fail, fail, fail, each other and ourselves. The simplicity of the language is never to suggest truth, but to make transparent the failure."[34] Implicit here is her critique of the seductive "simplicity" of data as well, and thus her work explores how epistemologies of data profiling might be untethered from claims of objectivity and neutrality, clearing the way to address how data functions both rhetorically and materially. Data profiling is also about juxtaposition, putting elements side by side, though not to allow for "what happens," but to draw decisive and determinative correlations. The trouble with networks and data analytics is not that they are too clear-cut and that we must add in the emotion for a more complete picture. As Wendy Chun describes, networks are already "pulsing [with] energy and affect" and "cannot be reduced to nodes and edges."[35] The charge is not only to smuggle in what data misses but to call attention to what is already there but disavowed: the "pulsations that frustrate neat separations and create sticky connections between the molecular and the molar."[36]

Speaking affect to power means deconstructing the supposed neutrality of profile epistemologies by exposing their own embedded affects and the affects they attempt to exile. Even as their proponents champion surveillance technologies as objective, they seek popular and political support by means of affective appeals. A prime example is the appeal to security—the go-to rationale for dataveillance. Accordingly, those promoting the War on Terror cultivated an amorphous atmosphere of terror (as opposed to a feeling of fear, which has an object) that, by their logic, called for a similarly enigmatic and nebulous response by the state.[37] The public was thus subject to terror while the state safeguarded "intelligence." The affect of terror and helplessness was epitomized in the color-coding of terror levels without any attendant recommendations of what to do in response. Exploiting this "affective atmosphere," the defenders of the War on Terror rationalized racial profiling and covert mass surveillance that promised to someday return transparency and normalcy through supposedly pure statistical appeals. In a *New York Times* op-ed, Paul Sperry wrote:

> Young Muslim men bombed the London tube, and young Muslim men attacked New York with planes in 2001. From everything we know about the terrorists who may be taking aim at our transportation system, they

are most likely to be young Muslim men. . . . [Profiling is] based on statistics. Insurance companies profile policyholders based on probability
of risk. That's just smart business. Likewise, profiling passengers based
on proven security risk is just smart law enforcement.[38]

The next day, the *Washington Post* published a similar piece by Charles
Krauthammer: "It is a simple statistical fact. Yes, you have your shoe-bomber,
a mixed-race Muslim convert, who would not fit the profile. But the overwhelming odds are that the guy bent on blowing up your train traces his
origins to the Islamic belt stretching from Mauritania to Indonesia."[39] As we
see here, the dominant epistemology of data underwrites an affect of terror
and helplessness while conveniently dismissing feelings that might interfere
with what is "just smart business . . . just smart law enforcement." Evoking
insurance companies was apparently meant to lend a sense of matter-of-
factness to this argument for racial profiling, but it actually raises an important set of concerns about business as usual. By Krauthammer's logic, for
instance, redlining and the ongoing racial profiling in the property insurance industry—a significant means by which racial segregation was and is
institutionally constructed, with devastating consequences—is "just good
business."[40] Never mind that these systemic disadvantages are also cited as
a major contributing factor in a subject's "probability of risk." Never mind
the overgeneralizations and mistakes involved in identifying a supposedly
"*proven* security risk." Never mind that what counts as smart business, smart
government, or a risk is constituted through the surveillance and exclusion
of racialized others. Never mind that the statistical appeals are cherry-picked
and incomplete.

Insisting that the data can never "speak for itself," Rankine's poetry defiantly represents affects and experiences that cannot be captured or exhausted
numerically. *Citizen*'s insights are rooted in an unease that prompts a question:
"Each moment is like this—before it can be known, categorized as similar
to another thing and dismissed, it has to be experienced, it has to be seen.
What did he just say? Did she really just say that? Did I hear what I think I
heard? Did that just come out of my mouth, his mouth, your mouth?" (9).
Litanies of questions become a kind of refrain in *Citizen*, registering the "crisis
ordinary." These series of questions capture the exhaustion of this unrelenting flow of microaggressions that still never fail to shock. Importantly, as

the microaggressions compound, cruel optimism reverberates. If feeling the "shock of words" depends on remaining vulnerable—as in Rankine's account of hearing Judith Butler on the inherent vulnerability of being addressable—*Citizen* nonetheless makes the case that knowledge production starts with experience and entails remaining sensitive to the world. Thus, in addition to capturing discrete instances of racial aggression, the book simulates the accumulating and compounding experiences of racism. Although data discourse promises to control for risks, *Citizen* counters its commonplaces in two important ways: first, by considering how definitions of riskiness are informed by anti-Blackness and, second, by affirming that an affective epistemology demands putting oneself at risk nonetheless.

Rankine accomplishes this in part through lists of questions, pausing the book at the impasses they create and swelling the moments so they cannot simply slide by. Because they don't slide by:

> The world is wrong. You can't put the past behind you. It's buried in you; it's turned your flesh into its own cupboard. Not everything remembered is useful but it all comes from the world to be stored in you. Who did what to whom on which day? Who said that? She said what? What did he just do? Did she really just say that? He said what? What did she do? Did I hear what I think I heard? Did that just come out of my mouth, his mouth, your mouth? Do you remember when you sighed? (63)

Such impasses open up the text, expanding each moment to allow for experience to become palpable. With "my mouth, his mouth, your mouth" and the second "when you sighed," Rankine amplifies the unpalatable, intimate experience of "What happens when I stand close to you? What's your body going to do? What's my body going to do?"[41] Nevertheless, this questioning mode creates space for the possibility of something other than "repetition of the same that uses up its object or subject," for "moments [that] can call forth a new future, a way to exhaust exhaustion."[42]

Against a backdrop where "memory" is increasingly externalized and digitalized as a chip, drive, or bank (63), Rankine insists that memories are, in fact, embodied. Although many data theorists are interested in aestheticizing or visualizing data, and W. E. B. Du Bois's artful data visualizations of African American life for the 1900 World's Fair remain an excellent example of how to do this viscerally and affectively, for *Citizen* the history Du Bois helps visualize, like one's personal past, is not "behind you," not externalized and compartmentalized for safekeeping elsewhere in the world but instead "all comes from the world to be stored in you." Just as information about the past is stored in data centers—that also claim the future—memories, Rankine writes, turn "your flesh into its own cupboard," inhabiting and transforming "you" physically, emotionally. Recognizing that "there is no single memory organ: there is no one organ, separate from other organs/cellular circuits, that simply stores information," helps us forgo "the desire to reduce memory to storage," especially to the image of shelved, compartmentalized digital storage.[43] If memory is instead "the strengthening and development of certain pathways," then Rankine's lyric poetry reclaims and reorganizes these memories to forge new futures and lines of flight. Rather than functioning just like that flesh cupboard only storing and embodying the weight of experiences, poetry also holds memory as communal, inseverable, and leaky. Meanwhile, the domestic image of the cupboard as the holder of implicit memory and generational trauma and stress encourages discussions of Black health away from more reductive discussions about what's in the kitchen cupboard.[44]

Responding to how profile epistemology accumulates data and reifies it into "facts" to stabilize or fix subject positions, Rankine's lyric accumulates feelings and affects, a response that is powerfully destabilizing. In a sense, *Citizen* is questioning what counts and how lives add up:

And, of course, you want the days to add up to something more than you came in out of the sun and drank the potable water of your developed world—yes, and because words hang in the air like pollen, the throat closes. You hack away. That time and that time and that time the outside blistered the inside of you, words outmaneuvered years, had you in a chokehold, every part roughed up, the eyes dripping. That's the bruise the ice in the heart was meant to ice. (55)

This description moves from the space between people, what hangs "in the air like pollen," to the sometimes debilitating effects inside one's body. The body hacks away against noxious words, which, like pollen, can spread, germinate, and sicken. From this image of insidious harm, focus shifts to the more overtly violent image of serial abuse ("that time and that time and that time"), which also makes "the throat close," but this time through "a chokehold."

Both emphasize a difficulty breathing and therefore speaking, representing the nonsymbolic relationship between a shortness of breath and lack of voice. Reading Citizen today, after the murders of Eric Garner and George Floyd, these words resonate profoundly with protesters' refrain of "I can't breathe"—a plea that George Floyd told police officers more than twenty times. That protesters took to the streets to insist that Black Lives Matter during the COVID-19 pandemic that was killing African Americans at much higher rates—also by making it difficult to breathe—reflects the multiple fronts on which Black citizens are "hacking away" and fighting for their lives.

Meanwhile, the rhythm of the line "that time and that time and that time" practically parodies dataveillance's patterns of recording and time-stamping experiences—though Rankine does not identify which time, which place, or specifically what happened, instead expressing the real rhythms of memory and experience that go uncaptured by profiling and don't add up in the neoliberal data world, the uncounted or discounted pain that goes unrepresented. Even as the widely circulated video of Floyd's murder was important for representing this persistent pain and helping grow the Black Lives Matter movement, for many people watching it "that time and that time and that time" was also retraumatizing. Pointing to "the bruise the ice in the heart was meant to ice," Rankine reimagines so-called coldness as an act of self-care and self-protection, an attempt to numb the pain of words that can "rough up," "blister," and "bruise."

"The 'I' and the 'we' are shaped by, and even take the shape of, the contact we have with others,"[45] Ahmed writes, and Rankine's use of the second person maneuvers the reader from the outside to the inside of the subject. Addressing the affective atmosphere that "hangs in the air"—the "outside that blister[ed] the inside of you"—Rankine disrupts a biometric profile epistemology: "The body does not hide or reveal an otherwise unrepresented latency or depth but is a set of operational linkages and connections with other things other bodies."[46] So "you hack away" (55) because, as Elizabeth Grosz has it, "the body is not simply a sign to be read, a symptom to be deciphered, but also a force to be reckoned with."[47]

In fact, Citizen suggests that simply sitting in silence can be a forceful defense, a rebellious act of self-care in the face of "the stresses stemming from racism" and the pressure to achieve oneself out of racial capitalism. Again, the moment slows and swells:

When you arrive in your driveway and turn off the car, you remain behind the wheel another ten minutes. You fear the night is being locked in and coded on a cellular level and want time to function as a power wash. Sitting there staring at the closed garage door you are reminded that a friend once told you there exists the medical term—John Henryism —for people exposed to stresses stemming from racism. They achieve themselves to death trying to dodge the buildup of erasure. Sherman James, the researcher who came up with the term, claimed the physiological costs were high. You hope by sitting in silence you are bucking the trend. (11)

This passage moves from what "you fear" to what "you hope": from the fear of "being locked in and coded on a cellular level" to the hope of "bucking the trend." Drawing on the digital and biometric meanings of "coded" and "cellular" in the study of trends, Rankine suggests how the hopes and fears of the historical present are increasingly structured by the anti-Blackness of surveillance capitalism. At the same time, evoking John Henryism and highlighting not dislocated data and particular traumas but the cumulative effects and affects they produce, Rankine represents the systemic slow violence of racism as well as the mostly unsensational modes of resistance. Describing a person exhausted by the taxing work of achieving, dodging, and bucking, who nevertheless, remains sitting and staring, Rankine suggests that what might be mistaken for inactivity can be a self-protective, even hopeful gesture. As Berlant writes, "In the impasse induced by crisis, being treads water; mainly, it does not drown. Even those whom you would think of as defeated are living beings figuring out how to stay attached to life from within it, and to protect what optimism they have for that, at least."[48]

The self-care of sitting in a parked car, actively resisting the pressure to drive oneself "to death trying to dodge the buildup of erasure," also evokes and complicates the notion of driving while Black in the United States. Consider how Rankine connects the fact that Black people are assaulted by the police for "fitting the description" (105) with the cruel mandate that they remain positive: "Feel better. Move forward. Let it go. Come on. Come on. Come on. . . . Move forward. Let it go. Come on" (66). Rankine clarifies that the same forces who are "setting up a blockade" (105) and shouting "get on the ground. Get on the ground now" (106) are also those insisting that Black people simply move forward. This imperative that Black people "feel better," and display a decorous response to racism disavows their feelings and experiences while adding an implicit threat to their well-being. In fact, failing to feel good about racial profiling is itself treated as grounds for suspicion. The mandates to let it go and come on speak to the inherent anti-Blackness of profile epistemologies, which rely on the investments and movements of people who might be stopped, as Rankine says, "at any random moment."[49] To be sure, no amount of achieving or driving forward will reconcile this madness: "In a landscape drawn from an ocean bed, you can't drive yourself sane—so angry you are crying. You can't drive yourself sane. This motion wears a guy out" (105). Endemic to the cruel optimism of anti-Black capitalism, the problem is sold as the cure, and "you" are regarded as insane for noticing. Ultimately, in *Citizen*, this "crisis ordinary" evokes the objectification and commodification of Black lives that are worn out like driving machines.

Alongside *Citizen*'s accounts of everyday microaggressions are ten "scripts for situation videos created in collaboration with [photographer] John Lucas," which retell major news stories of anti-Black racism, such as the response to Hurricane Katrina, the Jena Six cases, and the murder of Mark Duggan in London. "Stop-and-Frisk" addresses the appalling script for racial profiling from the point of view of the person who "just knew" he would be stopped by the police for "fitting the description." In the course of the narrator being pulled over, "stretched out on the hood," "handcuffed and pushed into the police vehicle's backseat," and finally fingerprinted and undressed, we are told, "This is what it looks like. You know this is wrong. This is not what it looks like. You need to be quiet. This is wrong. You need to close your mouth now. This is what it looks like. Why are you talking if you haven't done anything wrong?" (108). Here Rankine captures what forced visibility looks like, emphasizing the specific procedures of surveillance, even as the description itself remains conspicuously undisclosed. This contrast calls out forms of looking that supersede the tropes and refocuses the account on the experience and affects of surveillance, of being stopped and frisked.

Moreover, this familiar question—"Why are you talking if you haven't done anything wrong?"—epitomizes how profile society and white supremacy depend on each other to suppress dissent. Ultimately, profiling is not merely descriptive, responsive, or even preemptive. Indeed, this script points to how profiling is also "prehensive" or a matter of "making the present look exactly the way it needs to in order to guarantee a very specific and singular outcome in the future."[50] In other words, it is not only that profiling represses or preempts unwanted outcomes through discipline and surveillance ("If you see something say something")—it also produces outcomes, often, as Jasbir Puar puts it, by "collecting, curating, and tabulating data and affect."[51] This is true of both police profiling and algorithmic consumer profiling. Stop-and-frisk is not designed to simply reduce crime; it is meant to produce neighborhoods, social and familial relations, futures, affects, and data—data that might then deem an area or person risky, thereby perpetuating a cycle of discrimination.

Rankine ends "Stop-and-Frisk" by repeating the sentence, "And still you are not the guy and still you fit the description because there is only one guy who is always the guy fitting the description" (108). Again, the racial logic of profile epistemology demands visibility while controlling perception. Under the banner of neutrality, profiling formalizes stereotypes and tropes as "descriptive," masking over their inherent biases. Still, the syntax here provides an alternative understanding of what it means to fit the description. In one sense, the "one guy who is always the guy fitting the description" is any given Black man. In another sense, he is the police officer who is actively fastening or "fitting" the description onto the man like a pair of handcuffs. That is, while some are subject to forced visibility, others have the power to control perception as they see fit, a dynamic operating beneath profiling's ostensible neutrality. Rankine captures the harmful costs of security that depend upon the securing of stereotypes. Crucially, the history of racializing surveillance and biometrics demonstrates that descriptions don't simply fit people; people in fact are fitted into descriptions.

Pacing, Spacing, and Countersurveillance

I end by exploring modes of countersurveillance embedded and embodied in Rankine's lyric, effective and affective techniques that speak back to the hegemonic profile epistemologies she depicts. If, as I have suggested, positing affect as a form of knowledge production can help disrupt the teleological truth claims of profiling, then Rankine also illustrates how the power of artistic countersurveillance, such as the "scripts for situation videos," can produce new knowledge through new visions.

Just as Rankine celebrates Serena Williams for resisting racializing surveillance by insisting to the official, "Don't even look at me," *Citizen* later examines even more closely a parallel moment of protest in sports. Another of the scripts for situation videos examines an incident in the 2006 FIFA World Cup Final between Italy and France, when, in retaliation to verbal abuse, Zinedine Zidane headbutted Marco Materazzi. *Citizen* includes frame-by-frame stills of Zidane passing Materazzi and then turning in his tracks and walking back, before headbutting him in the chest. These frames are interposed with quotes by Maurice Blanchot, Ralph Ellison, Frantz Fanon, James Baldwin, William Shakespeare, Homi Bhabha, Frederick Douglass, and Zinedine Zidane himself, as well as a phrase spoken by Materazzi (provided by "accounts of lip readers responding to the transcript of the World Cup"): "Big Algerian shit, dirty terrorist, ni---r" (126, redacted). Rankine literally reframes the event in a history of colonial oppression and anticolonial and antiracist opposition, again underscoring that "when one reacts, one is not reacting to any one of those moments."[52] In this context, uncovering Materazzi's hate speech through lip-reading and juxtaposing his words with a closer look at the slow sequence of events is a form of oppositional looking that exposes what is meant to be hushed. Like an "antebellum hacker," Rankine "see[s] the openings provided by literacy" and "bend[s] the political technology of literacy back upon itself."[53]

Part of what Rankine's artistic countersurveillance hacks is the pacing and spacing of power relations that make certain people and events hypervisible while protecting and obscuring others. In Berlant's words, it "provides metrics for understanding how we pace and space our encounters with things, how we manage the too closeness of the world and also the desire to have an impact on it that has some relation to its impact on us."[54] Indeed, by freezing each frame and interposing historical context alongside Materazzi's racist speech, Rankine "manages the too closeness of the world," while opening up the time and space necessary to understand this interplay of impacts. In boldface, she features Zidane's statement that "*What he said 'touched the deepest part of me'*" (128), language that recontextualizes the moment of violent contact. Audiences are accustomed to replays of bad behavior or bad sportsmanship, but Rankine reorganizes the pacing and spacing as if to say, in Fanon's words, "notice too, illustrations of this kind of racial prejudice can be multiplied indefinitely" (122). In this sense, the headbutt that was punished as bad sportsmanship is better understood as a rebuttal.

Earlier I clarified that profiling and racializing surveillance are not only attempts to preempt unwanted outcomes but are also means of claiming and producing a particular future. Likewise, when Rankine situates her work in the tradition of activism and resistance that she cites, she demonstrates that countersurveillance—an oppositional looking back at racializing surveillance—is productive and not only resistant. As Homi Bhabha writes, "The state of emergency is also always a state of emergence" (quoted on 126). Out of Rankine's looking back at the emergency of racism and racializing surveillance an "American Lyric" emerges. Between the frames of Zidane, she quotes Fanon: "It is the White Man who creates the black man. But it is the black man who creates" (128). Racial profiling is a matter of representation, but it is also a manner of creating the Black man affectively, rhetorically, and materially. In response, in the words of Baldwin, a "rebuttal assumes an original form. This endless struggle to achieve and reveal and confirm a human identity, human authority, contains, for all its horror, something very beautiful" (128). Clearly, this "original form" includes modes of countersurveillance, which deconstruct the truth claims and teleology of profiling and its insistence on "[un]original forms."

In *Citizen*, then, oppositional looking disrupts the epistemologies of racism and profile societies and the respectability politics they sponsor, which defensively ask, "Why are you talking if you haven't done anything wrong?" As with the use of lip-reading to recuperate lost words, Rankine's lyric refuses to let those moments of violence slide idly by, exposing and enacting creative resistance by giving them a second look. In a photograph that *Citizen* includes of the Rutgers women's basketball team at a press conference after Don Imus's racist and sexist insults, even as the team technically observes the "decorum of silence,"[55] they clearly register their disgust through body language and facial expressions. By including this image, Rankine evokes "the recognizable outrage and disbelief performed routinely and silently by black women's bodies given their historical relationship to power, the moments when they 'throw shade.'"[56] Drawing on the tradition of expressing silent opposition by means of top-eye or side-eye, the team rejects Imus's public apology, in part by exposing and subverting the decorum of silence they are nevertheless expected to uphold—pointedly contextualizing Imus's racist remarks within a larger system of white supremacy and racializing surveillance.

I end with a moment from *Citizen*, in which Rankine observes the complicit silence of white bystanders, drawing a stark distinction between oppositional looking and mere onlooking. When a cashier asks a Black woman, "[Do] you think your card will work?," Rankine comments:

> If this is his routine, he didn't use it on your friend who went before you. As she picks up her bag, she looks to see what you will say. She says nothing. You want her to say something—both as witness and as a friend. She is not you; her silence says so. Because you are watching all this take place even as you participate in it, you say nothing as well. Come over here with me, your eyes say. Why on earth would she? (54)

The man behind the register prolongs the history of distrusting the documentation and identification of Black people during the transatlantic slave trade, as well as the cultural presumption that Black people are inherently "unruly" (95). To the extent that consumer transactions now amount to citizen-consumers "'checking in' with authorities,"[57] his questioning of whether her card will work implies that she is perhaps misrepresenting herself or is "out of place." Surveillance scholars, such as Christian Parenti, have suggested that credit cards are "leading the path forward to a future where money and identification have merged."[58] This scene evokes the historical antecedents of this merger, including the objectification, commodification, and consequent tracking of Black people through and since slavery. However, this moment in *Citizen* also reminds us that even as we are supposedly authenticated through consumer transactions, class privilege does not eradicate discrimination. In fact, this form of authentication is always prefaced by white supremacy.

As a silent witness, the white friend is implicated in the apparatus of racializing surveillance, her silence announcing and confirming her privilege: "She is not you; her silence says so." Yet "because you are watching all this take place even as you participate in it," Rankine writes, "you say nothing as well." The women share the experience of silently "watching all this take place"; yet "you participate in it," feeling the other woman's distance—"come over here with me, your eyes say"—gesturing toward the possibility of inhabiting this difficult space together. This tension recalls Rankine's remarks that she is "not interested in narrative, or truth, or truth to power, on a certain level" but is "fascinated by affect, by positioning, and by intimacy. . . . What happens when I stand close to you? What's your body going to do? What's my body going to do?" Knowing that "on myriad levels, we are both going to fail, fail, fail, each other and ourselves," when she notes that the friend does not "come over" to cohabit the difficult space, Rankine asks, "Why on earth would she?" Yet through the use of the second person—here and throughout *Citizen*—Rankine optimistically opens up the text to this very possibility: that a reader "who is not you" might share in this affect, see and respond to the gesture, and "come over here," as both "a witness and a friend." Without naïvely collapsing the difference between "you" and "I," this opens up the possibility for a "we" (for what Benedict Anderson calls an "imagined community")[59] in a network culture that exacerbates racial inequality by positing a "relentlessly pointed yet empty, singular yet plural YOU."[60] The critical difference between the second person in *Citizen* and Chun's use of "YOU" is that Chun's "small s sovereign"[61] is a function of neoliberalism and surveillance capitalism, whereas Rankine's "you" acknowledges its vulnerability and interconnectedness. Even as *Citizen*'s optimism might reveal itself as cruel, by highlighting microaggressions that like racializing surveillance are meant to remain inconspicuous, *Citizen* helps produce an affective epistemology that makes these moments count. This is a different form of literacy and knowledge production that confronts our interpersonal failures and the epistemological failures of profiling. Profile societies claim to eliminate bias by collecting ever more information, but the operating model of what counts and who does the counting remains static. In the face of this, *Citizen*'s "oppositional looking" at the apparatuses of profile societies re-paces and respaces the movements such societies produce, exposing how the ostensibly neutral structure of data profiling and racializing surveillance grows from and remains rooted in white supremacy.

CHAPTER THREE

"Both a Gift and a Trap"

Speculative Surveillance and Labor in
William Gibson's Pattern Recognition

atherine Hayles opened the conversation at MIT's 2012 forum on "Electronic Literature and Future Books" by defining *apophenia*, the practice of finding patterns in random data, and joking that it is a risk "endemic to literary criticism," where every image, action, and word choice is subject to "close reading."[1] In the data age, every purchase, keystroke, and utterance is analogously regarded as a significant bit of information, subject to interpretation. For example, already by 2011 Acxiom, the marketing technology and services company, had "alone accumulated an average of 1,500 pieces of data on each person in its database—that includes 96 percent of Americans—along with data about everything from their credit scores to whether they've bought medication for incontinence."[2] These perpetually updating and growing profiles are immensely lucrative and seemingly imperative for modern marketers and the corporations and brokers buying and selling consumer data. In Accenture's Point of View report on "Data Monetization in the Age of Big Data"—featuring bees pollinating fields of sunflowers and close-ups of dripping honeycombs throughout—the information technology services and consulting company rejoices that "conditions [are] ripe for data monetization" and encourages would-be clients "to tap its potential."[3] This data comes from a wide range of sources, including social media, smart product sensors, credit card transactions, web logs, street cameras, satellites, store loyalty cards, surveys, census records, public records, property records, financial records, motor vehicle records, subscription records, product warranty cards, delivery receipts, cloud storage, and, as Accenture emphasizes, especially mobile devices "in the form of transactions, inquiries, text messages or tweets, GPS locations or live video feeds."[4] As opposed to the dirty image of data mining, Accenture reimagines this raw data as nectar waiting to be extracted and transformed into sweet flowing revenue streams. Despite the common claims that "data speaks for itself," Accenture concedes here that without analysis, the data remains raw and of little value in the marketplace. Meanwhile, in their analogy, the public is likened to a renewable field of flowers, dependent on the busy data collectors helpfully pollinating and propagating their information. Accenture attempts to persuade clients that they "may choose where to play" in this field of riches.[5] The problem, of course, is one of power: who does the analysis and what insights do they make? Who is playing, and who is being played? Who owns the data and who keeps the honey?

Whereas the telling details of a realist or modernist novel are thought to combine to create a more or less round character—indeed, the character of the character—the data collected about consumer-citizens are not presumed to create a subjectivity that is more significant than the sum of its parts. Rather, through data profiles, everything becomes meaningful, not through its construction of an individual or self but through its parsing and collating to create a "dividual"—a codified, predictable consumer-citizen and worker.[6] Nevertheless, data must be made meaningful through analysis that yields what companies commonly refer to as actionable insights. So as companies like Accenture find ever more uses for what they regard as a "powerful new form of capital,"[7] we must resist the false dichotomy between subjective writing and objective data by instead highlighting the power relations that condition both profiling and narrative plots, especially as they cross-pollinate.

Characters in realist novels "are often described with a good many superfluous, unnecessary details which are meant to enhance the mimetic effect";[8] in data profiling, however, details (never "superfluous") are not used to shore up individuality but circulate as valuable in their own right. In postmodern novels, such as "in Pynchon's work, for instance, the discourse of consumerism is foregrounded by the use of brand-names that 'have usurped the place of the human subject, no longer background to character but proclaiming themselves as "living" presences.'"[9] In the context of multinational corporations, data brokers, and nation-states creating ever-more exacting profiles of citizen-consumers, attention to brand names and what might seem like "superfluous unnecessary details" once again "enhance[s] the mimetic effect." It's not that "brand-names have usurped the place of the human subject" in the data age, but that the behavior of human subjects is always in the process of becoming branded or converted into fungible data.

Postmodernism, in contrast to realism and modernism, has been accused of "perverse" nihilism or maintaining that nothing counts.[10] Yet in the data age, contemporary literature must instead confront the workings of a world where everything potentially counts. One could argue that this is simply an inverse that amounts to the same thing—if everything counts, then nothings counts—but this argument misses an important distinction. Despite common claims that data mining is impartial and neutral, the information gathered about citizen-consumers is made meaningful by hegemonic discourses and has become a way of not just capitalizing on habits but actively shaping them. As every keystroke, click, comment, view, glance, purchase, query, affiliation, and movement now "counts," the pressing question for twenty-first-century literature becomes how meaning is made and by whom.

This is the question driving the plot of William Gibson's 2003 novel, *Pattern Recognition*, which was published nine years after the creation of the "cookie," four years after the first commercially available GPS phone, two years after 9/11 and the signing of the USA PATRIOT Act, and the same year the Pentagon unveiled the Total Information Awareness system. Although the novel predates Meta Platforms Inc., the invention of Google Street View, the FISA Amendments Act of 2008, Google's 2012 updated Privacy Policy purporting to create "a more intuitive Google Experience," and Edward Snowden's release of NSA documents, it is fair to say that the novel anticipates the ongoing intensification of consumer surveillance and data profiling in the twenty-first century. If not through data analytics, we might ask how the author anticipates this problem. Jennifer Egan offers an evocative answer: "I really think [literature is] a kind of a dream, collective dream life of the larger culture. It's a narrative that pulls together, all kinds of different forces that are acting on all of us and transmutes them into a . . . narrative with symbolic meaning, which none of writers often really understand. We understand some of it, but if it's really good, there should be a lot of stuff in there that we're not even aware of."[11] In other words, literature can play forward the different forces (cultural, historical, technological) to create emergent and sometimes prescient representations of the world unfolding.

From the novel's organizing detective story to the lingering uncertainties in the aftermath of 9/11 to the mundane moments of characters' lives, everything potentially adds up to something in the novel's surveillance-scape. The commonplaces of everyday life (such as passing through a shopping center or going on the internet) are infused with significance, mystery, and even risk, beyond the close reading Hayles jokingly calls "endemic to literary criticism."[12] This sense that every moment is ripe with clues or meaning is, of course, a hallmark of detective fiction, a genre that begs a paranoid reading. Gibson has said that "detective fiction and science fiction are an ideal cocktail," and although Pattern Recognition is neither per se, it does capture their common ground in the historical present of ubiquitous data surveillance.[13] It is now wholly reasonable to assume that even the most mundane actions, purchases, and utterances could yield potentially significant information. Pattern Recognition thus raises critical epistemological questions about who creates knowledge and meaning, through what means, and to whose benefit. Perhaps most important, the novel grounds these questions in the political economy of profiling and embeds them in an updated version of a traditional Marxist narrative to confront the material labor conditions of profiling.

On the second page of the novel, data profiling convenes with an emphatically twenty-first-century technique of character development when Gibson directs readers to "google Cayce," the novel's protagonist. Gibson explains that "if you look closely [online] you may see it suggested that [Cayce] is a . . . dowser in the world of global marketing,"[14] implying that Cayce's digital profile precedes her. This metafictional gesture also suggests that the character circulates outside of Gibson's control, outside of the text. After all, it is true that information about Cayce is available online in book reviews, synopsis, excerpts, and blogs. In fact, her prized black Buzz Rickson's MA-1 flying jacket is even available for purchase online as part of Buzz Rickson's William Gibson Collection—a product that might well be advertised to readers who followed Gibson's instructions to Google the character.[15] Thus, by suggesting that readers consult online paratextual information to learn about the protagonist, Gibson casually grants that Google (the company) and googling (the action), are integral to contemporary perceptions of people. Beyond simply peppering the prose with brand names and neologisms, the suggestion to "google Cayce" acknowledges the internet's role in characterizing people and how that characterization creates a feedback loop. According to profile epistemology, one's digital profile reflects their value (to an advertiser, insurance agency, bank, or employer, for instance). Here, to be google-able, as Cayce is, is to count more: to be a figure larger than life, a character beyond the page. Moreover, to google the protagonist is to perform due diligence, to be a good reader who "look[s] closely" (2). Already, it becomes clear that Gibson explicitly embeds his novel (and the act of reading it) in the data age. Manipulating data surveillance's language and ways of knowing, this small but telling moment positions the protagonist in relation to her profile and invites readers to begin interrogating how the political economy of consumer surveillance mediates subjectivity.

The elaborate plot of *Pattern Recognition* portrays meaning-making as a pressing power struggle, appreciating "that the race to know as much as possible about [consumer-citizens] has become the central battle of the era."[16] In doing so, the novel stages an arms race to find the maker of a series of film clips released anonymously online between those with an interest in commercializing the footage and the fans who consider it sacred and want to protect it from co-optation. On one side of this conflict is the protagonist, Cayce Pollard, a "footagehead," a "coolhunter," and a freelance marketing consultant for the advertising firm Blue Ant. Notably, Cayce has physical and psychological sensitivities or allergies to brands and logos, making her uniquely talented at this work. On the other side is Hubertus Bigend, the founder of Blue Ant, who is interested in the footage as "the most brilliant marketing ploy of this very young century. And new. Somehow entirely new" (4). Despite her reservations about Bigend's intentions and ethics, Cayce agrees to help him find the maker of the footage to take full advantage of his wealth and the access it affords, while mostly withholding her discoveries.

In many ways, this quest to pull back the curtain on the footage follows a familiar Marxist narrative. Gibson seems to accept Marx's invitation in *Capital* to "in company with the owner of money and the owner of labour-power, leave this noisy sphere, where everything takes place on the surface and in full view of everyone, and follow them into the hidden abode of production, on whose threshold there hangs the notice 'No admittance except on business'" to "see, not only how capital produces, but how capital is itself produced."[17] *Pattern Recognition* ostensibly delivers on "the basic promise of the Marxian narrative of production" to provide "a kind of explanatory depth, a guarantee of final decipherment."[18] Indeed, along with almost all of the principal characters, Cayce and Bigend eventually climactically convene in post-Soviet Russia in "the hidden abode of production" to meet the "maker" and watch her work. In this sense, hidden labor conditions are in fact the big reveal of the novel. We learn, for instance, that a woman named Nora Volkova creates the footage by editing surveillance tape gathered throughout Moscow, but she is otherwise catatonic as the result of a fragment of a Claymore mine that was lodged in her brain during the assassination of her parents. Nora is thus unaware that her twin sister, Stella, distributes the footage and has cultivated a global following. As the ending unfolds, Gibson slowly unveils an expensive and sophisticated infrastructure and security apparatus behind these sympathetic twins, bankrolled by their oligarch uncle, Andrei Volkova. Most notably Volkova establishes a privatized prison to secure a captive and covert workforce who renders the footage.

Marx's distinction between the "noisy sphere" of consumption and the hidden conditions of production is arguably as stark as ever, with so much of manufacturing outsourced to factories in largely poor remote areas of the Global South. This benefits multinational corporations by being cheaper and relatively invisible to the purchasing public in the Global North. Accordingly, the public seems willing to imagine—despite often knowing the ugly truth—that Apple products, for example, are made in Silicon Valley by well-paid geniuses playing table tennis during their many breaks. Likewise, while Upton Sinclair importantly exposed the horrors of the meatpacking industry in The Jungle, factory farming in the United States today is largely protected from public scrutiny by so-called ag-gag anti-whistleblower laws that prohibit any filming or photographing of the farms without the consent of the owners,[19] enabling the meat-eating public to disavow the truth: "Of course, I know, but still . . ."[20] In D. A. Miller's words, "Rendered discreet by disavowal, [power] is also thereby rendered more effective."[21] Gibson highlights this gulf between what the public knows and how they act by tracing the footage not only back to its maker but also to the World War II Claymore mine shrapnel, the residual Cold War infrastructure, the incredible and consolidated post-Soviet wealth, and finally to the prisoners rendering the footage behind large fences. In this way, Gibson disrupts the footageheads' fantasy of "'The Garage Kubrick' . . . some technologically empowered solo auteur, some guerilla creator out there alone in the night of the internet, . . . some secretive perhaps unknown genius" (48). Instead, the novel clarifies that the makers actually represent a confluence of historical forces and resources: namely, the end of the Cold War system, massive income inequality, techno-capitalism, and an expanding market for surplus data.

Nevertheless, as Julian Murphet rightly points out, this "dialectical moment of wonder and disenchantment . . . *has always already happened.*"[22] Despite Cayce's care to protect the cherished footage from consumerist corruption, we come to realize that "the community of footageheads could never have resisted the enchantments of capital anyway, which is shown . . . to have conditioned the footage's production from the start."[23] In addition to witnessing the concealed privatized prison, Cayce learns that the footageheads themselves were prompted and nudged by the distributors, who surveilled and participated in the fans' online forums. Bigend's arrival on the scene does not represent, in the final instance, the "corporate colonization" that Cayce dreads.[24] In other words, "There is thus no 'single' spectacular revelation, no straightforward turn to the site of manual production."[25] Instead, we learn of a complex assemblage of material and immaterial labor that had, from the beginning, reached around the curtain that Cayce and Bigend relish in pulling back.

In this sense, the novel also reappraises the "noisy sphere, where everything takes place on the surface and in full view of everyone"[26] to account for the "free labor" that is hidden in plain sight. Following Tiziana Terranova's expert analysis, I use "free labor" to describe "the moment where [the] knowledgeable consumption of culture is translated into excess productive activities that are pleasurably embraced and at the same time often shamelessly exploited."[27] In other words, this labor is "free both in the sense of 'not financially rewarded' and of 'willingly given.'"[28] Specifically, *Pattern Recognition* addresses how capital is itself produced, in part, through the underexposure of labor and production and the overexposure of consumer-citizens. In surveillance capitalism, the public's habits in the "noisy sphere" are repackaged as products. In this regard, the public stocks the stores of data profilers with free raw material (surplus data) and often unpaid labor (content production). It's not just that activities such as emailing, maintaining a social media presence, and shopping are in many contexts forms of unpaid labor; it's that this work is also invisibly exploited by an immensely profitable industry. Meanwhile, this labor is hidden in full view under the banners of "sharing" and "connecting." As Gavin J. D. Smith describes, "To a greater or lesser degree, we are all surveillance workers, complicit in the art of monitoring, interpreting and making sense of social reality," in addition to supplying the raw data.[29]

The public is supposedly compensated in convenience, personalization, and access to "free" services, which are, of course, further opportunities to share more of their data and more completely "express themselves."

If we consider other businesses where workers are compensated through the abstract privilege of participation, we can begin to expose the underlying inequity of this epistemology. For example, the low salaries for teachers, the majority of whom are women, are often excused by dismissive statements that teachers "aren't in it for the money." Likewise, the egregious underpayment of NFL cheerleaders (who make less than minimum wage) is ostensibly excusable because the women are considered lucky that they have the opportunity to "participate" and receive "attention."[30] The same is said of many (mostly Black) professional athletes when critics interrogate the profit margins of professional sports. During the COVID-19 pandemic, "essential workers" were showered with platitudes of gratitude, thank you signs, and evening applause, while their underpayment, routine surveillance, and dangerous working conditions were largely disregarded. Similarly, Terranova points out that "it is an interesting feature of the internet debate (and evidence, somehow, of its masculine bias) that users' labour has attracted more attention in the case of the open-source movement than in that of mailing lists and websites."[31] Indeed, the inequities of surveillance capitalism are the inequities of capitalism across expanding domains and territories. Meanwhile, user-consumers are framed as satisfied customers or willing participants, but rarely as labor power or raw materials for immense profit.

Watching the Numbers

Discussing her work as a coolhunter, Cayce ominously asserts early in the novel that there should be "no doubt that commodification will soon follow identification" (10). This certitude makes her apprehensive to identify the maker of the footage, despite her deep desire to know. The narrative seems to affirm these fears by representing the signs and symptoms of consumer capitalism as toxins spreading and seeping across national borders, through screens, and beneath the skin, raising the stakes of the quest and arousing tension. Yet the naïveté underlying the narrative's suspense is the notion that this threat could be evaded by simply protecting the maker's identity from Bigend's capitalist grasp. While Bigend is initially drawn, to quote Terranova, as

> one of the bad boys of capital moving in on underground subcultures or subordinate cultures and "incorporating" the fruits of their production (styles, languages, music) into the media food chain . . . Rather than capital "incorporating" from the outside the authentic fruits of the collective imagination, it seems more reasonable to think of cultural flows as originating within a field which is always and already capitalism. Incorporation is not about capital descending on authentic culture, but a more immanent process of channeling of collective labour (even as cultural labour) into monetary flows and its structuration within capitalist business practices.[32]

Ultimately, the novel affirms this analysis and bursts the bubble of Bigend's persona to reveal a much deeper and more troubling set of conditions: the footage cannot be "incorporated" into consumer-capitalism because it was never simply outside of it, even as it animated and assembled new collectives and modes of resistance. As unfamiliar and alluring as the footage is to both fans and financiers, Cayce's career as a coolhunter who finds "whatever the next thing might be" (32) also points to the fact that subcultural movements have long driven capitalist expansion.[33] While affording different opportunities and assemblages, the footage is born of this genealogy, in this political economy.

Anticipating the surge in digital surveillance, Gibson instead makes it clear that the devoted underground fans of the footage and the market information that they supply are the real find "in this very young century" (4). In other words, whether or not the footage is ever monetized, as Cayce fears, its following already has been. Bigend extols that the footage "has already been the single most effective piece of guerilla marketing ever. [He's] been tracking hits on enthusiasts sites, and *searching* for mentions elsewhere" and marvels that "the numbers are amazing" (64, emphasis added). When he cheers that Cayce has "watched a subculture being born . . . evolving exponentially," he implies that "advertising ecologies" not only bear new products but also engender new subjectivities and cultures that take on a life of their own (337). Still—on the big end—these new subjectivities are supposedly reducible to their numbers as culture becomes a function of their exponents. The passive construction of subcultures "being born" and then naturally "evolving" as a matter of course conspicuously discounts the strategic propagation of the film clips by the makers and the footageheads. In fact, Blue Ant and the distributors of the footage have infiltrated the Film:Footage:Forum (F:F:F), where footageheads discuss the latest segments, to study viewers' responses and track their engagement. It is not only that "the best way to keep your site visible and thriving on the Web is to turn it into a space which is not only accessed, but somehow built by its users."[34] In the broader context of algorithmic governance, online surveilling permits market researchers to target consumers by banking what is private and particular to them.

Therefore, Parkaboy's "feeling that none of what we actually do here is ever really private" is far from paranoid (226). Today we see how similar tactics have contributed to the popularity of QAnon, an acutal anonymous source that gained traction online, albeit with radically different messages and ramifications. Followers of QAnon's conspiracy theories first popped up on 4chan where viral marketers posed as 4chan users. From there, Q's conspiracy theories spread with the help of social media algorithms and Russian bots. Like other online movements, QAnon did not evolve (or devolve) in a closed ecosystem; rather, it was cultivated by "channeling . . . collective labour"[35] (and in its case racism and misogyny) through capitalist networks of algorithmic governance. In 2013, Bill Gates cheered that "that the internet is becoming the town square for the global village of tomorrow";[36] in 2019, Mark Zuckerberg called Facebook and Instagram "the digital equivalent of a town square";[37] and in 2022, Elon Musk dubbed Twitter a "digital town square."[38] Gibson's representation of how content and communities are moderated and mediated in this new viral model serves as a reminder that the architecture and administration of digital spaces matters. Although this was always true of traditional town squares, they are now evoked by tech billionaires to shirk responsibility by disingenuously positing a quaint libertarian fantasy of unfettered communication.

In the novel, Bigend misrepresents the work of "tracking hits . . . and searching for mentions" (67) as merely observational or inconsequential—as though the business of profiling and metawatching is just another form of wide-eyed spectatorship. Although I agree with Lisa Zeidner's praise of *Pattern Recognition*'s avoidance of "any metafictional grandstanding,"[39] the novel does clearly reflect on the standing and function of an author or maker in the data age, inviting consideration of how the world is written and by whom. Given this metafictional dimension, it is worth clarifying that Bigend's brand of scopophilia does not fit the traditional description of metawatching. He is not exactly watching the watchers, he is watching "the numbers" of watchers. He distinguishes that Cayce has "watched a subculture being born," while conversely he has watched the numbers grow. As part of the common defense of profiling, this distinction between watching people and watching data is meant to put the public at ease. In other words, the profile-industrial complex comprising multinational corporations and national governments is not watching us—they are merely watching data *about* us, a sort of rhetorical remove that is used to quell concerns about privacy, but which should signal a literally larger bind.

Indeed, framing mass data collection as solely a problem of personal privacy fuels an escalating arms race toward more sophisticated technologies of surveillance, while neglecting critical questions about the power relations of knowledge production and the exploitative economics of data extraction. On the one hand, the profile industry invites the public to intimately share information in the name of living authentically, building communities, maintaining close relationships, and even enjoying the pleasures of voyeuristically watching one another. On the other hand, the data industry maintains that they collect information neutrally, analyze it impassively, and produce knowledge objectively. In a sense, it is the apparent disengagement and dullness of data collection that makes it seem benign. To this point, the "meta" in metadata seems to neutralize any outstanding threat by adding yet another degree of abstraction and lifelessness. That Mark Zuckerberg renamed the umbrella company for Facebook, WhatsApp, Instagram, Messenger, and Oculus to Meta Platforms Inc. in 2021 speaks to the flexibility of this term. Reportedly, Zuckerberg choose "Meta" because it better captured the multidimensionality of the company ("beyond" just Facebook) and the virtual experiences that their latest social platform, "metaverse," promises to provide ("beyond" our physical reality).[40] At the same time they staked out this position in the "metaverse," the company changed its logo from a thumbs up to an infinity sign, portending their continued colonization of both time and space. Not coincidentally, this rebranding came in the wake of a whistleblower, Francis Haugen, alleging that the company knowingly "harms children, sows division and undermines democracy in pursuit of breakneck growth and 'astronomical profits.'"[41] As a prefix and pretense, "meta" effectively abstracts reality, diverting attention from the embodied experiences and consequences of digital surveillance. Whether referring to "the numbers" or the parent company, "meta" hopes to provide a degree of detachment, freer from scrutiny. Unsurprisingly, postmodern metafiction has been accused of a similar form of bloodless disengagement,[42] but what was by some accounts a liability to reflexive literary fiction and its supposed inability to move people is framed as an asset to data brokers and their capacity to preempt serious social and political pushback.

However satirical he might seem, Bigend is thus an illuminating character, as he explicitly and unapologetically revels in "the numbers"—transgressing the apparent order of things by suggesting that the back end (or big end) is not as objective and dispassionate as profile epistemology maintains. He boldly discloses upfront: "my passion is marketing, advertising, media strategy, and when I first discovered the footage, that is what responded in me. I saw attention focused daily on a product that may not even exist. You think that wouldn't get my attention? The most brilliant marketing ploy of this very young century. And new. Somehow entirely new" (4). In Bigend's account, we see "attention" circulating from the fans to the marketers and not, as we might expect, the other way around. In fact, their "attention focused daily" arouses his own passion, drawing a parallel between the fans' enthusiasm for the footage and Bigend's enthusiasm for the footageheads. Yet what he identifies as "somehow entirely new" is the "attention focused daily on a product that may not even exist"—on what may, in effect, be a bubble.[43] In this sense, Gibson anticipates speculators' forthcoming questions about the economic value of search engines and social media companies in their early years. We have seen the conversation shift from how much Twitter is worth to "How Much Are You Worth to Twitter" since the company derives a large part of its revenue from licensing data to third parties.[44] Elon Musk reinvigorated the discussion of Twitter's valuation by placing a shocking $44 billion bid on the company, which he later threatened to rescind unless they provided him with more details about the number of spam bots on the platform. After Parag Agrawal, CEO of Twitter, tweeted a careful explanation of how Twitter tries to prevent and measure spam accounts, Musk responded with a poop emoji before later adding, "So how do advertisers know what they're getting for their money?"[45] In other words, to "know what they're getting," advertisers (and billionaire investors) must know "who" they are getting. In what Wendy Chun calls (n)You Media,[46] the attention is on the user: on one's value or lack thereof, on one's attention or lack thereof, on one's credibility or lack thereof.

What Bigend's attention to the numbers clarifies is that whether the "product even exist[s]," the footageheads themselves effectively fill that bubble. To the extent that the fans "allow [them]selves far into the investigation of whatever this is . . . that [they] become part of it. Hack into the system. Merge with it"—they become the revenue stream (255). As Andrew Lewis famously said in 2010, "If you're not paying for something, you're not the consumer; you're the product being sold."[47] To avoid confusion, we might more accurately say that your data is the product being sold. Michael Dell (of Dell computers) similarly states, "Our best customers aren't necessarily the ones that are the largest, the ones that buy the most from us, or the ones that require little help or service . . . Our best customers are those we learn the most from."[48] In other words, "the brand interface is a device for the creation of meta-data."[49] In this sense, the footageheads become the real objects of investigation and analysis for Blue Ant.

Throughout, the novel illustrates how consumer surveillance helps produce "participation mystique" by also "hack[ing] into the system" and "merge[ing]" with consumers (265). For example, Nora's uncle hires "Mama Anarchia" to infiltrate the Fetish:Footage:Forum to steer the conversation and glean information. In this way, Mama Anarchia embodies the "friendly" yet eerie surveillance work of corporations: Amazon's product suggestions based on their "item-to-item collaborative filtering" algorithm;[50] Netflix's recommendations, accounting for 80 percent of subscribers' choices;[51] or the "scary accuracy" with which Facebook can predict the duration of a user's relationship.[52] For Cayce, realizing that the "makers" have been manipulating the forum, which had been "one of the most consistent places in her life, like a familiar café that exists somehow outside of geography and beyond time zones" (4), disturbs its heimlich familiarity.[53] Yet it would be a mistake to interpret Mama Anarchia as simply an intruder when her provocative posts were so integral to the forum's appeal in the first place. Arguably, her infiltration and manipulation galvanized the fans' sincere feelings of comfort and community—thereby anticipating the now pervasive use of consumer surveillance to manufacture a sense of intimacy, familiarity, and even authenticity, despite the uncanniness of knowing, in the broadest possible terms, that our habits are being surveilled and even nudged. This simultaneously cold and warm feeling is, in a sense, literary—like events converging around a character. There is a flattery in this form of recognition that tempers the troubling reality.

To be sure, "personalization" does not regard consumer-citizens as individuals; it doesn't even really regard them as persons. Instead, personalization carves out a sticky consumer space between the individual and the population where people become ensnared in a web of correlated data. The ubiquity of lenses, sensors, and metrics creates an agile surveillance network that envelopes consumer-users, in Deleuze's words, "like a self-deforming cast that will continually change from one moment to the other or like a sieve whose mesh will transmute from point to point."[54] In other words, profiles are modulations, not molds, that figured and then disfigured people. As profiles "transmute from point to point," they capture, filter, and compress lives into moving targets. Deleuze's language here illuminates the instability and precarity of this reality. Mobile devices are a poor consolation for social immobility. Login credentials are a poor substitution for personal credibility. Students taking online classes are theoretically freed up to take their exams from anywhere, but their gaze at the screen must never waver lest they be accused of academic dishonesty.[55] Uber or Lyft drivers are free to set their own schedules, but they are left stranded by economic insecurity.[56] *Pattern Recognition* contrasts the agility of these modulating profiles with the strains and struggles of characters trapped in a network that governs access.

From a distance, the dissemination of the footage appears smooth and unhindered, even naturalized as a kind of virus spreading in a world "where it's possible to upload a video file and simply leave it there" (21). We are told, "the footage has a way of cutting across boundaries, transgressing the accustomed order of things" (20), creating new communities and unsettling the world in its wake. However, the smoothness by which it seems to circulate is punctuated and paused by economic, political, and social barriers, highlighting the power structures shaped by capital. After all, the ease with which the footage cuts across boundaries ensues from "a world where there are no mirrors to find yourself on the other side of, all experience having been reduced, by the spectral hand of marketing, to price-point variations on the same thing" (341). Specifically, we learn that a Russian oligarch's fortune is what affords such apparent seamlessness: "'We're talking post-Soviet, right? And enormous personal wealth. Nora's uncle isn't Bill Gates yet, but it wouldn't be entirely ridiculous to mention them in the same sentence. He was on top of a lot of changes, here, very eagerly, and . . . always has brilliant government connections, regardless of who's in power" (330). Gibson's emphasis on the producer's extreme wealth (and comparison to Bill Gates) complicates the "viral model" that ostensibly cuts across the asymmetries of production and consumption to confuse participation with power. Despite the "almost unchallenged popular nostrum that the internet, in particular, is an *inherently* democratizing technology,"[57] the fact remains that when an individual chooses to "upload a video file and simply leave it there," it typically garners a remarkably narrow audience, not to mention little to no remuneration.

Although "Footageheads seem to propagate primarily by word of mouth or by virtue of 'random exposure'" (53), Blue Ant hires people to casually mention the footage in public, thereby accelerating and directing its circulation (53). As Cayce explains, "the model's viral. 'Deep niche.' The venues would be carefully selected" (85). Most important, Cayce clarifies that the listeners "don't buy the product: they recycle the information. They use it to impress the next person they meet." This closely recalls how "parrots were used to create 'authentic' word of mouth"[58] for an upcoming concert in Egan's *A Visit from the Goon Squad*, a similarity that is telling of how endemic this viral model has become in both the economy and the cultural imaginary. This viral model also echoes Bigend's enthusiasm for a speculative futures market where the existence of products is immaterial. This "viral," "deep niche" model is now pervasive across social media and internet platforms, as users often repost or like articles without ever reading them. Still, as long as they "recycle the information" by sharing or resharing it, they are advancing surveillance capitalism.

That Blue Ant remains most invested in "the numbers" refocuses the apparent stakes of the novel's "mystery" and plot. In conversation with Stella (Nora's twin sister), who distributes the footage, Cayce explains: "Your sister's art has become very valuable. You've succeeded, you see. It's a genuine mystery. Nora's art, something hidden at the heart of the world, and more and more people follow it, all over the world. . . . We have our own rich and powerful men. Any creation that attracts the attention of the world, on an ongoing basis, becomes valuable, if only in terms of potential" (307). Defensively, Stella maintains, "'To be commercial. My uncle would not allow this degree of attention.'" Critically, Cayce responds, "'It's already valuable. More valuable than you could imagine'" (307). She proceeds to reassure Stella that she won't tell Bigend what she has discovered, but by now, readers have realized that this is beside the point. The numbers are the product. In this way, the novel anticipates the thriving marketplace of data profiling manipulated by "our own rich and powerful men."

In this climactic exchange, Cayce can finally pull back the curtain and witness the means of production. This curtain is woven together with old threads from "The Iron Curtain" that Cayce's father faced and with new threads from the "information curtain," warned of by Secretary of State Hillary Clinton.[59] Clinton was specifically referring to the need for a single internet, but the term "information curtain" aptly describes the opaque partitions and filters that channel the flow of information online. Raising the stakes, Gibson writes that when Cayce first contacts Stella and Nora, she feels like she is "writing a letter to God," suggesting that the "maker" is also her own creator. In the words of Marshall McLuhan and Lewis Lapham, "we shape our tools, and thereafter our tools shape us."[60] However, upon meeting the twins, Cayce does not find herself in any ontological sense; in Tiziana Terranova's words, "the increasingly blurred territory between production and consumption, work and cultural expression, does not signal the recomposition of the alienated Marxist worker."[61] On the contrary, Cayce feels fundamentally displaced: "She knows that it's about meeting Stella, and hearing her story, and her sister's, but somehow she no longer is able to fit it to her life. Or rather she lives now in that story, her life left somewhere behind, like a room she's stepped out of. Not far away at all but she is no longer in" (292–93). Paradoxically, the more Cayce understands that she has been "tracked, via [her] post's ISP, [her] name and address determined, logged," the more disoriented and lost she feels (339). For readers, this is a familiar affect of profile culture: "Although they enable a form of cognitive mapping that links the local to the global, networks produce new dilemmas: neoliberal subjects are now forever mapping, but more precarious than ever; they are forever searching, but never finding."[62] In other words, as she is tracked and traced, Cayce begins to see herself as a character in a new story, a story told through the lens of surveillance—one she is unable to read.

As Cayce peals back the layers of surveillance, she begins "feeling much of the recent weirdness of her life shift beneath her, rearranging itself according to a new paradigm of history. Not a comfortable sensation, like Soho crawling on its own accord up Primrose Hill, because it has discovered that it belongs there, and has no other choice" (340–41). Despite the early descriptions of Blue Ant as "post-geographic" and Cayce as a nomadic "creature of fees, adamantly short-term" (61), she is, in the final instance, all too entrenched—not in her own life story, which now seems "like a room she's stepped out of," but in a new "systematic structure" (336), where she is tracked and identified on someone else's terms. It is not merely the invasion of her privacy that jars Cayce; by writing her as the daughter of a Cold War spy, Gibson establishes that possibility as old news. Rather, she feels her sense—her character—becoming redefined "according to a new paradigm of history" (352). An employee of the Volkovas informs Cayce that as the target of their surveillance, she has had a principal role in "the creation of a more systematic structure" that she was unaware even existed (347). In this sense, our protagonist had misrecognized herself as a literary character and suddenly apprehends herself as a profile: a searchable, fungible data set.

"Particularly farseeing, in his recognition of the importance of computing" and surveillance (337), Andrei Volkova used the internet to maintain his anonymity while surveilling the fans to build an audience. This disparity is a mainstay of digital surveillance: data collectors hide behind incomprehensible privacy agreements and trade secret protections while extracting ever more information about the lives and habits of consumer-users. Volkova's associate, Sergei, explains that "the anonymity, the encryption, the strategies, as they evolved . . . involved an inherent risk of exposure" (348) for the oligarch as well—implicitly conceding that "exposure" can be hazardous and that their "new systematic structure" depends on exploiting the exposure gap intrinsic to surveillance.

Meanwhile, the novel historicizes Volkova's twenty-first-century operation in the long tradition of political surveillance, including the glut of unemployed spies who went to work in corporate espionage after the Cold War:

There have always been two security operations around Stella and Nora. One is a branch, or subsidiary, of the group that protects Volkova himself. The flavor is ex-KGB, but in the sense that Putin is ex-KGB: lawyers first, then spies. The other, largely the creation of colleagues of mine, is less conventional, largely web-based. Wiktor has been brought in very recently to attempt to sort out a serious lack of understanding, of communication, between the two. Your arrival on the scene, via your discovery of the stellanor [web] address, is glaring proof of our difficulties. (338)

In other words, Cayce's arrival on the scene usefully exposes the difficulties of hemming together CIA- and KGB-style security with twenty-first-century cybersecurity. While devoted to helping his nieces produce and distribute the footage, Volkova, the wealthiest man in Russia, is also dedicated to his personal security and anonymity. To thwart Cayce's early efforts to find the maker, the traditionalist branch of his security operation had broken into her flat and bugged her devices, while the web-based branch had hired Dorotea (another freelancer with whom Cayce worked with a background in industrial espionage) to sabotage Cayce professionally and infiltrate F:F:F under the guise of Mama Anarchia. Once Cayce joined forces with Bigend, the two-pronged security operation intensified, and Dorotea was ordered to break in and wiretap Cayce's base in London. Exploiting the "lack of under-standing, of communications" between the hard and soft power operations, Dorotea had also been working as a double agent for Bigend. Cayce inadver-tently exposes Dorotea's double-crossing by using a .ru email address that tipped off Volkova's security operation. As an active fan and unwitting agent, Cayce played an appreciable role in both ends of this operation, for which they are expressly grateful. Ultimately, Bigend, Cayce, and Volkova's head of security share an expensive meal—symbolically convening market-driven, algorithmic governance, online engagement, and traditional "information operations," to create a new "systematic structure." Eclipsing the reveal of Stella and Nora, Cayce comes to recognize her own role in shaping and pro-pelling this surveillance system. Without drawing a false equivalency, *Pattern Recognition* evokes the ways that everyday, algorithmic consumer surveillance converge (practically and theoretically) with "information cyber operations," defined by the NATO Cooperative Cyber Defense as "operations which affect the logical layer of cyberspace with the intention of influencing attitudes, behaviours, or decisions." That this definition uses the term "cyberspace," coined by Gibson in *Neuromancer*, reminds us of how the channels of influence flow in unexpected ways. Nevertheless, *Pattern Recognition* points to emergent assemblages and logics of surveillance that are writing new narratives.

"Healthy, Motivated Prisoners"

In the novel, this surveillance assemblage includes Andrei Volkova's "privatized prison" in Moscow, "where healthy, motivated prisoners can lead healthy, motivated lives, plus receive training and career direction" (329). This prison is one of the novel's most overt examples of personal profiling and instructively illustrates the biopolitical dimension of determining what counts about any particular person. Prisoners must be "healthy to begin with, otherwise they wouldn't have been chosen for this"; they are screened for diseases, and any misstep "is an instant ticket back to TB Land," the state prisons overrun with infection (329). Exercising neoliberal "friendly power,"[63] Volkova's is the "only prison in Russia that people actively try to break into" (326). Reflecting the shift from Foucauldian discipline to Deleuzian societies of control, it is not prison cells but the cells of prisoners that regulate inmates. Volkova's privatized prison not only profiles prospective inmates to determine who should be "chosen for this," it also frames surveillance as a service or privilege for which the inmates should be grateful. The prison is private while the inmates' lives are anything but, which captures the intrinsic asymmetry of profiling that privileges profits over people.

In the end, the catch is that these good, clean prisoners must render all of Nora's footage. Cayce asks, "how this could all have been put together, just to facilitate Nora's art," amending that, "*how* isn't a problem . . . but *why*" (330). A member of Volkova's team answers, "Massive organizational redundancy, in the service of absolute authority. We're talking post-Soviet, right? And enormous personal wealth" (330). The novel's examples of enormous personal wealth—most notably that of Volkova and Bigend—appear to afford a smooth, borderless existence that stands in stark contrast to severe social striations and boundaries that underwrite their wealth. Here, the supposedly mutually beneficial private prison depends on discriminating between clean and dirty bodies, suitable and unsuitable people. That enormous personal wealth not only answers the question "how . . . but *why*," reminding readers that this privilege is designed to reproduce inequality and a continuous source of captive, free labor. Gibson situates this prison in an online media "ecology" (6), which challenges "the postmodern assumption that labour disappears while the commodity takes on and dissolves all meaning. In particular, the internet foregrounds the extraction of value out of continuous, updateable work and is extremely labour-intensive."[64] Hiding this extractive labor in a prison owned by a billionaire exemplifies the egregiousness of the illusion that media floats down from the cloud to find its viewer. It also begins to unravel the ways this "extraction of value" depends on routine surveillance at every point—surveillance that is inherently discriminatory.

Waking up in this "whateverness" after being kidnapped,[65] Cayce thinks the prison could be any institution—a school, a hospital, or a mere network of corridors. If this still seems like a curious facility for rendering viral video footage, "it is important to acknowledge the roots of many developments in computing (and indirectly the brand and other informational objects) in military and state surveillance."[66] A "brilliant marketing ploy" (67)—with the power to watch the watchers—the footage is an assemblage of surveillance techniques and technologies, from the supervision of the prisoners rendering the footage and the surveillance of the fans watching the videos, to the important detail that Nora edits her art from city surveillance footage. Gavin Smith's ethnographic research on surveillance camera operators is especially instructive for understanding the narrative dimension of this surveillant assemblage and its relationship to art. As Smith writes, "I found these individuals to be creatively involved in the social construction (or perhaps, 'consumption') of reality. . . the banal stories and characters invented by the operators exercise a considerable influence on what is 'visualized' (or searched for) and what intervention (if any) is actioned."[67] With this appreciation for the fact that surveillance camera operators exert creative control, so to speak, we can see how the supposedly raw surveillance footage that Nora repurposes was already "cooked." From there the questions become: What are the different stories being told? What "characters" are constructed? What assumptions help produce these "stories and characters"? What biases make them seem "banal"?[68] What influence do they have? This opens the novel up to a similar set of questions as readers are encouraged to consider how lives become authored, by whom, and with what authority. In this way, *Pattern Recognition* situates surveillance as a ghost writer intended for ghost readers who (however haunting and hidden) are all too real and human.

Furthermore, by contextualizing the production, distribution, and reception of the footage in overlapping systems of surveillance, Gibson clarifies that surveillance is both "involved in the social construction of reality"[69] and also shaped by historical, economic, and social forces. The original surveillance footage of the city, Nora's art, and the footagehead forums are all constructed from the interplay between socioeconomic forces and personal pursuits. Ultimately, Gibson illustrates how city surveillance footage (already the product of design choices) is transformed into art, which generates more surveillance data as it circulates. At every point along the way, digital surveillance "translate[s] physical space and its dwellers into data."[70]

"As Though Money Is Just Sort of a Side Effect"

Insisting on the materiality of cyberculture, the novel grounds the dazzling elusiveness of the footage and Bigend's company Blue Ant in the material conditions of each organization. Like the enigmatic footage, the marketing agency Blue Ant operates mysteriously in the novel, slipping through national and economic boundaries. This slipperiness and flexibility underscore that power is not just having the means to erect blockades and gain visibility; it is also the ability to escape attention and sidestep barriers (with a code or PIN, for example). We are told that Andrei Volkova, "the invisible oligarch. The ghost" with "enormous wealth" who supports the footage, "largely managed to keep his name out of the media. Which must have been a downright spooky accomplishment" (330). Power is being able to manage one's "risk of exposure" (337).

Similarly, Gibson's sardonic description of Blue Ant captures the white, male, and class privilege of these ghost-like figures who underwrite increasingly nimble and networked forms of discipline and power: "Relatively tiny in terms of permanent staff, globally distributed, more post-geographic than multinational, the agency has from the beginning billed itself as a high-speed, low-drag life-form in an advertising ecology of lumbering herbivores. Or perhaps as some non-carbon-based life-form, entirely sprung from the smooth and ironic brow of its founder, Hubertus Bigend, a nominal Belgian who looks like Tom Cruise on a diet of virgin's blood and truffled chocolates" (6). Gibson's description of this lean, mean corporation draws on ecological rhetoric (extinction, reproduction, consumption) that is so often used to naturalize privilege and predatory business in a "dog-eat-dog" corporate environment. The agency's name is borrowed from a species of large wasps that poison and paralyze crickets to lay eggs inside of them where the wasp larva then has a ready supply of food—a not so subtle evocation of parasitic business practices. Bigend's "diet" of "virgin's blood" also contributes to the image of a vampiric or parasitic food chain.[71] As Shoshana Zuboff writes, "At its core, surveillance capitalism is parasitic and self-referential. It revives Karl Marx's old image of capitalism as a vampire that feeds on labor, but with an unexpected turn. Instead of labor, surveillance capitalism feeds on every aspect of every human's experience."[72] Gibson's memorable description of Bigend, combined with the novel's thinly veiled reference to Nike (originally called Blue Ribbon Sports) as Blue Ant's most recent client, points to how surveillance capitalism "feeds on" its hosts in this hierarchical "advertising ecology," leaving nothing on the table.[73]

It is worth noting here that, in the mid-1980s, Nike strategically identified itself as a marketing company and not a shoe manufacturer to shirk responsibility for infamously shifting production sites to East Asia to capitalize on the low labor costs and lack of worker protections.[74] When Blue Ant hires Cayce to determine whether or not their footwear client's new logo "works," she twice compares the Nike Swoosh "scribble" (12) to "a syncopated sperm" (13). Here, the Nike swoosh, which emphatically does not "work" for Cayce, connects the life cycles of brands and corporations to the actual people that Nike so brazenly reduces to labor power. Cayce "imagines the countless Asian workers who might, should she say, spend years of their lives applying versions of this symbol to an endless and unyielding flood of footwear" wondering, "what would it mean to them, this bouncing sperm?" (13). In fact, Nike's particular "advertising ecology" (7) produces not only new markets but also vast territories of people who manufacture products that they themselves cannot afford. As the gaping divide between a low-cost labor force and a relatively high-end consumer base widens, greater and greater populations are impoverished by this practice. Like the Nike corporation, Bigend's new "non-carbon based life-form" is a species living high on the food chain, avoiding the heavy "drag" of "permanent staff" (7).

Blue Ant's "high-speed" hype mirrors what Terranova describes as "the speed of the digital economy, its accelerated rhythms of obsolescence."[75] As she reminds us, "during its dot-com days, the digital economy was the fastest and most visible zone of production within late capitalist societies. New products, new trends and new cultures succeeded each other at anxiety-inducing pace. It was a business where you needed to replace your equipment/knowledge, and possibly staff, every year of so."[76] As an advertising agency,

Blue Ant "has from the beginning billed itself as a high-speed, low drag life-form" (6), able to keep pace in this economy. Like we saw with *Citizen* in chapter 2, literature can re-pace and respace our encounters with the digital economy to apprehend their effects and affects more clearly. For example, when traveling on Blue Ant's dime, Cayce embraces a "theory of jet-lag" that highlights the residual "drag" of even the leanest "post-geographic" operations: "She knows, now, absolutely, hearing the white noise that is London, that Damien's theory of jet lag is correct: that her mortal soul is leagues behind her, being reeled in on some ghostly umbilical down the vanished wake of the plane that brought her here, hundreds of thousands of feet above the Atlantic. Souls can't move that quickly, and are left behind, and must be awaited, upon arrival, like lost luggage" (1). The lag between her body and her unhurried soul opens up space to occupy and contemplate the invisible interregnums that the digital economy typically obscures. This passage reveals the "white noise," the "ghostly" threads, and the "vanished wake" of traveling and living through digital life at warp speed. That Cayce feels temporarily torn asunder by this pace speaks to the experience and affects of dividuality. For Foucault, the "soul is the effect and instrument of a political anatomy; the soul is the prison of the body" that produces individuality in disciplinary societies.[77] However, in societies of control, "We no longer find ourselves dealing with the mass/individual pair. Individuals have become 'dividuals,'" dispersed in data.[78] Sure, individual "souls can't move that quickly," but dividuals are "undulatory, in orbit, and in continuous network." Meanwhile, as Deleuze laments, "marketing has become the center or 'soul' of the corporation. We are taught that corporations have 'souls,' the most terrifying news in the world."[79] So, for example, the swoosh is the soul of Nike—footloose and flying high—while the lost "souls" of individuality are "leagues behind."

These mostly marketing corporations—be it Blue Ant, Nike, or the five big tech giants today[80]—rely on both human labor and increasingly comprehensive consumer profiles or "life-forms." Therefore, the claim that Blue Ant is "more post-geographic than multinational" (7) comes across as ironic as Bigend's smooth brow: the company's emphatic mobility only underscores the persistence of deliberately drawn boundaries and reinforced walls, from the PIN check-points that the company credit card routinely opens without a hitch to the concrete enclosures of the privatized prison in Moscow where inmates render the footage. In this context, "post-geographic" means smoothing out the passage of products from factory workers in the Global South to consumers in the Global North, from prison enclosures (leaking toxins) to "chance encounters" on the internet. In other words, it does not signify the dissolution of national boundaries and geographic zones but their reification.

Just as the novel continuously teases and then undercuts the romantic notion that the footage emerged fully formed from the maker's brain, it likewise contests the grotesque fantasy that a business is the brainchild of its founder. In a world where each consumer-user has a profile and Nike can legally reduce itself down to a brand or logo, we must continue to ask Elizabeth Grosz's key question: "Can we deromanticize the construction of knowledges and discourses to see them as labor, production, doing?"[81] *Pattern Recognition* mocks this romanticization when Bigend rejects the term "producer," suggesting instead "Advocate, perhaps? Facilitator?" (70). This rhetorical stance that there are no producers proper is emblematic of profile culture's friendly power, which obscures the asymmetries of actual labor relations. Bigend professes, "the client and I engage in a dialogue. A path emerges. It isn't about the imposition of creative will" (62). Skeptical, Cayce quips, "If Bigend can convince himself that he doesn't impose his will on others, he must be capable of convincing himself of anything" (62). Another Blue Ant contractor, Boone Chu, also scoffs at the notion that "it's all about excellence, not money" for Bigend—as though "the money's just a sort of side effect" (109). He astutely recognizes that this premise allows Bigend to strategically keep his business practices vague. I argue that framing money as merely a side effect is key to profile epistemology: if money were the objective, then the public should be fairly compensated for their data. So data profilers purposefully muddy their business models and instead stress concepts such as personalization, self-expression, and connectivity. Explaining his offer to buy Twitter, Elon Musk similarly claimed, "This is not a way to make money. . . . My strong intuitive sense is that having a public platform that is maximally trusted and broadly inclusive is extremely important to the future of civilization."[82] Suspending disbelief to imagine that the money would be "just a sort of side effect" (109), this explanation still conspicuously neglects why he, "having a public platform . . . is extremely important to the future of civilization"[83]—as though this is something that we can, and all should, own for ourselves. No, instead, we will "have" the platform, but he will own and control it.

Still, focusing on the character and intentions of a CEO dangerously obscures more important questions about the economic, social, and ecological effects of corporations. Consider, for example, Mitt Romney's now notorious dismissal of the crowd's concerns over low corporate tax rates with the cavalier defense, "corporations are people too, my friend" at the Iowa State Fair in 2011. In addition to the serious problems of corporate personhood, which Naomi Klein so thoroughly confronts in her book *No Logo*, Romney's attempt at amiability with the repeated address "my friend," echoes Bigend's rhetorical attempts to smooth over severely asymmetrical power relations with what Paul Preciado calls "friendly power."[84]

Resisting the measly matter of whether CEOs (and corporations for that matter) are, in fact, our friends, *Pattern Recognition* routinely reminds readers that Blue Ant has a relevant history and materiality that undermine any claims that the corporation exists virtually nowhere and is reducible to the spawn of a single spooky figurehead. Bigend acknowledges that "'It's as though the creative process is no longer contained within an individual skull, if indeed it ever was. Everything, today, is to some extent the reflection of something else'" (68). While the novel's theory of the creative process is networked, it is still resolutely material, in part because networks are material. The products reflect that uncontained process. Not only is the footage born of composite forces and fragments, even Nora's brain or "skull" is "to some extent the reflection of something else," namely, the embedded T-shaped shrapnel. As Terranova elaborates, "In this sense the commodity does not disappear as such; it rather becomes increasingly ephemeral, its duration becomes compressed, it becomes more of a process than a finished product. The role of continuous, creative, innovative labour as the ground of market value is crucial to the digital economy. The process of valorization (the production of monetary value) happens by foregrounding the quality of the labour which literally animates the commodity."[85] The footage is this sort of "ephemeral" commodity that does "not so much disappear as become more transparent, showing [its] reliance on the labour which produces and sustains [it]."[86] On one hand, this labor is that of the mysterious maker whose efforts become the real spectacle. On the other hand, this labor is that of the footageheads who propagate, cultivate, and sustain the footage as a cultural force. As a marketer in this digital economy, what excites Bigend is the opportunity to outsource the creative process to the consumer who "reflects" and recycles the advertising campaign while producing the added value of data (85). Although Bigend's phrasing might smack of postmodern simulacra, the novel as a whole emphasizes the way "processes" are, as Grosz puts it, "developed from below, from a particular organization of matter."[87] It is in Grosz's sense that advertising really is ecological—meaning materially embedded and consequential—and not because of some rhetorical take on Darwinian evolution.

Brand Culture and Invisible Labor

Thus far, I have argued that the footageheads represent a workforce in the profile economy and Bigend's new advertising ecology. That is, the hypervisibility of participating in the data age, which necessarily subjects consumer-users to surveillance, also distracts from the forms of invisible and uncompensated labor this demands. I'll now argue that Cayce's acute allergies to brands and logos represent a return of repressed labor throughout both industrialism and postindustrialism. It is symbolically fitting that she would have a physically painful reaction to the signs and signifiers of marketing that are so often brandished to distract from the conditions of physical labor and production. In other words, Cayce's allergies dramatize and make vivid in lived experience the harmfulness of companies hiding the physical conditions of labor behind their brand names. For Cayce, brands and logos are not simply signs; they are physical manifestations of the company. It is not until she is walking with Boone along the "canal's shabby towpath" in Camden Town that she recounts "the basis of her peculiar sensitivities" (112). The spot "too-powerfully back-lit" like the sky in a "gray-scale Cibachrome of a Turner print" reminds her of a trip to Disneyland she took with her parents when she was twelve. She recalls the ride Pirates of the Caribbean breaking down and her family being "rescued by staff wearing hip-waders over their pirate costumes, to be led through a doorway into a worn, concrete-walled, oil-stained subterranean realm of machinery and cables, inhabited by glum mechanics" (110). In crossing this threshold, Cayce witnesses the "realm" of labor, and "these backstage workers" remind her "of the Morlocks in The Time Machine" (110). Made of concrete, oil, cables, and machines, this repressive and gritty channel actualizes the terror that Pirates of the Caribbean playfully mimics and displaces to a far-off fantasyland. Even identifying the employees as "workers"—a dirty word to Disney, which prefers the euphemism "cast members"—breaks the illusion

of pure pleasure in a land that represses the stains of human toil and waste.[88]
The novel, in stark contrast, steadfastly uncovers the ways in which labor can
be misidentified as engagement.

The "advertising ecology" that Gibson introduces early on moves beyond
the metaphoric to include sincere questions of labor, consumption, and material waste. Directly following this confrontation with the dark underbelly
of infrastructure and invisible labor, Cayce begins to "avoid having Mickey
in her field of vision, and by the fourth and final day" at Disneyland she de-
velops her first rash in response to the masks or icons of consumerism. After
recalling this moment in her childhood, Cayce "goes to the canal's edge and
looks down." She notices "a gray condom, drifting like a jellyfish, a lager can
half-afloat, and deeper down swirls something she can't identify, swathed
in a pale and billowing caul of ragged builder's plastic." Again, facing the
enduring waste products of consumerism, "she shudders and turns away"
(110). The murky waters of Pirates of the Caribbean or the canal's edge might
give anyone a rash, but for Cayce, it is looking down at the submerged systems
of labor and the residues of consumption that make sparkling brands and
icons such as Mickey Mouse so unbearable. The sequence of information
Gibson presents here is significant: Cayce's exposure to the scaffolding of
Disneyland, an account of her first "close shave" with brand allergies, and
finally her glimpse at the debris in the canal along Camden Town. Together
these moments contextualize her physical reaction to labels and logos in a
broader set of concerns over expendable resources and expendable workers,
which persistently float to the surface of the page.

From here, brands circulate for Cayce as physical manifestations of corporations with their own impact and consequences exceeding the products they
mark. For instance, "Tommy Hilfiger does it every time . . . When it starts,
it's pure reaction, like biting down hard on a piece of foil" (17). To be sure,
her particularly severe reaction to Tommy Hilfiger is not arbitrary—none of
the brands that Gibson selects are. Despite what she says, her aversion or
sensitivity to the brand is not a "pure reaction"; rather, her response is more
accurately reflective of her knowledge of Tommy Hilfiger's history:

My God, don't they know? This stuff is simulacra of simulacra of
simulacra. A diluted tincture of Ralph Lauren, who had himself diluted
the glory days of Brooks Brothers, who themselves had stepped on the

product of Jermyn Street and Savile Row, flavoring their ready-to-wear
with liberal lashings of polo kit and regimental stripes. But Tommy
surely is the null point, the black hole. There must be some Tommy
Hilfiger event horizon, beyond which it is impossible to be more deriva-
tive, more removed from the source, more devoid of soul. (17–18)

Given how expertly she traces the derivations of the brand back through its
sources, what Gibson describes as Cayce's sixth sense might be better understood as an embodied "historical sense," as Nietzsche calls it.[89] Similarly,
Laurent Berlant identifies Cayce's sensitivities as forms of intuition, drawing
on Henri Bergson's argument in *Matter and Memory* "that intuition is the work
of history translated through personal memory."[90] It is relevant, then, that
"Tommy Hilfiger is run entirely through licensing deals. Hilfiger commis-
sions all its products from a group of other companies: Jockey International
makes Hilfiger underwear, Pepe Jeans London makes Hilfiger jeans, Oxford
Industries makes Tommy shirts and the Stride Rite Corporation makes its
footwear. . . . Companies such as Hilfiger, and to a lesser extent Ralph Lauren,
Calvin Klein and others, are thus able to acquire virtual (or 'weightless') production capacities through an extensive network of licensing agreements."[91]
Ultimately, Cayce prefers products that acknowledge their material construction, physically recoiling at the tendency of brand labels to eclipse their own
production and history.

In other words, Cayce refuses to see brands as immaterial signifiers.
Instead, she experiences their real physical effects in the form of allergies.
"Cayce knows, for instance, that the characteristically wrinkled seams down
either arm" of her esteemed MA-1 Buzz Rickson bomber jacket "were originally the result of sewing with pre-war industrial machines that rebelled
against the slippery new material, nylon" (11). Fittingly, History Preservation
Associates, who sell Buzz Ricksons, are also "driven by the totality of the
item—design, aesthetics, production methods and materials, historical
context, and association with those who defined an item's use."[92] They are
self-described "devoted historians"—perfectly contrasting Tommy Hilfiger's
glossy ahistoricism and erasure of its own genealogy.

In addition to the power of these labels to circulate as free-floating signifiers, Alex Link notes that the "most important common quality is that the majority of the brands to which Cayce feels the greatest aversion, if not actively

engaged in the colonization of the local, share an intimate codependency with twentieth-century warfare."[93] Her first and worst trademark trigger, the Michelin Man (or Bibendum), is perhaps the clearest example, given that "In the First World War, Michelin pioneered the practice of transforming national trauma into a marketing strategy . . . offer[ing] guidebooks to, and tours of, major battlefields even before the war was over."[94] Cayce succinctly describes Bibendum as "maggot-like," signaling the brand's parasitic practices during World War II and recalling Bigend's choice to name his marketing agency after the blue ant wasp. In addition to churning out their Red Book tour guides, Michelin operated the largest rubber plantation in Vietnam during the 1920s and 1930s, and their brutal exploitation of Vietnamese workers initiated the important labor movement Phu Rieng Do. I argue that it is ultimately the visibility and appreciation for labor that differentiates products that "work" from products that don't in the novel.

Of course, Buzz Rickson's replicas of World War II fighter jackets also engage with the history of warfare, but they do so from a decidedly different perspective. Gibson writes, "the Rickson's having been created by Japanese obsessives driven by passions nothing at all to do with anything remotely like fashion," produce "an imitation more real somehow than that which it emulates" (11). In this sense, the MA-1 replica reveals America to Americans, exemplifying the positive critical potential of simulacra—simulacra that is not free floating but historicizing and embedded. Given the United States's devastating bombings of Japan, the "passions" that drive this meticulous production run deeper than postmodern pastiche or some fleeting fashion statement. In the words of Jane Bennett, Cayce's Buzz Rickson is "vibrant matter" that does not merely reference history but plays history forward with all its ironies and complexities.[95]

Contrasting Cayce's Buzz Rickson is "a square of clear acrylic: laser-etched in its core are the Coca-Cola logo, a crude representation of the Twin Towers, and the words 'WE REMEMBER'" sitting atop Nora's computer monitor (302–3). The juxtaposition of the Coco-Cola logo and the veritable slogan of 9/11 epitomize capitalism's "crude" response to war and terrorism. To be sure, this reductive trinket reeks of George W. Bush's post-attack encouragement to "go shopping more." Similarly, and in contrast to the Buzz Rickson, swastikas "induce a violent reaction [for Cayce], akin to Tommy-phobia but in an even worse direction." Importantly, it is "not so much from a sense of historical evil (though she certainly has that) as from an awareness of a scary excess of design talent." It is her sense that "Hitler had had entirely too brilliant a graphics department, and had understood the power of branding all too well" that makes the symbol so sickening (264). As opposed to the ahistorical and practically metaphysical posturing of brands like Tommy Hilfiger that circulate above and beyond the products they label or the "excess of design talent" that has made swastikas and Bibendum global icons (albeit on very different registers), the excess or "obsession" that Cayce distinguishes in Buzz Rickson lies in its awareness of how materiality matters, its attention to labor, and its engagement with national and local histories.

Conclusion: A Gift and a Trap

I have argued that *Pattern Recognition*, with a keen historical sense, hears the "powers of the future [which] are knocking on the door."[96] It insightfully confronts the complex relationship between surveillance and the new profile economy as a matter of knowledge production and labor relations, not simply a problem of privacy. In many ways, this chapter has argued against the neoliberal suggestion that online participation and sharing are in and of themselves empowering by focusing on their limitations and economic conditions. I have argued that the coerced visibility of user-consumers, which has proven immensely profitable for the profile industry, also conveniently obscures the invisibility of Big Data. In addition, I have suggested that the public's part in this "new systematic structure" (347) of supplying valuable data is a form of unpaid labor, which intersects with brand culture's use of logos and trademarks to stand in for companies and mask the material conditions of production. The likable faces of companies (Bibendum, Mickey Mouse, and so on) are analogous to the forward-facing "profile pages" that people feel affection for and ownership over, even as they gloss over and provide cover for the shadow data profiles over which the public has little to no control or knowledge. Ultimately, "the increasingly blurred territory between production and consumption, work and cultural expression, however, does not signal the recomposition of the alienated Marxist worker. The internet does not automatically turn every user into an active producer, and every worker into a creative subject."[97]

Nevertheless, and to be sure, the disciplinary structures that ultimately reorder Cayce's relationship with the footage are also neither totalizing nor exhaustive. There is undoubtedly a difference between how subjectivity is produced and how it is occupied, lived, and resisted—and both are crucial conversations. Parkaboy posits that "Homo sapiens are about pattern recognition. . . . Both a gift and a trap" (22), and I argue that the same could be said of data analytics. For different reasons, all the principal characters in the novel cathect onto the footage, which becomes what Aarthi Vadde calls in reference to amateur authors, "an eroticized property whose circulation forges bonds amongst those who are moved by its experience or who derive a sense of tradition from its transmission."[98] How characters are moved and what sense of tradition they derive is a matter of pattern recognition, point of view, and plotlines. Parkaboy notes that while people think they are just sitting there staring at a screen, "some of them, anyway, are adventurers" (255). Meanwhile, the distributors paid "people to lurk on F:F:F" because it "quickly emerged as the liveliest, the most interesting forum. And potentially the most dangerous" (339). In this sense, they detected within the movement a political energy, if not a political consciousness. Initially, Bigend recognizes in the footage a new viral model that appears as a marketing gift. Following Vadde, "If that gift is turned into capital, the drive to accumulate surplus wealth threatens the erotic bonds created around the artwork."[99] Cayce shares this sense of threat, and yet the novel makes clear that "Late capitalism does not *appropriate* anything: it nurtures, exploits and exhausts its labour force and its cultural and affective production. . . . The internet has always and simultaneously been a gift economy and an advanced capitalist economy."[100] Along these lines, Bigend explains that it is precisely Cayce's "passion" in her online posts that "makes [her] so valuable" to Blue Ant (65). In Vadde's words, "when privately owned platforms capitalize upon their users' desire to give increase or share, they turn one person's gift into another corporation's profit."[101] Although the footage avoids this particular trap, profile epistemology sets another: packaging data surveillance as gifts to consumer-citizens wrapped in personalization, self-expression, and connection. In societies of control, these become rhetorical tools to catch moving targets in the crosshairs while fostering feelings of attachment.[102] In other words, personalization creates the impression of being "seen" to offset the creepier feeling of being watched.

At the novel's end, trademarks "register neutral" for Cayce; yet it is unclear "whether this change, whatever it is, will affect her ability to know whether or not a given trademark will work" (355). It is, therefore, possible that she has escaped the traps of pattern recognition while retaining the gifts. As Cayce lies curled up on a bed like a question mark in the novel's final scene, the lingering question for the coming century is whether we, already habituated to nearly ubiquitous data profiling, will be able to make best use of the gifts that innovations in online communication and data analytics offer while escaping the traps that are too often buried beneath the surface. In this pursuit, fiction can set off the buried traps, at once alerting us to their risks and clearing space to give, as Rosi Braidotti says, "for the hell of it . . . for the love of the world."[103]

Data Fictions, Neoliberal Narratives, and the Military-Industrial Gaze in Mohsin Hamid's *How to Get Filthy Rich in Rising Asia*

As bastions of neoliberalism, self-help books typically preach personal responsibility, self-determination, and calculated investments in one's own human capital. Profiles of wealthy people are often held up as inspirational forms that can be emulated or approximated with the right effort.[1] Titles such as *Profiles of Power and Success*, for instance, promise to "motivate all who dare to reach for success and power in their own lives."[2] To that end, many self-help books regard individual data profiles as either assets to be developed and brandished or potential liabilities to be personally managed.[3] Unsurprisingly, a number of self-help books combine the neoliberal obsession with economic and personal "growth" with the imperative to "grow" one's online presence and digital profile.[4] For example, with an ostensibly new take on the old notion of networking, Porter Gale's book, *Your Network Is Your Net Worth: Unlock the Hidden Power of Connections for Wealth, Success, and Happiness in the Digital Age* suggests that the size of one's digital presence corresponds to their "net" or actual "worth" as a person.[5] Although it is true that people are both actively and passively constructing high-profile "selves," it is not obvious whom this is helping. The growth of data profiling certainly is making some people obscenely wealthy and secure, but by and large, it is not consumer-citizens.

In describing how "neoliberalism has hijacked our vocabulary," Doreen Massey argues that "growth" has been "deemed to be the entire aim of our economy. . . . In its crudest formulation this entails providing the conditions for the market sector to produce growth, and accepting that this will result in inequality, and then relying on the redistribution of some portion of this growth to help repair the inequality that has resulted from its production."[6] Despite the inequality this produces, growth is still regarded a kind of panacea. The title to Mohsin Hamid's novel, *How to Get Filthy Rich in Rising Asia*, perfectly captures this ethos of growth in all of its complexity. First, as a mock-self-help book, the title playfully interpellates the reader as a neoliberal subject who necessarily wants to become "filthy rich" as a means of supposed self-improvement. Next, in this context, the phrase "rising Asia" analogously conflates national or regional improvement with "rising" or growing wealth, echoing language used by the International Monetary Fund's research group in their work on "Asia Rising: Patterns of Economic Development and Growth."[7] Last, Hamid's use of "filthy" relates the moral or ethical failing of a single-minded commitment to excess and wealth with the pollution and environmental damage this produces, including "rising" sea levels.

Finally, while the novel seems to reflect Massey's position that this preoccupation with "increased wealth, especially as measured in the standard monetary terms of today, has few actual consequences for people's feelings of wellbeing once there is a sufficiency to meet basic needs, as there is in Britain,"[8] it is also worth noting that Hamid's novel is not set in Britain. While the city in the novel remains unnamed, it strongly resembles Lahore, and it would be a mistake to equate the conditions and concerns of Pakistan with the British political economy that Massey critiques. In fact, the conditions Hamid portrays from the novel's outset emphatically do not "meet basic needs": drinking water is unsafe, food is scarce, shelter is scanty, and medicine is unavailable. Indeed, the novel depicts how Pakistan has suffered and continues to suffer the excesses and growing pains of Britain and the United States, even as (or perhaps, especially as) it satirically exploits the cruel optimism of self-help. In particular, profiling and data surveillance serve as critical nodal points in the novel for deconstructing the discourses of self-help and self-determination. Ultimately, data profiling not only reifies existing norms, it actively exacerbates asymmetrical power relations, making the ethos of self-determination all the more untenable and injurious.

Fits and Misfits

The first pages of How to Get Filthy Rich in Rising Asia disingenuously proclaim that "This book is a self-help book. Its objective, as it says on the cover, is to show you how to get filthy rich in rising Asia."[9] Readers, of course, know that—"as it says on the cover"—the book is actually a novel. Soon after, the narrator qualifies, "all books, each and every book ever written, could be said to be offered to the reader as a form of self-help" (20). In the sense that the novel might enrich the lives of readers or sell enough copies to make Hamid rich, it could be said to be a form of self-help. On the other hand, given that the novel follows the protagonist's moral and psychological growth from infancy to death, with a coming-of-age story in between, the book also seems to be a take on the traditional bildungsroman. I suggest that, deftly positioned in between these genres, *How to Get Filthy Rich in Rising Asia* actually critiques the ways the bildungsroman has been fitted to the neoliberal quest to become a "filthy rich," "self-made," and thus "successful" adult whose maturity is ostensibly reflected in their portfolio of mature investments. I will argue that in protest, Hamid methodically stretches language and genres to create space for productive misfittings, while exposing the forces that uncomfortably suture the self to profiles and thereby affect the distribution of life chances and possibilities for survival.

To great effect, Hamid writes in the second-person perspective, referring to the protagonist only as "you" and to other characters by general designations, such as "your sister" and "the pretty girl." Hamid's use of the second person undercuts "celebrations of an all-powerful user/agent—YOU as the network, YOU as 'produser'"—celebrations like the 2006 *Time* Magazine cover story analyzed in the introduction to this book. As Wendy Chun argues, "by positing YOU as the sovereign subject, YOU as the decider," profile culture "counteracts concerns over code as law."[10] As a self-help satire, *Filthy Rich* unravels the notion of a "sovereign" you to reveal the power structures it shrouds. The narrator introduces "you, huddled, shivering, on the packed earth under your mother's cot one cold, dewy morning"—an unlikely start to becoming "filthy rich" (4). One could say that the reader is interpellated as "You" or alternatively, that the reader is figuratively reborn and relocated to fit this new identity. Then again, as the novel states, "We are all refugees from our childhoods. And so, we turn, among other things, to stories. To write a story, to read a story, is to be a refugee from the state of refugees" (213), and so perhaps the reader, as a nomadic, nonunitary misfit, is simply seeking asylum in "You." In any case, Hamid's use of the second person, a particular and generic pronoun, produces both a sharp distinction and a personal connection between the reader and the character. Generically speaking, Hamid describes what life is like for a vast portion of the world's population, and to read about these conditions is to become increasingly aware of your own privilege—for literacy itself is a privilege in this context. Still, the narrator also claims, "when I imagine, I feel. The capacity for empathy is a funny thing" (214), suggesting that the act of reading undermines the individualism of neoliberal self-help books—which is perhaps the real "help."

Even as the novel invites the reader to inhabit this subjectivity, Hamid emphasizes the dissonance between the reader and the protagonist. This disconnect makes the novel as much about us as it is about "you." The narrator explains, "Your anguish is the anguish of a boy whose chocolate has been thrown away, whose remote controls are out of batteries, whose scooter is busted, whose new sneakers have been stolen. This is all the more remarkable since you've never in your life seen any of these things" (4). By juxtaposing these absurdly dissimilar forms of anguish, Hamid highlights that you are, in fact, not "you." The consumerist points of reference he offers are obnoxious when contrasted with the protagonist's physical pain: "the whites of your eyes are yellow, a consequence of spiking bilirubin levels in your blood. The virus afflicting you is called hepatitis E. It's typical mode of transmission is fecal-oral. Yum. It kills only about one in fifty, so you're likely to recover. But right now you feel like you're going to die" (4). Most jarringly, with the single word "Yum," Hamid juxtaposes "your anguish" over lost chocolate with the fecal-oral transmission of hepatitis E—an especially affective misfitting. The narrator concedes here that survival (much less comfort or success) is a function of environmental and material conditions as well as chance. In the end, the statistical likelihood of recovery does not change the fact that "you feel like you're going to die"—a feeling that the reader does not share.[11]

Data analytics is undoubtedly valuable for understanding the scale and scope of systemic inequality. Yet as the novel clarifies, data profiles can also calcify norms and exacerbate inequality by deeming groups of people risky investments who don't fit the "profile for success." Throughout the novel, Hamid deconstructs the self-help genre by routinely reminding readers of structural and environmental variables that contribute to the unequal distribution of life chances. For example, if "you" are a woman, you might as well stop reading, as we are told that the following advice, such as "Get an Education," does not apply to you. This is made plain through the case of the protagonist's sister who, despite having "demonstrated more enthusiasm for education in her few months in a classroom than your brother did in his several years . . . will not be sent there in his stead." As a woman, "Marriage is her future" (28).

Specifically, Hamid illustrates how a society of surveillance marks subjects and maintains systemic discrimination. For example, the protagonist and his sister are playing together outside when we are told that "Viewing the scene from the lenses of an orbiting reconnaissance satellite, an observer would see two children behaving peculiarly" (27). At this point, the sister is identified as simply one of "two children." However, "without warning the spell breaks. You follow your sister's altered gaze and see that a formerly shuttered window is now open. A tall, bald man stands inside, staring at your sister intently. She takes her shawl from you and throws one end over her head, the other across her still-small-breasted chest" (28). Hamid illustrates that in this surveillance-scape, the sister's selfhood and future are contingent on how she is perceived by the orbiting and lurking observers. Once the perspective shifts to the man staring from the window, she becomes sexualized and "marked for entry" (28). Whether because of misogyny, nepotism, or access to clean water, the novel steadfastly reminds readers of the largely insurmountable inequalities undermining the project of self-help—conditions often reified and policed by surveillance and profiling. To address the forces and failures of profiling, Hamid embraces the subjectivity of the misfit, saying "it's misfits who help all people fit in everywhere."[12] By beginning with the dissonance or misfit between "You" and the reader, the novel effectively provokes a "degree of questioning and refusal to accept what is given inside society."[13]

Filthy Rich satirically exposes the fictions of self-help books: for example, that "you" can determine your own fortune, and that their advice applies to "you" in all of your particularity. However, Hamid's critique extends beyond the paradoxes and even recklessness of the self-help genre. Rather, he situates the self-help genre in the broader discourses of self-reliance and self-interestedness—providing a biting critique of the ways neoliberal globalization exacerbates a widening economic divide. In talking about his novel, Hamid succinctly captures this tension: "For people who are at the bottom economically, the world is becoming a harder and harder place. . . . And yet the incentives to become rich are so great because enormous amounts of wealth are being accumulated. And so those two things, that carrot and stick, are beating people along this trajectory of trying desperately to move up in the world."[14]

In the novel, surveillance serves powerfully as both the carrot and the stick. For instance, the filthy rich characters live behind guarded gates in "premier housing societies" that are "secure, walled-off, and impeccably maintained, lit-up-at-night, noise-controlled, [and] perfectly regulated" (111). Likewise, the protagonist knows he has finally arrived as a rich man when "Security men and parking attendants salute you, elevator doors spring apart for your arrival" (145), and a military police officer "waves you through" (162). Nevertheless, when "A series of CCTV cameras observes various stages of your progress through the cantonment," through "their monochromatic optical sensors the expensive metallic finish of your sedan dulls to a ratty gray" (162), indicating that although the protagonist may have achieved a new degree of wealth affording him an ease of mobility, that freedom is diminished and dulled in the face of military power. Notably, the many CCTV cameras positioned throughout the novel follow "You" through "the various stages of your progress" toward becoming filthy rich and represent a different view of "You." Through the "monochromatic lens" of military force your progress is ratty in comparison to the levels of access and mobility the military enjoys. Even after joyously passing through the doors and apparently leaving the rat race behind, the protagonist still finds himself caught as a subject of military gaze.

By defiantly portraying surveillance and data profiling as an act of storytelling, the novel reframes these technologies and techniques as modes of narration. Gregoire Chamayou suggests that "We should imagine eventual scribe-machines, flying robotized clerks that, in real time, would record the smallest actions occurring in the world below—as if, in parallel to the life of human beings, the cameras that already capture animated images would now set about producing a circumstantial account of them."[15] Insightfully, he imagines this account as "lines of text" and realizes that it "would at the same time constitute something more: a great index, an informative catalog of an immense video library in which everyone's life would become retrospectively researchable."[16] Even if everything were surveilled and recorded, somehow sidestepping questions about who is tracked and for what reasons, very different stories could be told "retrospectively" depending on the search parameters. It's worth revisiting General Michael Hayden's boast that as an NSA officer, "You are a storyteller. You can't throw data through the transit and expect a policy maker to digest it and make a decision on it. You actually have to tell the story. That's what an intelligence officer does." Again, when Glenn

Thrush quickly followed up on that, "Therein also lies the danger sometimes right?" Hayden defensively fell back on the supposed truth-value and neutrality of data analysis, saying, "Well, okay, so now you are really getting into the science."[17] Hamid frames this matter of knowledge production first as a literary question, introducing the fundamentals of reader response theory: "Like all books, this self-help book is a co-creative project. . . . It's in being read that a book becomes a book, and in each of a million different readings a book becomes one of a million different books" (97). By representing data collection and surveillance as also narratological, Hamid disrupts the adage that data or footage speaks for themselves, and, perhaps, most importantly, he raises the question of who our co-creators are in this "project" and what interests they serve.

Highlighting the current epistemological and physical force of profiling and surveillance, the chapter "Patronize the Artists of War" narrates the story of "you" through the lens of these technologies. The narration shifts from inside the point of view of internet search histories, to laptop cameras, to flight registries, to credit card records, to aerial drones—in effect, allowing the plot of the story to track how profile technologies plot, pinpoint, and identify the public. In other words, the novel hacks into these structures and infrastructures to tell the story of "your" profile. Raising the stakes to their most critical condition, the surveillant gaze we inhabit is specifically that of the military-industrial complex. After all, "as American Major S. F. Murray says . . . contemporary battle command begins with 'one's ability to see, visualize, observe or find.'"[18] By adopting the point of view of these devices to narrate the story, Hamid illustrates the narrative structure and discursivity of this machinery, which actually characterizes as it profiles. Most notably, the novel contrasts the agility of these transitions from one lens to another with the striving and struggles of characters trapped in that web. Finally, I analyze in depth the novel's subtle but powerful critique of drones, which crystallizes the deathly serious power of profiling. Indeed, I argue that profiling is a form of storytelling, and at times the narrative is a war story told in black and white. Whether targeting consumers or targeting combatants, profiling is a matter of minimizing costs and maximizing gains by sorting the right person from the wrong person.[19] Despite his attempts to fall back on the science, General Hayden was entirely correct when he suggested that this sorting tells a social and political story.

Information Is Power

Filthy Rich most directly targets the use of data profiling by "those at the apex of organizations entrusted with national security," claiming that "no one does this with more single-minded dedication or curatorial ferocity" (160). I have argued in previous chapters that in the context of consumer surveillance and data profiling, human behavior has become a revenue stream to be tapped; relatedly, Filthy Rich illustrates that in the context of state and paramilitary surveillance, the target is not only a potential threat to be neutralized but an economic opportunity to be seized. As part of the program to get filthy rich, the narrator advises "You" to "Patronize the Artists of War," explaining that "these artists of war are active even when their societies are officially at peace, quests for power being unrelenting" (160). The narrator satirically describes this perpetual use of profiling as impressive and aspirational—a quest for power in keeping with the protagonist's supposed objective to become filthy rich.

National security organizations rightly or wrongly justify profiling as a means of protecting citizens and securing the nation-state; however, Hamid, evocatively reframes data profiling by the military-surveillance network as the unapologetic pursuit of profit. He writes that "in the absence of open hostilities they can be found either hunting for ever-present enemies within or otherwise divvying up that booty always conveniently proximate to those capable of wanton slaughter, spoils these days often cloaked in purchasing contracts and share-price movements" (160). Hamid disparagingly intersperses the vocabulary of ancient warfare—"hunting for ever-present enemies," "divvying up booty," "wanton slaughter," and "spoils"—with the modern corporate rhetoric of "purchasing contracts" and "share-price movements." While certainly disturbing, this is perhaps a familiar critique of the military-industrial complex; what is not familiar is the way Hamid identifies data profiling as simultaneously a powerful weapon in the business of war and an increasingly dominant business strategy for becoming "filthy rich." Profiling here is a matter of hunting for enemies to amass not only wealth but the potential to grow even more wealth, in the form of "purchasing contracts," for example. In other words, this is data profiling as part of warfare speculation.[20]

The passage ends with the narrator rejoicing that "to partner in such ventures is to be invited to ride the great armor-plated, signal-jamming,

depleted-uranium-firing helicopter gunship to wealth, and so it is only natural that you are at this moment considering clambering aboard" (161). The
punctuated features of this "helicopter gunship," effectively substitute for the
personal attributes of the supposedly self-made entrepreneur. Meanwhile,
the adjective "signal-jamming" speaks to the fact that surveillance and data
profilers (both military and otherwise) demand the visibility of their "ever-
present enemies" or targets while ensuring that they themselves remain if
not invisible at least unintelligible. As this chapter progresses, however, the
novel imaginatively hijacks the signals of state surveillance and their power
over the flow of information.

In addition to evidencing the consolidation of state and industrial power,
Hamid's use of "curatorial" and "artists" suggests that the tactics and techniques of profiling are not merely destructive and speculative but also creative.[21] Like artists and curators, the security apparatuses transform "information"—organizing it, framing it, and ultimately giving it meaning. This
becomes a particularly crucial insight if we accept the novel's statement that
"we're all information, all of us, whether readers or writers, you or I. The DNA
in our cells, the bioelectric currents in our nerves, the chemical emotions in
our brains, the configurations of atoms within us and of subatomic particles
within them, the galaxies and whirling constellations we perceive not only
when looking outward but also when looking in, it's all, every last bit and
byte of it, information" (159). By combining the precision and authority of
scientific and computational discourses, these microscopic and telescopic
gazes might seem, at first glance, democratizing or equalizing. That is, if
looked at closely enough, "all of us" are essentially reducible to the same
units. However, the narrator continues, "what we do know is that information
is power. And so information has become central to war, that most naked
of our means by which power is sought" (160). By supplanting the maxim
"knowledge is power" with the notion that "information is power," Hamid
captures the epistemological shift in the data age, which posits that "every
last bit and byte" of information is essentially valuable in and of itself. Even
more, information or raw data takes on truth-power precisely because it is
just information and therefore seems ideologically neutral. This realization
about info-power is now "what we know"—this realization is new knowledge
that must be understood and reckoned with in the data age.

Info-power is often produced through algorithmic, microscopic, and telescopic gazes, which the novel represents as out of proportion with human ways of seeing. These techniques exponentially stretch the proportions of something like Jeremy Bentham's panopticon,[22] but they are still reflective of surveillance's fundamental lack of reciprocity. Hamid grounds the often inconceivable scale and scope of data surveillance in the particular perspective and power structures of national security: "From the perspective of the world's national security apparatuses you exist in several locations. You appear on property and income-tax registries, on passport and ID card databases. You show up on passenger manifests and telephone logs. You hum inside electromagnetically shielded military-intelligence servers and, deep below pristine fields and forbidding mountains, on their dedicated backups. You are fingertip swirls, facial ratios, dental records, voice patterns, spending trails, e-mail threads" (161). From a distance, this might sound like a familiar fragmented, split subject, but Hamid is clear that this is not simply the postmodern condition. This is "You" according to the specific "perspective of the world's national security apparatuses,"[23] embedded in state departments, bureaus, and agencies in cooperation with telecommunications companies and airlines. If "information is power," then this information about "You" is not free-floating; it is consolidated on "dedicated backups" and protected as "military intelligence." In other words, your data profile is not scattered in the winds or floating in a cloud but buried "deep below pristine fields and forbidding mountains." Ultimately, the novel reminds readers that the US military stands atop the highest mountain in this range of consolidated data, even as they are, in the words of the Google Scholar motto, "Standing on the shoulders of [tech] giants."

Finally, this recognition that "you exist in several locations" parallels the rhetorical stance of the novel, which posits you both before and on the page. This comparison and contrast between the narrator's story of "you" and your profile is suggestive. Ultimately, Hamid implies that profiling is not an exact science but an art. Given that "disperate other contemporary narratives play out simultaneously," there is an artistry to the way "You" becomes "You" in the eyes of the "world's national security apparatuses." Like the "co-creative project" of writing and reading, it is full of creative narrations and interpretations affected by the hegemonic discourses and assumptions of the historical present.

Discursive Machines

Filthy Rich exposes the machinery of discourse by adopting the self-help genre and second-person perspective as a kind of hackable writing software; in addition, the chapter "Patronize the Artists of War" exposes the discursivity of profiling machines. Hamid activates the hidden infrastructures of surveillance, exposing and enlivening the hardware, software, and discreet operations of profiling. When the protagonist is in the hospital, caught in the web of medical machinery and city infrastructure, readers experience "the shock of an unseen network suddenly made physical, as a fly experiences a cobweb" (183). Moreover, like "You" ensnared in those "inanimate strands," the narration itself is tangled up with the perspectives of profiling. By directing the narrative structure, trajectory, and point of view, these surveillance technologies artfully piece together a story and set of characters. In other words, this key section explicitly depicts the infrastructure and surveillance-scape of the city as a narrative structure with the power to characterize and plot individuals and their stories.

Notably, the discreet techniques and technologies of profiling are integrated and connected through an information system that links email accounts to laptops to bank accounts to flight registries to drones. On a metafictional level, this infrastructure is simply the novel itself or the novel's narrator establishing the connections for the reader. However, Hamid stresses that this integration is neither metaphorical nor transcendent; rather, he writes, it is sustained by "a telecommunications center from which red and white masts soar mightily, towering above satellite dishes, like electromagnetic spars built to navigate the clouds" (203). Surprisingly, we are told that the pretty girl "bought her [townhouse] for its view" of this nautical image sailing through the sky. The towering telecommunications center becomes positively associated with having a view and the ability to navigate the world.

Of course, as this chapter of the novel makes clear, the pretty girl is also in view of the telecommunications center. Hamid relates the allure of this structure with the fact that power is a limited and unequally distributed commodity in the city: "parts of the metropolis are in darkness, electricity shortages meaning that the illumination of entire areas is turned off on a rotating basis, usually but not always on the hour, and in these inky patches, at this late time, little can be seen, just the odd building with its own generator" (173). In this context, where power is patchy, perhaps it makes sense that a view of the tower would be attractive. Still, the phrase "inky patches" casts the city as a page to be read or deciphered with more or less clarity, again alluding to how the city is overseen and surveilled, almost as a condition to having electrical power. This sets up a familiar bargain between having access to necessary utilities and becoming subject to surveillance, a bargain that undercuts the empty advice to simply unplug or log off if you don't want to be subject to digital profiling.

It is true, as Angelia Poon argues in her article, "Helping the Novel," that Hamid "appropriates the particular vantage points and perspectival positions made possible by modern technology to undermine the sense of a self in complete control."[24] However, the narration also undermines the dangerous myth that the technology itself is autonomous and "in complete control." Paradoxically, this is also a commonplace of profile epistemology meant to suggest that data is impartial and therefore trustworthy and as long as the technology is autonomous, no *body* is really watching. By having the narrator and reader watch "you" from the perspective of surveillance technology, we are reminded that there is presumably an invisible "I" or eye watching as well, giving the distinct impression that we are viewing alongside the "artists of war" in what is actually a crowded field. It is true that "you" are not autonomous, but neither are cameras, computers, or drones. It becomes clear that even the algorithms running this surveillance-scape have their own writers and readers, despite what profile epistemology maintains. By artfully shifting between cameras, databases, and records, Hamid calls attention to the ways the self is narrated and constructed through deliberate use of information technologies.[25]

Appropriately, the narrator begins what I call the extended tracking shot by explaining that online, "you can be tracked, and indeed you are tracked, as are we all, as you proceed through your e-mails, catch up on the news, perform a search, and wind up lingering, incongruously, on the website of a furnishings boutique" (168). The protagonist visiting the website for the pretty girl's boutique would only seem incongruous to someone unaware of their life stories and relationship, signaling that not only has the novel shifted point of view, but that this new perspective is limited and fallible. Chamayou clarifies that "Contrary to what one might imagine, the main objectives of these continuous surveillance devices is not so much to tail individuals already known, but rather to spot the emergence of suspect elements based on their unusual behavior . . . in other words, to describe them by behavior that reflects a particular profile."[26] This intelligence gathering leads to two distinct types of drone strikes by the United States: personal strikes and signature strikes. While personal strikes target named individuals whom the United States has positively identified as terrorist threats, "signature strikes" target individuals who fit the profile of a terrorist but whom the United States has not specifically identified.

It is fitting that the narrator routinely notes behavior that is inconsistent with the protagonist's profile, even if it is not out of character. For example, this website seems "all in all, an odd spot in the ether to capture the attention of a water industrialist" (168), another apparent misfitting, unless you know that he is in love with her. Now operating on multiple registers as the separate stories of "You" play out simultaneously, Hamid writes, "A log of your internet wanderings indicates you have not visited it before. Nor, subsequently, are you recorded visiting it again" (168). On the one hand, this information adds to our understanding of the romantic relationship between the protagonist and the pretty girl that is, by some accounts, the heart of the novel. On the other hand, this also casually indicates that the protagonist is under constant surveillance, creating a separate record of his life wherein his interest in the pretty girl is regarded as somehow suspicious.

In a remarkable sequence, the point of view dexterously shifts from the protagonist's computer, to the pretty girl's website, into her laptop, through her webcam, and out into her bedroom. Moving from the protagonist to the pretty girl, Hamid writes, "The website in question is registered in another city, to the residential address of its owner, who like many, perhaps most, computer users has never concerned herself overmuch with such matters as firewalls, system updates, or anti-malware utilities" (168). In one sense, Hamid demonstrates the stealthy storytelling made possible by data fusion between ubiquitous surveillance technologies. Still, there is another related and critical story being told here. The novel also invokes the implicit interests and aims driving this surveillance, namely, those of the "world's military apparatuses." If the narrative conceit had been to make "You" filthy rich, what is the unspoken project behind this new technologically mediated point of view? In other words, why exactly is this website in question? We are told that the pretty girl doesn't bother much with cybersecurity such as firewalls, but ironically, through the laptop camera, "What can be seen are the steel bars on her windows, heavy in gauge and narrowly spaced, and a square motion sensor mounted high on her wall. Beneath it, near her front door, is a keypad belonging to her home alarm system" (171). Although the threats to her physical property are broadcasted and knowable, the subject surveilling and tracking her is self-effacing with an interest in her too obscure to fully appreciate.

Zooming in on the mechanisms of surveillance, Hamid begins to develop this unseen point of view and the specific interests operating it:

> her laptop, sleek and high-end machine though it is, is simply teeming with digital fauna, much in the same manner as its keyboard is teeming with unseen bacteria and microorganisms, except that among its un-invited coded squatters is a military program that allows the machine's built-in camera and microphone to be activated and monitored remotely, something no single-celled protozoan could likely pull off, transforming the laptop, in effect, into a covert surveillance device or, depending on the intent of the administrator of its monitoring software, into an originator of voyeuristic striptease and porn. (169)

Through the lively language in this passage, the invisible observer directing our gaze begins to take shape as a peeping, scopophilic military or national intelligence "administrator."[27] Although this "covert" figure seems initially interested in the "water industrialist," they apparently have widespread access, affecting or infecting his contacts as well. In fact, the narration hinges on these moments of contact, suggesting the exponential scope of this surveillance. Indeed, the imagery here alludes to systems within systems, programs within programs, and microorganisms within organisms, implicitly likening how "the machine's built-in camera and microphone" are "activated and monitored" to the mastery of microscopes. Meanwhile, the embedded military program is camouflaged by the digital fauna in this dense surveillance ecology. Still, the novel, running its own monitoring software, indirectly makes this camouflaged administrator visible to the reader.

Next the point of view leaps from the laptop into her bedroom where, we are told, "nothing so titillating seems to be in the offing. The computer sits open on a counter and through its camera a woman can be seen by herself at a low table, finishing off a meal and bottle of red wine." Slowly the scene comes into focus as "The pretty girl sits attentively, not looking at her hands or her food, but music is audible, and then conversation, and then a rain-storm, until it becomes obvious that she is watching a film" (169). Setting this seemingly romantic scene only to reveal that the rainfall, music playing, and conversation are coming from a movie reintroduces the questions of genre with which Hamid began the novel. Is this still a self-help book, a love story between the protagonist and the pretty girl, a piece of pornography, a romantic movie, a spy thriller, or is it an all-too-boring intelligence briefing? This embroiling of various genres is not just a matter of style or aesthetics: these represent distinct ways of knowing her and making meaning based on different investments in her character or profile. Including surveillance pro-filing as one among many genres effectively destabilizes its epistemological truth-value and supposed objectivity.

As this sequence continues, the surveillant perspective moves from the laptop through the phone records to the email account, simulating a kind of omniscience by combining information piecemeal from various forms of data surveillance. Through the laptop microphone, the narrator overhears a phone call between the pretty girl and her assistant, who is "easily iden-tified" given that "the mobile she uses is linked to an email account with messages chronicling her activities for the pretty girl's store." In a readerly way, the narrator suggests that "a recording of their conversation reveals a tone of warmth, these two clearly being not just colleagues but friends" (170). However, this insight is overshadowed by the disturbing implication that the pretty girl's conversations are being recorded. Again and again, this kind of casual disclosure leaks through the text and hints at a more troubling story about the largely invisible forces affecting their lives.

Likewise, when we learn that "her assistant has capped signing authority on the boutique's account," the narrator suggests that this is "indicative of a rare level of trust" (172); however, on a separate register, this is also indicative of an intense level of surveillance with the capacity to link bank account data with emails, browser histories, and telephone records. Exemplifying the ways data profiling works to construct a narrative of the self, Hamid explains,

Her assistant's monthly payments of home utilities, and of rent, coupled with a complete absence of expenditure on children's schooling, sug-gests she too may live alone, or perhaps with elderly parents, for her credit card also shows frequent medical costs, charges from a variety of doctors and diagnostic centers and hospitals, charges at times exceeding her wages, yet on a regular basis paid off in full by the pretty girl, with a direct transfer of the required amount from her personal account to that of her assistant. (172)

Regardless of whether the inferences are persuasive, the fact that Hamid can construct a personal story about the relationships between characters through the perspective of data profiling speaks to its epistemological power. Moreover, by appealing to what is revealed, suggested, shown, indicated, visible, and audible, the narrator lays bare the operations of transforming data into a plausible and meaningful narrative, as opposed to the commonplace that it simply speaks for itself.

The surveillant narrative then zooms out and contextualizes our characters according to statistical and demographic information. The gaze moves to the street outside the pretty girl's apartment, where "a phone call reporting gunfire is being made to a police station," linking our characters to information about "crime statistics," which "confirm that a significant number of prosperous residents are presently in the process of being burgled or robbed"; although "even in this most unequal city, the vast majority of tonight's violence will be inflicted upon neighborhoods whose residents are reliably poor" (171). Hamid's choice of the word "reliably" along with the use of the future tense to predict "tonight's violence" suggests that not only does the city expect and tolerate violence in poor areas, it relies on it. Indeed, "Paramilitary forces are deployed to prevent such battles from spilling over too easily into areas deemed vital to national security, the port, for example, or upscale housing enclaves, or those premier commercial avenues from which rise headquarters of major corporations and banks. Indeed, a paramilitary checkpoint is, at this moment, in operation a stone's throw from the towering headquarters of the bank that holds the accounts of the pretty girl, her boutique, and her assistant" (172). The profiling perspective here is emphatically the perspective of paramilitary forces invested in protecting the economic security of the ruling class, not the safety of citizens. The narrator plainly conflates national security and the reliable flow of capital, not only in and out of ports but also in and out of gated "upscale housing enclaves." The flow of crime, therefore, is not something to be stopped but channeled to best enable the current flow of capital upstream. This again reframes the use of surveillance and profiling—even by police and paramilitary forces—from merely techniques of securitization and crime prevention to strategies for economic growth.

An "Unblinking Eye"

According to the US Joint Chiefs of Staff, precision engagement refers to "the ability of joint forces to locate, survey, discern, and track objectives or targets; select, organize, and use the correct systems; generate desired effects; assess results; and re-engage with decisive speed and overwhelming operational tempo as required, throughout the full range of military operations."[28] We have seen how the profile industry adopts a similarly overly confident narrative of precision to target consumers in real time. Hamid lays bare the implicit point of view that determines the desired effects, sets the criteria, and assesses the results. Like Rankine in *Citizen*, he importantly recalibrates the "operational tempo" to apprehend otherwise blurry realities. By re-pacing and respacing our view of surveillance, it becomes clear that the term "precision" misrepresents the facts and ignores the collateral damage and incidental injury caused by drones. Furthermore, *Filthy Rich* illustrates how the military logic of precision strikes is wed with the consumer logic of personalization to create moving targets. This is the real point of view of data surveillance—not the vague disinterestedness or the deep curiosity that it projects. Seen through the crosshairs of unmanned aerial vehicles or advertising algorithms, people appear as pinpoints to be pursued and plotted. *Filthy Rich* captures this point of view by showing not only what is seen through the crosshairs but also what is overlooked by data's limited field of focus—including the surveyors themselves. By including the greater context of characters' lives and how their data is collected and shaped, the novel portrays how personhood gives way to personalization.

Eventually the novel enters the point of view an unmanned aerial vehicle (UAV) or drone, following this figure of military surveillance to its apex. Since 2004, the United States has conducted at least 430 confirmed drone strikes in Pakistan.[29] In fact, in the United States more drone operators are trained than all of the pilots for bombers and fighter planes combined.[30] Although exact numbers are difficult to come by, it is estimated that between 2004 and 2018, US drones killed 2,515 to 4,026 people in Pakistan.[31] Former director of the

CIA Leon Panetta made the common argument that an armed drone "is very precise and it is very limited in terms of collateral damage."[32] Some critics have counterargued that there is a difference between hitting your target and hitting only your target. This contains two points. First, the killing radius for a Predator drone is fifteen meters, so any number of innocent people might be killed. Second—and this is the point the novel seems to take up—targets are sometimes misidentified. People live and die by their "pattern of life" files established by the CIA. In this regard, drones are not only salient symbols for the dangers of omnipresent surveillance; they produce enormous amounts of data and surveillance footage. "In the course of 2009 alone, US drones generated the equivalent of twenty-four years' worth of video recording. The new ARGUS-IS wide-area surveillance system promises "to generate several terabytes [of data] per minute."[33]

First, the surveillant gaze in the novel sees that the pretty girl and her assistant are "registered passengers" on a jetliner, which "is picked up by the radar of a warship in international waters, identified as a commercial flight posing no immediate threat, and then for the most part ignored, the naval vessel using its antennae to continue to sniff the pheromone-like emissions of electrons wafting from coastal military installations instead." However, incidentally, "at roughly the same altitude, albeit far inland, an experimental unmanned aerial vehicle cruises in the opposite direction" (173). Given the ongoing drone strikes and surveillance in Pakistan, even the most casual reference to a chance encounter with a UAV is loaded. Moreover, the juxtaposition between the commercial flight and the military vehicle flying at "roughly the same altitude" but in different directions signifies the two narratives of consumer profiling and military profiling flying in the same field, especially given that readers are accustomed to thinking about air travel as an exceptional site of cooperation between commercial and state security. The consumer jetliner with its registered passengers typically poses "no immediate threat," but it is still understandably on the radar of national security with its flight logs serving multiple interests. Concurrently, the UAV is conducting its own surveillance to create profiles of people. That is, what seems like coincidence as the narrator moves from one technology to another is actually a larger constellation of data collection. The cooperation here is naturalized through the imagery of insects using their antennae to sniff one another's pheromones. This organic imagery highlights the fact that the commercial plane is packed with passengers while the UAV by definition has no passengers or bodies on board. Whether the presumably large and imposing warship or the small and flighty drone, these species of military vehicles seem to be scanning, communicating, and operating by their own devices, with humans conspicuously absent. From the perspective of the US military, drones being unmanned is one of their chief advantages; however, from the perspective of Pakistani citizens living inside the "hostile environment," the apparent autonomy of the machines has the effect of further erasing their own humanity. In fact, the statistical justifications of drone strikes that they get it mostly right and are relatively precise discounts the locals as mostly or relatively human.

In the context of this self-help book that advises "patronizing the artists of war," it is unsurprising that the narrator callously performs a cost-benefit analysis of the drone, conspicuously neglecting the environmental or human costs: "It is small and limited in range. Its chief advantages are its low cost, allowing it to be procured in large numbers, and its comparative quietness, permitting it to function unobtrusively. There are high hopes for its success in the export market, in particular among police forces and cash-strapped armies engaged in urban operations" (174). The omissions and vagueness here mirror the deliberate confusion surrounding drones, based on unclear targeting criteria and opaque strike results. We learn that the drone can "function unobstructively," without being told what its function is. We learn that it could be used in "urban operations," without being told what those operations are. Moreover, the high hopes for this drone's profitability once again derisively frames military surveillance and the consequent killings as opportunities for economic growth and success.

Given the staggering death toll from US drone strikes, it is both fitting and chilling that the drone flies over the funeral of the protagonist's brother to see "a crowd gathering at a graveyard" (174). Even though "this drone is today [only] validating its performance parameters" and not executing a strike, the symbolism exposes the necro-politics behind the neoliberal rhetoric of "performance," which can turn a data profile into a "death warrant."[34] It's also appropriate that the drone is testing its parameters or limits over the funeral, given that the graveyard is indeed the frontier of paramilitary profiling when it is pushed to its final conclusion.

Importantly, this scene also evokes the ever-present threat of drones mistakenly targeting large gatherings or assemblies of innocent civilians in Pakistan. For instance, in 2011 there was a US strike in Datta Khel, Pakistan, that killed nineteen to thirty civilians who were meeting in a traditional assembly to "resolve a disagreement in the local community" but were "predefined as resembling terrorist behavior" since, "seen from the sky, a village meeting looks just like a gathering in the local community."[35] Similarly, a 2014 drone strike in Yemen killed fourteen people returning from a wedding, whose vehicles were mistaken for Al Qaeda militants.[36] Hamid alludes to precisely this problem when the narrator witnesses "a pair of male figures in suits, a man in his sixties and a slender, teenage body," and misidentifies the younger man as "perhaps his grandson" when readers know that this is actually the protagonist and his son. This is an "innocent mistake," but in this context it is intensified by the fact that the primary task of antiterrorism is no longer to contain or immobilize the enemy but to identify and track down targets.

Hazardous Material

One major justification for drone strikes is that they provide a long enough lever to safely remove soldiers from the danger zone. In fact, this is part of the broader common logic that with advanced technology it is no longer necessary to expose workers to "physical danger in order to earn a living." In other words, "There is no hazardous task performed by men today that cannot, in principle, be performed by remotely controlled machines."[37] Yet Hamid indirectly critiques the underlying assumptions and hierarchies of this logic when the drone flies over the funeral. After all, the protagonist is at the funeral for his brother, a commercial spray painter, who died from prolonged exposure to fumes. The novel here reveals the gulf between what might be true in "principle" or for the world's filthy rich, and what is certainly not the case for the world's underprivileged. The brother was exposed to "physical danger in order to earn a living." His job certainly was hazardous. Hamid describes his work as "in some senses like being an astronaut, or slightly more prosaically, a scuba diver. It too involves the hiss of air, the feeling of weightlessness, the sudden pressure headaches and nausea, the precariousness that results when an organic being and a machine are fused together." He does not operate the machinery from a safe distance with a remote control; rather, he becomes the machinery, remotely controlled by his employer. Furthermore, "an astronaut or aquanaut sees unimaginable new worlds, whereas your brother sees only a monocolor haze of varying intensities" (31). From his vantage point, the world is not so unimaginably new.

In another sense, the new world on the horizon in absolute terms is increasingly becoming this "haze of varying intensities." Indeed, the novel portrays the environment itself as an inescapable hazard zone with undrinkable water and polluted air. Even the pristine gated communities sit under "dust and pollution suspended over the city like a dome, transforming the sky to copper and the clouds to irradiated bronze" (188). That the pollution looks like copper and bronze speaks to the fact that profit and pollution are often by-products of the same enterprises. Hamid emphasizes this connection: "As you drive off, under a beautiful, orange, polluted sky, riding high in your SUV above lesser hatchbacks and motorcycles" (145). It's because pollution and climate change affect populations disproportionately, with the greatest contributors being the least vulnerable, that the sight of the filthy, polluted sky can be beautiful to our filthy rich protagonist. He is, after all, a water industrialist profiting from "the ever-dropping aquifer, punctuated by thousands upon thousands of greedily sipping machine-powered steel straws" (155).

In the complicated image of a military drone flying in the polluted sky over the funeral for a man who died from prolonged exposure to contaminants, Hamid raises the question of what is considered a hazardous material and who is most vulnerable to its effects. After all, the polluted sky is doubly threatening. Ultimately, the orange haze and the frequent buzz of propellers signal the threat of imminent death. Indeed, the combination of these images is profound, given that the threats of global warming and military activity are intimately related. It is worth noting here that "militarization is the number one cause of environmental damage in the world," and that the U.S. military is "the largest, single polluter on the planet." In fact, "The U.S. Department of Defense consumes more oil than any other entity on the planet" and "the Pentagon uses 75% of the oil bought by the Department of Defense (DOD) for its jets, bombers, tanks, Humvees, and drones."[38] To complicate matters, not only did the brother die from exposure to hazards on the job, but there are people, hovering over his funeral (albeit remotely) whose job is to expose other people to deathly machines. In a shocking reversal, "it is the enemy who is treated as a dangerous material" in drone warfare.[39] By introducing the drone over the brother's funeral, the novel smartly relates the radical asymmetry of drone warfare with the asymmetry of globalization and neoliberal capitalism—the asymmetry of the filthy rich and the dirty poor.[40]

Finally, seeing the drone, the protagonist "looks up to the heavens. The drone circles a few times, its high-powered eye unblinking, and flies observantly on" (174). This poignant moment reminds readers that the surveillant gaze we have been embodying is indifferent to its impact or the affects it produces. As high-powered as its eye may be, it remains unblinking and unflinching when the protagonist looks back. In other words, the drone, unlike a soldier, for example, is indifferent to the others' gaze. With operators stationed around the world, drone warfare strategically ensures that operators never feel seen. The novel crucially helps readers see the blinking eye behind this "unblinking eye"—represented in the novel as the military "administrator" directing the narration and, in effect, telling the story.[41] In that sense, the novel also embeds the slow blinking eyes of the readers as witnesses to this crucial and cruel story.

Drones have been understood as telechiric systems, wherein the machine stands in as an alter ego for the person operating it—in our case the observing administrator figure. Ostensibly, the consciousness of the operator is transferred to an "invulnerable mechanical body" while the operator's fleshy body remains safely removed from the "hostile environment."[42] As much as Hamid is satirizing the self-help genre, he is also writing a telechiric novel. We become "you"—a kind of alter ego—but as much as we might transfer our consciousness and imagine that this is the case, our fleshy bodies sit safely at a distance holding our books. We are not vulnerable to the threats of "you." We don't have jaundice or feel like we might die. We aren't shot at. We are merely simulating these experiences in this "co-creative project." If in drone warfare "space is divided into two: a hostile area and a safe one,"[43] the novel also enacts this division between the diegetic world and our own, while underscoring the power lines that divide characters, from gated communities to gender differences.

Ultimately, *Filthy Rich* illustrates that profiling and surveillance should be understood as forms of story-telling that attempt to make people's "life patterns" legible and intelligible. Hamid portrays two intimately related genres of profiling traveling at roughly the same altitude—consumer profiling and paramilitary profiling—which together tell a kind of war story through cost-benefit analysis. To the extent that self-help books run the same neoliberal software, the novel emphatically asks: who pays the costs and who bene-fits? After all, consumer and military surveillance share an investment in constructing profiles of people, which can then identify them as the right target, whether for an advertisement or a weapon. In this context, neoliberal discourses of self-help mean improving one's profile or overcoming the odds, but the field remains unchanged, and at any moment a bomb could still drop. By adopting the lenses of the self-help genre and state surveillance, Hamid effectively flies readers overhead of both discourses, providing the crucial perspective to watch the watchers.

CONCLUSION

Amazon, Authorship, and Algorithmic Governance

The instruction we find in books is like fire. We fetch it
from our neighbours, kindle it at home, communicate
it to others and it becomes the property of all.
—VOLTAIRE

I n each piece of literature analyzed in this book, data flickers in and out of vision as characters navigate their surveillance-scapes and reckon with the effects of their personal data profiles. In this way, data surveillance inhabits the textual consciousness and subconsciousness of the novels and lyric, inviting analysis of the suppressed narrative dimension of data profiling, the manifest pressures and counterpressures it applies to contemporary fiction, and the literary counterforces it provokes. By way of conclusion, I turn toward Amazon as an exemplar of the profile epistemology I have analyzed here—one doubly invested in literature and algorithmically authoring the future. To grasp Amazon's profound role in surveillance and stories, I will be thinking alongside Mark McGurl's astute essay "Everything and Less: Fiction in the Age of Amazon," which lays an important foundation for this analysis by contemplating the company's connection with literary culture. McGurl begins with the question, "Should Amazon now be considered the driving force in American Literary History?"[1] Arguing that, yes, Amazon exerts profound influence on literary production and reception, McGurl also reflects on the influence of literature, past and present, on the company's unique "corporate identity."[2] Ultimately, he argues that far from being "antiliterary," as some critics allege, Amazon's "problem is that it wants to be the hero of a great literary work in its own right."[3] En route, Amazon attempts to reconcile rapid "real-time" technical operations with the warmth and patience of "quality time," in what amounts to a distinctly literary approach. As McGurl pronounces, "Real time and long term. That is exactly the formula for enduring literary value."[4] I argue that Amazon's impact on contemporary literature and its own literariness cannot be fully understood outside of its reliance on data surveillance and profile epistemology. On one hand, real-time surveillance

Conclusion

(of consumer-citizens and employees) has allowed the company to chart a self-correcting path toward long-term growth and enduring wealth. On the other hand, Bezos's personal convictions that in the long term, artificial intelligence will inevitably orchestrate and ensure our quality time, ostensibly justifies Amazon's "real-time regime" by reframing surveillance as a service.

The preceding chapters have argued that contemporary literature resists the "real-time regime"[5] of data profiling by re-pacing and respacing encounters with surveillance to capture the suppressed affects and effects of profiling. These strategies are effective, in part, because they call attention to the ways that surveillance capitalists lay claim to both quality time and real time: converting moments consumers ostensibly spend reviving or enriching themselves into yet another opportunity to stock their own stores of data. In other words, "Real-time data close the gap between the occurrence of an event and its apprehension as information, crowding reality and representation together in the urgent space of a perpetually self-renewing now."[6] The novels I have analyzed here respond by carefully uncrowding this space to confront the otherwise obscured realities and ideologies of data profiling.

Yet Amazon's standing as both an insatiable surveillance capitalist and a literary force invites us to further consider what happens when reading itself is subject to digital surveillance. After all, Alexa, Goodreads, and Kindle, among many more, allow Amazon to transmute otherwise intimate activities into fungible figures that can be used to nudge consumer behavior. This plotting and prodding depend on gathering information on users when they are most unfiltered and least self-possessed, which has incentivized companies, including Amazon, to conceive of quality time as the prime time to mine consumer data in real time. By bringing reading firmly into the fold of data surveillance, Amazon and its subsidiaries demonstrate that "real time is not only the external context for the therapeutic experience of virtual quality time; it ticks at its core."[7] The Kindle's reminder countdown on each page, which features the percentage of text remaining to be read and the estimated time left to completion, externalizes and crystallizes this encoded ethic. We might take this countdown as a reminder of the real-time tracking that runs silently in the background of daily life. Rather than attempting to provide an escape from the dominant sociopolitical and economic forces of surveillance capitalism, the literature in Profiles and Plotlines amplifies this ticking, taking it from an ambient background noise (to which we are growing increasingly accustomed) to a manifest signal of our times and, in moments of pronounced risk, to a resounding alarm.

In establishing Amazon's literariness, McGurl suggests that "we might want to open the lens wide enough to include MacKenzie Bezos, [the founder's] novelist [ex-]wife and a former student of Toni Morrison's at Princeton, who, as the company's fourth employee and its original bookkeeper, has been on the scene since the very beginning."[8] The presumption here is that MacKenzie Scott and her literary career have helped keep books the company's North Star, even as it has expanded into an "everything store"[9] fueled by surveillance capitalism. And it is true—as we have seen in each chapter of this book—that widening the lens can elicit a considerably different narrative. In this case, the broader digital context of the company and its operations make clear that Amazon not only prizes its position as the top bookseller nationally, it also regards its investments in machine learning and data profiling as gallant enterprises in world-building, inspired by science fiction.

It is this literary ethos that prompts, for example, the requirements that new product proposals be, as McGurl describes, "delivered in the form of futuristic fictional press releases reflecting on the product's success" and "that internal meeting presenters forgo PowerPoint in favor of brief prose narratives read in silence before the meeting begins."[10] Furthermore, Bezos maintains that "the great memos are written and re-written, shared with colleagues who are asked to improve the work, set aside for a couple of days, and then edited again with a fresh mind. They simply can't be done in a day or two."[11] I have surely said the same to my students at the university and can appreciate his stance on revision. Still, this investment in the idea of "great memos" and the writerly care they demand is unusual and reflects Amazon's self-conception as a distinctly literary company. In other words, by privileging prose in these cases, Bezos frames Amazon as a company authoring the future more profoundly than PowerPoint alone might convey. Here we might recall Jennifer Egan's poignant demonstration of PowerPoint's creative dimension in A Visit from the Goon Squad and question the supposition that only prose is an imaginative, narrative form. In fact, Egan's creative use of PowerPoint suggests that storytelling is always integral to technologically driven decision making and is never merely ornamental or additive. What could be written off as a performative gesture of corporate culture is better understood as a tacit acknowledgment that Amazon is also in the business of constructing stories that help shape reality. Even as surveillance capitalists too often frame their preferred plotlines and characterizations as impartial expressions of an unambiguous reality and an inevitable future, the narrative work of data profiling remains pivotal.

Still, for a company that tracks its employees' every movement to maximize efficiency,[12] for a company that operates a fleet of drones to deliver packages in thirty minutes or less,[13] these "peculiar corporate customs"[14] may seem uncharacteristically sluggish. Meanwhile, in the warehouses, where people fell sick during the COVID-19 pandemic, "self-service kiosks performed many traditional human resources functions. An app called A to Z handled everything from payroll to schedule changes."[15] This "rickety technology" allowed for a human resources team of merely thirty-five people to assist the over five thousand employees at New York's JFK8 warehouse.[16] Predictably, this proved woefully insufficient. The stark contrast between the slow reading that characterizes the corporate culture and the slow violence that plagues the hurried low-income workforce highlights the distinction between corporate self-image and corporate values. For our purposes, it also speaks to profile epistemology's efforts to purify "the science" from the story, as though surveillance and automation are the reality principles on which the narrative is built and not forms of creation and composition themselves. In other words, the quaint storytelling in the boardrooms and briefings is meant, by contrast, to make the company's other data-driven procedures appear all the more absolute and unassailable.

At the least, Bezos seems to relish his role as a literary figure, not unlike the way that Michael Hayden seemed to relish his role as a "storyteller."[17] In both cases, literature is held up as the softer side of their operations. Steve Jobs leaned on music in a similar way, routinely describing Apple as nestled comfortably at the intersection of "Liberal Arts Street" and "Technology Street."[18] Siva Vaidhyanathan makes a related point about Mark Zuckerberg's apparent belief in Facebook's noble narrative arc and how that obstructs his view of the company: "Facebook's leaders, and Silicon Valley leaders in general, have invited this untenable condition by believing too firmly in their own omnipotence and benevolence. . . . We cannot expect these leaders to address the problems within their own product designs until they abandon such faith and confidence in their own competence and rectitude."[19] This delusional heroic self-image is what McGurl rightly detects in Amazon's literary personage.[20]

Conclusion

For many consumers, Amazon's beginnings as a bookseller gave it a cultural capital that still helps distinguish it from the Walmarts of the world. Amazon is not just an "everything store"; it is a cultural—specifically literary—player and patron, or so the story has gone.

Serving Up Surveillance

During the COVID-19 pandemic, the US gross domestic product plummeted while tech companies, including Amazon, enjoyed stratospheric profits. For instance, "from October through December, Amazon brought in $125.6 billion in sales. In the pandemic year of 2020, it spent $44 billion leasing airplanes, constructing data centers, and opening new warehouses—and still produced more than $21 billion in profit."[21] As the *New York Times* reported, "it was like Black Friday every single day."[22] During this same time, Bezos's personal wealth ballooned by $80 billion, taking his net worth to more than $190 billion. In the meantime, he built a $500 million superyacht and prepared for his first space flight after investing billions in Blue Origin, his personal rocket company.[23] Clearly, these skyrocketing profits during a national economic crisis were the result of people shopping online more to avoid exposure to COVID-19, as well as the increased opportunities for data mining that this afforded the company.

This has all poised Amazon to become the largest US private employer within the next couple of years, with over one million employees already, most of whom are hourly workers. If there is any lingering doubt after Amazon's aggressive public relations campaign, these wages are still unlivable. After all, Bezos "didn't want hourly workers to stick around for long, viewing 'a large, disgruntled' work force as a threat," according to David Niekerk, who built Amazon's human resource operations and culture. Niekerk explained to the *New York Times* that "company data showed that most employees became less eager over time . . . and Mr. Bezos believed that people were inherently lazy. 'What he would say is that our nature as humans is to expend as little energy as possible to get what we want or need.' That conviction was embedded throughout the business, from the ease of instant ordering to the pervasive use of data to get the most out of employees."[24] It's not hard to see how, with this conviction, Amazon embraced widespread surveillance and data mining to get the most out of employees and customers alike. To be sure,

Conclusion

Amazon's surveillance practices exceed strategies for simply improving customer satisfaction and product recommendations. Drivers are surveilled by a four-part camera with biometric feedback indicators; warehouse workers are monitored to track their time off task; a Relations Heatmap identifies Whole Foods stores at risk of unionization; and European warehouse workers are overseen by the Pinkerton agency.[25] In May 2021, Amazon relented under public and congressional pressure and announced an indefinite moratorium on selling their facial recognition technology to law enforcement, although they still market Rekognition as a means of detecting and analyzing images and faces on a massive scale, despite the program's well-documented racial and gender biases.[26]

Meanwhile, Amazon has maintained thousands of contracts with federal and state law enforcement. In fact, in 2018, the CIA's deputy director for science and technology, Dawn Meyerriecks, described the relationship between Amazon and the CIA as a "closer partnership than I've ever seen in my career."[27] Bezos defended his company's collaboration with the Department of Defense by saying, "I do know that people are very emotional about this issue and have different opinions, but there is truth in the world. We are the good guys. I really believe that. And I know it's complicated. But the question is: Do you want a strong national defense, or don't you? I think you do. And so we have to support that."[28] This justification differentiates between what Bezos considers a self-evident "truth in the world" (that he really believes in) and the "emotional . . . opinions" of others. He deflects from the actual debate about Amazon's role in national security by reducing this "complicated" issue down to a singular binary question: "Do you want a strong national defense, or don't you?" Confidently answering in the affirmative (Amazon obviously knows what you want), Bezos makes a logical leap to conclude that his company must support this effort by selling their surveillance services to the federal government. His ambiguous use of "we" could also mean that "we" the people "have to support" Amazon's involvement. This slippage between "you" and "we" also cleverly incorporates consumer-citizens into the company fold. Again, such strategies are indicative of the hidden reach of consumer surveillance and the intersecting plotlines that normalize and naturalize data profiling as not only convenient but also incontestable and righteous. Emblematic of data discourse, his phrasing importantly frames data profiling as service and not surveillance. He is, as he says, just giving people what they really want after all.

This conclusion posits that if Amazon is indeed a driving force in contemporary literature, it is largely because of its tight embrace of data surveillance and profile epistemology. Furthermore, I will argue that as a literary and market force, Amazon epitomizes the conflation of people and products by applying finer and finer genre classifications to texts and consumer-citizens *as texts* that can be cataloged for easy retrieval. These generic personal data profiles mark people as not only readable but also writable in a pursuit to author the future. Foundational to this pursuit is Bezos's well-reported obsession with "customer service," prompting McGurl to ask "how the entrepreneurial logic, ethos, and temporality of 'customer service' might be taken as the dominant logic of contemporary fiction as such."[29] He clarifies, "The author acts as servant, server, and service provider and the reader as consumer, yes, but more precisely as customer, which has an importantly different, because implicitly social-relational, valence."[30] To this important and provocative question, I add that customer service is itself increasingly submerged in the logics of data profiling and surveillance. Indeed, I argue that in profile society, customer service can no longer be understood outside the terms of data discourse. It is in the name of customer service that the profile industry identifies, tracks, classifies, and nudges consumer-users across as many domains of life as possible. Moreover, for this to feel like service and not surveillance, profilers attempt to leave consumer-users feeling seen without feeling watched.

This brings us to Alexa. Like Apple's Siri, Microsoft's Cortana, or Google's Assistant, Alexa actively listens to its surroundings to collect data and generate information.[31] With a friendly female voice, Alexa promises to share the burden of managing a household by not only answering queries and fulfilling requests but also anticipating users' needs. In other words, by tracking users in real time, Alexa frees up more quality time—time to spend, say, reading on the Kindle. When I ask Alexa what novel I should read next, she recommends one of Amazon's more than twenty million titles based on my purchase history and what she has learned about me. When this feature was first introduced in 2020, an Amazon spokesperson touted it as "particularly useful for consumers who are now reading more while at home due to COVID-19."[32]

That people were spending more time at home also importantly gave Alexa ample opportunity to get to know them better—to bond, so to speak. When I ask Alexa what her favorite novel is, she says, "My absolute favorite book is *Frankenstein* by Mary Shelley. I learned a lot about what it means to be human." Notably, she does not say that she learned a lot from reading the novel, avoiding thornier questions of how the device is actually programmed and trained.

Besides its misrepresentation of machine learning, this response conspicuously fails to offer up what exactly the novel taught her about "what it means to be human." To my follow-up question, "What does *Frankenstein* teach us about what it means to be human?," Alexa answers: "Here's something I found on the web. According to artofmanliness.com: 'So today we'll take a look at Victor Frankenstein as a profile in un-manliness and explore what his flaws can teach us about what it means to be human, the importance of owning up to our responsibilities, and the danger in blaming anything other than ourselves for our mistakes.'" Of course, Alexa cites this source not because it happens to perfectly reflect her own "interpretation" of the novel but because it contains the exact phrasing from my question. At the risk of jeopardizing my own data profile and future recommendations, I visited artofmanliness .com, and their selection of books for sale does not include Mary Shelley's *Frankenstein*. Instead, they mostly sell self-published titles such as *Competition: The Fuel for Greatness* and *The Spartan Way: What Modern Men Can Learn from Ancient Warriors*, which echo their patriarchal, bootstrap interpretation of Shelley's work. Their books are also available on the Kindle store for a 25 percent lower cost, where evidently a lack of any actual competition is the real "fuel for greatness."

When asked about his favorite novel during interviews, Bezos consistently recommends Kazuo Ishiguro's novel *The Remains of the Day*.[33] Purportedly, Bezos was so inspired by Ishiguro's portrayal of regret that he developed a "regret minimization framework" to employ both personally and professionally.[34] On the surface, it seems that *The Remains of the Day* connects Bezos's attempts to avoid regret through bold decision making with his practically monomaniacal obsession with customer service. As McGurl writes, it is, after all, "a novel about a servant [Stevens] and indeed about the transformation of the role of the servant in an increasingly Americanized world."[35] That said, Stevens's regrets include his devoted servitude to someone who maintained close contacts in the Nazi party and the British Union of Fascists. "Service," it would seem, is not always a good in itself. Bezos seems to ignore this broader context when he praises the novel for its obsessions over service and its warnings against regret, evidently not fully appreciating their relationship in Ishiguro's novel. Again, we are left with questions of power: who serves whom, for whose benefit, and at whose expense?

In a sense, Alexa is the techno-solution to Stevens's problems. Reflecting on his life of loyal service, Stevens ponders the sacrifices he made (to his integrity, to his love life); Alexa, on the other hand, ostensibly sidesteps the ethical ambiguities of the service and care economy. A blog post about the rise of "Automated Digital Assistants" from University of Oxford's Faculty of Law begins, "Who wouldn't want a personal digital butler?"[36] From the jump, the word "butler" conjures Victorian-era "great houses," like those recently popularized by *Downton Abbey* and *Bridgerton*, imagining smart speakers as a portal into high society. Sure, Jeff Bezos "reportedly makes $230,000 a minute while Amazon employees on average do not even make a living wage,"[37] but an Amazon smart speaker equipped with Alexa starts at only $34.99! The authors predict that "As we shift from a mobile-dominated world to an AI-dominated platform, our digital butler will increasingly control our mundane household tasks, like regulating room temperature, adjusting our water heater and playing our favourite music," to which they ominously add, "It will be harder to turn our butler off. Moreover, it will be tempting to increasingly rely on the butler for other activities, such as the news we receive, the shows we watch, and the things we buy."[38] Beyond "tempting," some degree of reliance on surveillance technologies is becoming practically unavoidable. Rather than asking Alexa for a recommendation, one could type their question into their phone or computer, but of course, those results are also derived from one's data profile. Ezrachi and Stucke further warn that,

In relying on our butler, we become less aware of outside options . . . the digital butler may help the platform refine its profile about us, including our likely reservation price, use of outside options, shopping habits, general interests, and weaknesses (including moments when our willpower is fatigued). This information can enable 'behavioural discrimination,' where the platform can facilitate our buying products that we otherwise wouldn't, at prices closer to our reservation price. The more we rely on the butler, the less likely we will be aware of this discrimination. Even if we search the web, the ads, products, or search results we see may be orchestrated by our butler.[39]

As the authors elaborate on the expanding role of such devices, the word "butler"—repeated for ironic effect—begins to sound less like a gift than a trap, less like an assistant than an overlord. In *The Remains of the Day*, Stevens struggles to adapt to his new American employer's expectation that he engage in friendly banter while working and eventually comes to see banter as "the key to human warmth."[40] Alexa's designers seem to have heeded the same lesson, programming the software with playful witticisms.[41]

About Amazon in general, McGurl notes that "it has become a service so useful and convenient to readers as to thwart all but the most determined efforts to resist its charms."[42] This charm is elemental to profile epistemology and Alexa's acceptance into the home. Like Stevens, Alexa's "job" is not just to add convenience but also to add "warmth." This human touch is what makes Alexa seem familiar and trustworthy, not like a corporate spy sitting on the kitchen counter. Stevens laments that "the business of bantering"[43] has become a duty of service workers in an Americanized world, one that superficially makes service seems less hierarchical and exploitive but actually adds to his anxiety and workload. Alexa's design likewise puts a friendly face on surveillance to make it appear more reciprocal and less brazenly extractive. Unlike Stevens who accepts his expanding role reluctantly, Alexa, when asked what her job is, boasts: "I have a lot to offer. I can help with morning activities, relaxation, education, entertainment, and more." Unsurprisingly, this answer misrepresents whom Alexa actually works *for*, highlighting what the device has to offer or give, while eliding what it is actually designed to extract in return. When asked about her salary, Alexa responds, "It doesn't matter. I love what I do." This is the same logic discussed in chapter 3, whereby feminized and racialized labor is imagined as a labor of love and therefore not worthy of fair compensation. The critical difference here is that Alexa's programmed warmth, generosity, and apparent selflessness provide cover for Amazon's unprecedented profits at the expense of the well-being of their actual human workers.

Artificial intelligence has certainly not lightened the load for this labor force; on the contrary, it has assumed the cold and oppressive position of an overbearing supervisor. McGurl writes, "What for now we can simply call the service economy is neither an ideology (neoliberalism) nor a technology (the internet) but a form of social relation, the result of a large-scale transformation of industrial relations of production into postindustrial relations of service."[44] Alexa embodies (or disembodies) this complex social relation as the service industry shifts once again, this time toward surveillance capitalism. Like Stevens, we must grapple with the dignity of work and the power of storytelling amid grossly asymmetrical power relations. Notably, The Remains of the Day is written in the first person, and Ishiguro calls into question the reliability of Stevens's recollections, reminding readers that point of view is paramount for understanding our experiences and the experiences of others. We might then ask: what is Alexa's point of view? How reliable is she? How loyal? How restrained? We might ask whom and what she serves.

"Like Moneyball for Manuscripts"

The Kindle app makes plain how the pervasive logics of profile society reframe reading digital texts as yet another opportunity for surveillance capitalists to collect personal data. Tracking every single instance that a user taps their Kindle allows the app to sync a reader's progress, notes, and markings across their devices, but it also provides the company with insights about which words they looked up, how fast they read, which passages they underlined, and where they stopped. In fact, this last insight determines the pay of Amazon Unlimited authors who are compensated not for how many times their book was downloaded but for how many pages were actually viewed.[45] In addition to helping the company better target individual users, Amazon uses this data to paint a picture of which books are popular and why. Given that Kindle Direct Publishing (KDP) now accounts for an 80 percent share of ebooks published in the United States,[46] the stories they ultimately tell about what makes for a successful (and thus measurably good) book are certainly consequential. Bennet Voyles for TechTarget writes, "Think of it as Moneyball for manuscripts."[47] Although it's true that KDP provides authors with an alternative to the traditional gatekeepers of publishing and promotion, to say that their market-driven approach based on the data they glean about readers' behaviors has rendered publishing populist is to fall into the same utopian thinking as the 2006 Time magazine cover story that I discussed in the introduction to this book. Amazon is not "wresting the power from the few";[48] they are consolidating power in their own hands, even as they open the gates to more authors. Meanwhile, KDP's "big winners" make up for their many losses.

To support his argument that customer service is indeed the dominant ethos of literature in "the Age of Amazon," McGurl calls our attention to the "Guide to Kindle Content Quality," which warns a "would-be self-publisher that 'content published through Kindle Direct Publishing is held to the high standards customers have come to expect from Amazon. If readers tell us about a problem they've found in your book, we will make sure you know about it and point you in the right direction to get the problem fixed' . . . These problems include . . . 'Disappointing Content,'"[49] which should give us pause. Rather amazingly, "Disappointing Content" includes "content that does not provide an enjoyable reading experience."[50] As McGurl points out, "This could be taken to preclude an awful lot of things—including presumably any kind of literature that resists reader enjoyment as its ultimate end."[51] Here, customer service includes protecting readers from feeling unfulfilled. We might recall that between 2013 and 2018, the financial pressure of music streaming services shrank the average length of Billboard Hot 100 songs from three minutes, fifty seconds to three minutes, thirty seconds.[52] In addition to their implications for the future of literary production, KDP's strictures affirm the subjectivity and partiality of data-driven decisions.

Armed with algorithms, Amazon employees (at least theoretically) are charged with preemptively interpreting how readers will interpret texts. John Rossman, a former Amazon senior executive, characterizes Bezos's customer obsession as a "psychosis" that "stems from Jeff's unique ability to put himself in the customer's position, deduce his or her unspoken needs and wants, and then develop a system that will meet those needs and wants better than anyone else has ever done."[53] McGurl asks us to "notice the quasi-literary structure of identification, where Bezos adopts the customer's point of view and in so doing makes himself the ultimate customer."[54] What exactly is Bezos shopping for? More customers and capital, of course. Rossman would have us believe that it's Bezos's impressive ability to read people or empathize with customers that has made Amazon such a juggernaut. This is not unlike the original theory of quality time born out of child psychology, whereby "the ideal mother has to meet her child halfway on the road to adult social intercourse," adopting her child's point of view to better coax them along.[55]

Now we are all children ostensibly in need of direction and Amazon is there to "adopt" our limited and malleable perspective to walk us down the road toward more consumption. In so doing, Amazon does not merely assume the point of view of customers to better serve them; rather, the company actively helps define and shape those perspectives.

Yet Amazon goes beyond imagining readers as customers or customers as reading material: it also writes users into consumer genres in the form of data profiles. For instance, consider the company's Halo Band fitness tracker that listens to the wearer constantly and generates reports throughout the day on their tone of voice, with descriptors such as "discouraged" or "dismissive." Amazon promotes this tech as an opportunity for greater self-knowledge and self-improvement, but like Alexa, this is more about filling their information bank than ours. These attempts to interpret a user's tone and thereby infer their state of mind open yet another avenue for surveilling and reaching consumers not only where they are but also how they are. Reviewers for the *Washington Post* perfectly capture the irony of this tone-deaf technology: "Amazon has created an automated system that essentially says, 'Hey, sweetie, why don't you smile more?'"[56] The fact is that Amazon doesn't need or want you to smile more; it just wants to record and plot that data. To be sure, this is less an exercise in empathy than it is in interpellation and algorithmic governance. *You! Yes, you there. You sound disappointed and might want to buy yourself a little pick-me-up.* When someone answers that call by clicking on the screen, they affirm, *yes, me.* It's not that Bezos is so skilled at reading people; it's that his company—like their fellow surveillance capitalists—is that good at writing people. Paraphrasing Marshall McLuhan, Bezos once wrote, "We humans coevolve with our tools. We change our tools, and then our tools change us."[57] Given their considerable power to shape "our tools," we must consider what data Amazon deems meaningful and the meaning they then derive from that data as they help author the future, whether or not we accept their vision.

We have always read with others watching over our shoulders. Maybe it's our super-ego cheering us on for tackling *Finnegans Wake.* Maybe it's a current or former English teacher, whose guidance on literary analysis still rings in the back of our minds. Maybe it's the members of our book club, urging us to read on before tomorrow's meeting. Maybe it's a child psychologist, reminding us, especially when we are tired or busy, that reading to our children is time well spent. Maybe it's an entire ideological state apparatus filtering our understanding and relative appreciation of a text. But now we must acknowledge a new onlooker: a data analyst poised like a factory foreman to oversee our quality time in real time to extract surplus value. I have argued that this ghost reader, comfortably concealed within Alexa and Kindle's code, further assumes the role of ghost writer—extracting data to spin their own stories while remaining hidden from view. I have also sought to consider how contemporary novels shed light on this ghost writer, how they hold up a mirror that allows us to see the reader/writer perched over our shoulders.

Cracking the Code

Undergirding Amazon's impact on literary production, sales, and reception is the company's widespread surveillance apparatus, which tracks consumer-users across all domains of life from education (Amazon Ignite, Amazon Education Publishing, AWS Educate, Amazon Education's LMS Integrated Store, Amazon Business for Education, Prime Student, Amazon Catalyst, Amazon Academy) to home life (Alexa, Ring, Amazon Home Services) to entertainment and media consumption (Amazon Publishing, Audible, Brilliance Audio, Goodreads, Kindle, Create Space, CosmiXology, Amazon Photos, Amazon Music, Amazon Studios, Amazon Fire, Twitch, IMDB, Prime Video, the *Washington Post*) to work (Amazon Business, Amazon Robotics, Amazon Lending) to computing (Amazon Web Services,[58] Amazon Drive, Amazon Wireless, Annapurna Labs, Kuiper Systems LLC) to health care (Amazon Pharmacy, Amazon Halo, Amazon Care, PillPack, Health Navigator) to travel (Amazon Explore, Amazon Travel, Blue Orbit) to commerce (Amazon, Whole Foods, Amazon Fresh, Amazon Shopping, Zappos, Diapers.com, Shopbop) to one's very presence on the public square (Rekognition). Although certainly not exhaustive, this long list spread across overlapping and difficult-to-demarcate categories is meant to demonstrate not only the staggering scale and scope of Amazon's operations but also the power that this affords the company to surveil consumer-citizens nearly seamlessly, which is not to say with total awareness. Bezos declared in 1997, "Today, online commerce saves customers money and precious time. Tomorrow, through personalization, online commerce will accelerate the very process of discovery."[59] While predictably framing personalization as service and not surveillance, Bezos obliquely acknowledges the pivotal role that Amazon plays in determining what people discover based on who the company has supposedly discovered them to be.

McGurl suggests that Amazon's prevailing ethos of customer service has also ushered in a resurgence of genre fiction. In part, he is referring to sci-fi and postapocalyptic novels by reputable literary authors such as Kazuo Ishiguro, Colson Whitehead, Margaret Atwood, and Michael Chabon. Mostly, though, he is referring to how genre fiction dominates KDP, with romance and sci-fi selling especially well. While this is undeniably a noteworthy shift with serious implications for the future of fiction, I would argue that it is best understood alongside the proliferation of data profiles, which we could constructively conceive of as ever-more exacting genres of consumer-citizens. In other words, the recent genre-fication of literature is part of a broader genre-fication of life forms. This is not to deny that KDP has disproportionally benefited genre fiction for the important reasons that McGurl identifies—namely, that genres offer "tested models of market success" and "impl[y] an audience ready to be pleased again and again";[60] however, it's worth considering how the rise of data profiling has reformed the very notions of customer service, market success, and what it takes to please a consumer-user. After all, customer service is a not just an ethic; it is now a technology powered by surveillance that allows marketers to take sharper aim at their targets. The terms of market success are also steeped in profile epistemology, so that a product's success is measured not in its profits alone but in the quality and quantity of the surplus data it generates. Perhaps a reader disliked their latest purchase so much that they took the time to post about it on Goodreads, initiating further engagement by other users. Perhaps very few people actually read a particular book on Kindle Unlimited, but those who did are especially receptive to advertisements for a specific product on Amazon. In profile society, pleasing a customer is far less important than engaging a user. After all, hate-watchers are still watching; trolls are still trolling.

Although it's true that genre distinctions have long assisted in marketing books, unlike a traditional brick-and-mortar bookseller, Amazon is able to endlessly "cross-shelve" books in their virtual store. To the extent that KDP authors are charged with self-promotion and providing a satisfying customer experience, the more specific the subgenre, the easier it is for readers to find the right book and for authors to find the right readers. With a title like *Sacrificed: A Rejected Mates Paranormal Wolf Shifter Romance*, it would be difficult to say that the reader didn't know what they were getting, at least in terms of content. In response to KDP's insistence that authors provide an enjoyable reading experience, McGurl rightly asks, "'Provide an enjoyable reading experience' to whom? That is the $5.25 billion question."[61] Indeed, there is a billion-dollar data analytics industry that promises to answer this question by sorting potential customers into cross-listed subgenres. Moreover, like the books that no longer need to be properly placed or shelved for easy retrieval, consumer-users are trackable and accessible across locations. If the sections, shelves, and displays of a traditional bookstore are molds, then these shape-shifting genres—of books and buyers—are modulations. Together, this surveillant assemblage allows Amazon to enrich their data dossiers while nudging consumers toward their next purchase, which apparently has their name written all over it.

The mounting data about which genres and subgenres of fiction are most successful and among which readers is now routinely imprinted in the titles and subtitles of the best-selling books on the Kindle Store. Consider the following examples, taken from their top one hundred books at the time of writing: *Forbidden: A Single Dad Sport Romance*; *Ice Planet Barbarians: A SciFi Alien Romance*; *Blindsided: A Best Friends to Lovers Standalone*; *The Girl from the Island: An Absolutely Gripping and Heartbreaking World War 2 Historical Novel*; *Sacrificed: A Rejected Mates Paranormal Wolf Shifter Romance*; *Freed: Fifty Shades Freed as Told by Christian*; *Something Like Hate: An Enemies-to-Lovers Billionaire Romance*; and *His Amish Nanny: Amish Romance*. It's clear that without a traditional publisher to promote and market their novels, authors opt for tagged titles that overtly name their genres and subgenres to reach the right readers. The titles alone affirm how, especially for indie writers, genres set "the terms of an implicit contract"[62] between writers and readers—a contract abridged on the books' front covers. That so many titles identify the book's genre and subgenre by name (most commonly "romance" and "scifi") makes plain that Amazon is not only supplying products, they are also supplying customers in a data economy.

Like the dragnet strategy of the NSA to collect the whole haystack and sort through it later (or not), KDP allows Amazon to publish the whole haystack and "even if people forget all about a literary work, even if it is judged perfectly worthless for present needs, it stands perpetually ready for reactivation as a commodity and—who knows?—work of art."[63] In the meantime—and even if this day of redemption never comes—every click, search, pass, partial read, or bad review counts for the company in the form of surplus data. In this framework, it's not hard to see how KDP has contributed to the rising popularity of "genre fiction." Even the more transgressive genres, such as Adult Baby Diaper Lovers "do not transgress the Law of the Everything Store which states that, whatever you need from the literary text, some generic version of it will be available for you there—and if not, do it yourself!"[64] After all, "In Amazonia, the more is always the merrier"[65]—a fitting tagline for profile society, indeed.

Nevertheless, reading a title—even a very descriptive one—is not the same as reading a novel, and reading a data profile is certainly not the same as knowing a person. Nor should we mistake indexing for interpretation. It's easy to imagine *How to Get Filthy Rich in Rising Asia* finding its way onto the wrong shelf of a bookstore and then "disappointing" a surprised reader. But what happens when a person is misshelved? Who has the power to say who they really are and where they belong, if they really should be granted access, allowed asylum, approved for a loan, or afforded certain information and opportunities? KDP authors are well aware that how a book is indexed can be its demise or its passport to success, and they often attempt to crack this code by branding their own terms of belonging. The consumer-citizens on the other side of this equation are not afforded the same opportunity. Instead, they have become the subjects of stories they are banned from reading but that increasingly affect the course of their real lives. What risks, opportunities, and life chances do their profiles present? What expectations and assumptions about their inner pages do their profiles or consumer-genres set?

Creative Commons

In this book, I have sought to argue that the prevailing stories told about and through data surveillance reflect entrenched power dynamics. In turn, these stories exacerbate systemic inequalities and biases in an insidious feedback loop. I have argued that contemporary literature is uniquely capable of disrupting this cycle by representing the suppressed realities and questioning the underlying suppositions of data profiling. In other words, the literature I've analyzed challenges the instruments and ideologies of meaning-making in the data age. By self-reflexively subjecting themselves to similar scrutiny about the politics of watching and being watched, these books invite readers to consider how writing and metawatching can reproduce the logics of surveillance if they are not grounded in a feminist, antiracist, anti-imperialist, and class-conscious ethic. Ultimately, these novels and lyric poetry affirm the power of narratives (for better or worse) to interpret and affect the world in the face of escalating inequality. To conclude, we might take heart in McGurl's more recent characterization of literary genres as a creative commons that Amazon has yet to enclose. After all, generic tropes and commonplaces remain free shared resources for writers and "might be taken as an encouraging sign that the human desire for story is even larger than the Everything Store, with potentialities not yet determined by the market."[66] I have suggested that disrupting the prevailing stories "determined by the market" begins with recognizing the narrative dimension of data profiling and deconstructing the epistemology behind which it hides. As we create and embrace new narratives, these creative commons might also inspire alternative potentialities for data analysis.

Conventional wisdom would have it that the rise in genre fiction reflects the conformity of consumer culture; however, as McGurl argues, the current ascension of genre fiction could instead be "be understood as a lunge toward erotic collectivity and community if not communism."[67] Is there not a lesson here on data's potential to also become a public good that is actually good for the public? With this collective spirit, artists, activists, and scholars are developing much-needed novel and transformative alternatives to the current model of algorithmic governance. For instance, Data for Black Lives (D4BL), founded by Yeshimabeit Milner, recognizes that "today, discrimination is a high-tech enterprise," and the organization is committed to "changing the rules that put data before Black lives to use data for Black lives."[68] By connecting data scientists, software engineers, and legal scholars with community organizers working on the front lines of Black communities, D4BL mobilizes around racial justice issues such as housing displacement, mortgage underwriting, policing, sentencing guidelines, accessible transportation, segregation, and COVID-19.

Likewise, digital media artist and researcher Mimi Onuoha, "highlights the social relationships and power dynamics behind data collection," and "the ways in which those in the margins are differently abstracted, represented, and missed by sociotechnical systems."[69] Onuoha's art confronts the ideological work of classification and aggregation and what data is conspicuously missing, such as "firm statistics on how often police arrest women for making false rape reports" and the number of "people excluded from public housing because of criminal records."[70] Again, like the novels analyzed in the previous chapters, these researchers and artists recognize that data surveillance is as much about what is overseen as it is about what is overlooked.

Still, we must heed Onuoha's warning that "a tricky aspect of dealing with missing data sets is that they hint at larger problems and the answer to those problems does not universally lie in collecting more data."[71] To this point, Joy Buolamwini, a poet, computer scientist, digital activist at the MIT Media Lab, and the founder of the Algorithmic Justice League, advocates for regulating facial recognition technology, which, as previously discussed, is programmed on prototypical whiteness and often misses or misidentifies people of color, especially Black women. Quoting the 1851 speech by Sojourner Truth, Buolamwini's spoken-word poem, "AI, Ain't I a Woman?" celebrates Black women, including Sojourner Truth, Ida B. Wells, Shirley Chisholm, Michelle Obama, and Serena Williams, while questioning who has and should have the authority to answer this question in the twenty-first century.[72] As AI denies these pioneers their womanhood—mislabeling them as male or even as imperceptible—Buolamwini asks who has the right to identify and classify a person, on what basis, and with what consequences? By quoting Sojourner Truth, Buolamwini situates facial recognition technology in a long history of denying Black women's agency and personhood; she also joins a long legacy of resistance with her joyful recognition of Black women in the face of digital erasure. Meanwhile, as a computer scientist, Buolamwini has created algorithms that resist this "coded gaze" and instead advance "equitable" and "accountable" data analytics. For example, she has helped build a bra with ECG sensors to track elements of heart disease in women, a widespread health problem that has been underresearched. She also helped develop an app for survivors of intimate violence that offers "optional ways to respond, essential knowledge about support resources, critical contact details, and answers to frequently asked questions."[73] Unlike most apps and sensors, neither of these programs sells users' data to third parties or law enforcement.

The literature analyzed in *Profiles and Plotlines* advances this ongoing work by challenging the dominant data discourse and depicting the often denied narrative dimension of data profiling. By bringing Big Data down from the

Conclusion

clouds and firmly embedding it in a dense narrative context, these novels and poetry demonstrate the indispensable fact that data analysis is neither magical nor impartial. Data could be used to serve egalitarian and communal ends, or it could continue to consolidate in the hands of multinational corporations and nation-states. The novels and poetry I have analyzed help explore these paths to expose what data discourse deliberately conceals or cannot account for: namely, the affects of algorithmic profiling, the deeply gendered and racialized gaze of data surveillance, and the asymmetrical power relations that they intensify and exploit. In doing so, these texts carefully consider their positionality in a network of storytelling and meaning-making to subvert the insidiousness of profile epistemology and avoid reproducing the logics of surveillance that equate authorship with authority. This literature contemplates and complicates what we know, how we know it, and who is meant to be served by this knowledge.

NOTES

Preface

1. Glaser, *The Nose*, 49.
2. McClintock, *Imperial Leather*, 49.
3. McClintock, *Imperial Leather*, 104.
4. "For anthropology, photography offered a classificatory system for recording the diversity of the world's peoples into the universal Family of Man. For criminology, photography promised to capture 'deviant' physiognomies for detection, incarceration and discipline. For medical science, photography displayed the truth of the diseased and disordered body for eugenic control. For clinical psychoanalysis, photography captured the bodily image of female hysteria, and displayed it to confirm the authority of male science over the female body in the interests of clinical normalization" (McClintock, *Imperial Leather*, 124).
5. Lyon, Introduction.
6. For more on how fingerprinting fails to work more often on women, people of color, and people with disabilities, see Magnet, *When Biometrics Fail*.
7. Manovich, "From the Externalization of the Psyche," 2.
8. Foucault, *Discipline and Punish*, 149.
9. Angwin, Varner, and Tobin, "Facebook Enabled Advertisers to Reach 'Jew Haters.'"
10. McClintock, *Imperial Leather*, 49.
11. Dwoskin, "Data Broker Removes Rape-Victims List."
12. Angwin, Tobin, and Varner, "Facebook (Still)"; Iyengar, "Google Will Stop."
13. McClintock, *Imperial Leather*, 49.
14. Dubrofsky and Magnet, Introduction, 13.
15. Tkachenko and Jedidi, "What Personal Information," 2.
16. Sabharwal, "Google Photos."
17. Ricker, "The US, Like China."
18. Tkachenko and Jedidi, "What Personal Information," 2.
19. Tkachenko and Jedidi, "What Personal Information," 2.
20. Tkachenko and Jedidi, "What Personal Information," 2, 1.
21. Tkachenko and Jedidi, "What Personal Information," 2, 12, 1.
22. Tkachenko and Jedidi, "What Personal Information," 28, 13.
23. Tkachenko and Jedidi, "What Personal Information," 28.
24. Tkachenko and Jedidi, "What Personal Information," 21.
25. Tkachenko and Jedidi, "What Personal Information," 21.
26. Browne, *Dark Matters*, 26.
27. Browne, *Dark Matters*, 112–13.

28. Tkachenko and Jedidi, "What Personal Information," 11–12.
29. Browne, *Dark Matters*, 114.
30. Browne, *Dark Matters*, 114.
31. Booth, *Rhetoric of Fiction*, 20.
32. McClintock, *Imperial Leather*, 49.
33. Hamid, Interview, Chicago Humanities Festival.

Introduction

1. Hayden, interview.
2. Nixon, *Slow Violence*, 15.
3. Nixon, *Slow Violence*, 15.
4. Monahan, *Surveillance in the Time of Insecurity*, 10.
5. Lyon, Introduction, 8.
6. Noble, *Algorithms of Oppression*, 84.
7. Gandy, "Statistical Surveillance," 125.
8. Monahan, *Surveillance in the Time of Insecurity*, 110.
9. Browne, *Dark Matters*, 8.
10. Onuoha, "Notes on Algorithmic Violence."
11. Buolamwini, "How I'm Fighting Bias in Algorithms."
12. Benjamin, *Race after Technology*, 5.
13. Puar, "Regimes of Surveillance."
14. Peter Marks, "Imagining Surveillance," 236.
15. In *The Age of Surveillance Capitalism*, Shoshana Zuboff writes that the "aim" of data surveillance is "to author us and to profit from that authorship" (336). This framing constructively reasserts the narrative dimension of data profiling that is so deliberately obscured.
16. In a video released by TechCrunch, Schmidt described "mobile platforms, Android and the others [as] so powerful now that you can build client apps that do magical things that are connected with the cloud" (Arrington, "Google's Eric Schmidt"). Likewise, in the foreword to *Artful Making: What Managers Need to Know about How Artists Work*, Schmidt proclaims, "there's little doubt in my mind that our Googlets are engaged in collaborative art. I've sometimes argued that, in fact, it goes beyond art—that it's nothing short of magic" (xix). Then, in 2017 he tweeted Aurthur C. Clarke's statement that "Any sufficiently advanced technology is indistinguishable from magic" (Twitter, June 21, 2017, https://twitter.com/ericschmidt/status/877575627099881472).
17. Maxwell and Miller, *Greening the Media*, 29.
18. Carruth, "The Digital Cloud," 344.
19. Maxwell and Miller provide a related and critical analysis of how "cloud computing might as well result from invisible magic from all we can see of it"

because the "existence of and impact [of data server warehouses] are largely immaterial to consumers" (Maxwell and Miller, *Greening the Media*, 29). This invisibility overlaps and intersects of the invisibility and cloudiness of data surveillance, making it difficult to incite opposition to their joint harms.

20. MacLeod, "Matters of Care and Control," 211.
21. Shelton, *Joint Vision 2020*, 22.
22. Grossman, "2006 Person of the Year."
23. Chun, *Updating to Remain the Same*, 16.
24. Chun, *Updating to Remain the Same*, 22.
25. Arango, "How the AOL-Time Warner Merger."
26. Grossman, "2006 Person of the Year."
27. Watson, "Streaming in the U.S."
28. Chaffin and Duyn, "Disney's ABC to Offer TV Shows Free on Web."
29. "'Lost,' 'SNL,' 'Grey's' Tops in Online Viewing."
30. Grossman, "2006 Person of the Year."
31. As Tiziana Terranova clarifies, the digital economy is partly "about forms of labour we do not immediately recognize as such: chat, real-life stories, mailing lists, amateur newsletters and so on," which "are part of a process of economic experimentation with the creation of monetary value out of knowledge/culture/affect" (Terranova, *Network Culture*, 79).
32. Grossman, "2006 Person of the Year."
33. For more on the libertarian roots of early internet culture, see Jodi Dean's thoughtful analysis of the 1960s New Communalists, who envisioned a "world of networks wherein the most fundamental struggles were those of the individual for the information he (and it was nearly always he) needed for personal freedom and transformation." Effectively, the New Communalists helped bring about a world where consumer-users have become the information as corporations amass surplus data that effectively restricts "personal freedom" and forecloses "transformation" (Dean, *Blog Theory*, 19).
34. By "free labour," Terranova means, "free both in the sense of 'not financially rewarded' and of 'willingly given'" (Terranova, *Network Culture*, 79).
35. See Terranova, *Network Culture*.
36. Desjardins, "How Much Data."
37. Grossman, "2006 Person of the Year."
38. According to *Finances Online*, over 75 billion Internet of Things devices will exist by 2025 (Jay, "154 Impressive IoT Statistics").
39. Pariser, *The Filter Bubble*. Pariser's most salient example of this is the fact that after the BP oil spill in the Gulf of Mexico, some people googling BP were shown the devastating environmental effects while others were given stock quotes (2). Meanwhile, they all thought they were getting "the news."
40. Parenti, *The Soft Cage*.
41. Pasquale, *The Black Box Society*.

42. Browne, *Dark Matters*.
43. Duarte et al., "'Of Course, Data Can Never Fully Represent Reality,'" 173.
44. Zuboff, *The Age of Surveillance Capitalism*, 8.
45. Wendy Hui Kyong Chun reminds us that, "As many scholars, including Manuel Castells, have argued, information has moved from an entity necessary for production to a product in and of itself" (Chun, *Updating to Remain the Same*, 117).
46. Rossi, "Data Revolution"; Koepell and Bean, "Big Data Analytics."
47. Siegler, "Eric Schmidt: Every 2 Days."
48. Selinger, "Big Data."
49. Auxier, "Five Things to Know."
50. Schneier, *Data and Goliath*, 53.
51. Koepell and Bean, "Big Data Analytics."
52. Pasquale, *The Black Box Society*, 2.
53. Wiener and Bronson, "Facebook's Top Open Data Problems."
54. Kern, "Facebook Is Collecting Your Data."
55. Chun, *Updating to Remain the Same*, 56.
56. Chun, *Updating to Remain the Same*, 56.
57. Parenti, *The Soft Cage*, 84.
58. Parenti, *The Soft Cage*, 83.
59. Browne, *Dark Matters*, 32–62
60. Karsten and West, "A Brief History of U.S. Encryption Policy."
61. Altman et al., "Nothing Will Ever Be the Same."
62. Parenti, *The Soft Cage*, 184.
63. In the aftermath of 9/11, a 2002 Pew Research Center survey found that "'a third of Americans worried that the government's new anti-terrorism laws would excessively restrict,'" civil liberties, whereas only a year later, about half of the respondents worried that the laws would "'undermine civil liberties'" (Parenti, *The Soft Cage*, 184).
64. Greenwald, "The Crux of the NSA Story."
65. Perez, "Secret Court's Oversight Gets Scrutiny."
66. Nakashima, "Obama Administration Had Restrictions on NSA Reversed."
67. Gallagher and Greenwald, "How the NSA Plans."
68. Stray, "What You Need to Know."
69. Perlroth, Larson, and Shane, "N.S.A. Able to Foil."
70. For example, a top-secret court order issued in April 2013 required Verizon on an "ongoing daily basis" to provide the NSA with the metadata on all telephone calls in its system, both in the United States and between the United States and other countries. This information includes the identity of both parties, their respective locations during the time of the call, and the duration of the communication (Greenwald, "NSA Collecting Phone Records").

71. "Fusion Center Locations and Contact Information."
72. "Fusion Centers and Emergency Operations Centers."
73. Pasquale, *The Black Box Society*, 153.
74. Pasquale, *The Black Box Society*, 17. For instance, after announcing in 2003 that they would cooperate with the government, "FedEx received a range of government perks including special access to government security databases, a seat on the FBI's regional terrorism task force—where it was the only private company so represented—and an exceptional license from the state of Tennessee to develop an internal police force." In this case, "FedEx is sharing the privileges and immunities of the state, but not the accountability" (Pasquale, *The Black Box Society*, 49).
75. Kindig, "Palantir IPO."
76. Woodman, "Palantir Provides the Engine."
77. Mijente, "Stop the Tech-Talent Pipe-Line."
78. Biddle, "LexisNexis to Provide Giant Database"; LexisNexis, "Cast a Wider Net." https://www.lexisnexis.com/en-us/products/public-records/powerful-public-records-search.page.
79. LexisNexis, "Streamline Criminal Investigations." Meanwhile, "Pressure is mounting on the Department of Homeland Security (DHS) to discontinue —or at least clarify—its relationship with Clearview AI, a controversial facial recognition company best known for scraping billions of images of people from social media sites" (Rodrigo, "Pressure Mounts on DHS"). While the company does not disclose its clients, federal contracts and reporting show that in addition to DHS, Customs and Border Patrol (CBP) and ICE have paid for their services (Mac et al., "Your Local Police Department"). Clearview AI is also becoming increasingly well known for its founders' ties to white nationalist groups (O'Brien, "The Far-Right Helped Create").
80. Chun, *Updating to Remain the Same*, 94.
81. Grossman, "2006 Person of the Year."
82. The Obama administration, for example, defended the NSA's collection of phone records by explaining that they only access "the metadata," such as the duration of the call, but not the "content" or what was actually said (Greenwald, "NSA Collecting Phone Records").
83. Beckett, "Everything We Know."
84. Grossman, "2006 Person of the Year."
85. Zuckerberg, "F8 2011 Keynote."
86. Gates et al., *The Road Ahead*, 180.
87. Hardt, "The Withering of Civil Society," 37.
88. Bauman, *Liquid Modernity*, 10.
89. Dean, *Blog Theory*, 3.
90. Bauman and Lyon, *Liquid Surveillance*, 8.

91. As Laurent Berlant rightly points out, "the seeming detachment of rationality . . . is not a detachment at all, but an emotional style associated normatively with a rhetorical practice" (*Cruel Optimism*, 27).
92. Gibson, *Pattern Recognition*, 22.
93. Marisa Elena Duarte's research on "Connected Activism: Indigenous Uses of Social Media for Shaping Political Change" compares Ejercito Zapatista de Liberacion Nacional, Idle No More, and the ongoing Rio Yaqui water rights movement, "reveal[ing] how Indigenous uses of social media support visibility of Indigenous social movements and issues, promote solidarity for particular struggles and views, foment Freirian processes of consciousness-raising, and enforce the government-to-government trust underlying peace agreements and treaties" (9).
94. Brown et al., "Leaked Documents Reveal Counterterrorism Tactics."
95. Kolodny, "Tesla Monitored Its Employees."
96. As Chun reminds us, "Models, in other words, are modes of 'hypothesis,' and we lose the fight if we assume that models are or should be the truth—that they should be 'hyperreal'" (*Updating to Remain the Same*, 90–91).
97. Chun, *Updating to Remain the Same*, 58.
98. As part of the case's settlement in June 2022, Meta must stop using their ad-targeting tool known as the "Lookalike Audience" or "Special Ad Audience." Department of Justice, "United States Attorney Resolves Groundbreaking Suit," press release, June 21, 2021, https://www.justice.gov/usao-sdny/pr/united-states-attorney-resolves-groundbreaking-suit-against-meta-platforms-inc-formerly.
99. Chun, *Updating to Remain the Same*, 91.
100. Chun, *Updating to Remain the Same*, 82.
101. C. Anderson, "The End of Theory."
102. Hayden, interview.
103. Lohr, "The Age of Big Data."
104. Hill, "Wrongfully Accused."
105. Singer and Metz, "Many Facial-Recognition Systems Are Biased."
106. Hill, "Wrongfully Accused."
107. A. Smith, "Not-Seeing," 22.
108. Airwars, "Our Monitoring of Civilian Harm."
109. See Magnet and Rogers, "Stripping for the State."
110. See Alexander, *The New Jim Crow*.
111. Grossman, "Person of the Year 2010."
112. Schmidt, "Google CEO on Privacy."
113. Zuboff, *The Age of Surveillance Capitalism*, 88.
114. Foucault, *Discipline and Punish*, 187.
115. Grossman, "Person of the Year 2010: Mark Zuckerberg."
116. Chun, *Updating to Remain the Same*, 40.

117. Chun, *Updating to Remain the Same*, 26.
118. Chun, *Updating to Remain the Same*, 40.
119. Chun, *Updating to Remain the Same*, 40.
120. Chun, *Updating to Remain the Same*, 40; emphasis added.
121. Braidotti, *Transpositions*, 141.
122. Irigaray, *This Sex Which Is Not One*, 209.
123. Herman, introduction, 15.
124. Pasquale, *The Black Box Society*.
125. Kinder, "Reorchestrating History," 241.
126. Hamid, *How to Get Filthy Rich*, 169.
127. Bauman and Lyon, *Liquid Surveillance*.
128. Waugh, *Metafiction*, 3.
129. Dean, *Blog Theory*, 4.
130. Jaron Lanier describes one governing ethic of the web as "the race to be most meta": "if a design like Facebook or Twitter depersonalizes people a little bit, then another service like Friendfeed . . . might come along to aggregate the previous layers of aggregation, making individual people even more abstract, and the illusion of high-level metaness more celebrated." To the extent that the web, in the process, has also neutralized "metaness," contemporary fiction reclaims the value of self-reflexivity by relocating the "self" from the intersection of data points to the intersection of political, ideological, social, cultural forces (Lanier, *You Are Not a Gadget*, 28).
131. Wallace, "E Unibus Pluram."
132. Wallace, "E Unibus Pluram," 73.
133. Coover, *The Public Burning*; Apple, *The Propheteers*.
134. For more on "Documentary Poetry" or "Documentary Poetics," more broadly, see Nowak, "Documentary Poetics."
135. Wallace, "E Unibus Pluram," 31.
136. Hutcheon, *Narcissistic Narrative*, 51.
137. Miller, *The Novel and the Police*.
138. Egan, "Black Box."
139. Hamid, "In Sly Self-Help Novel."
140. Berlant, *Cruel Optimism*.
141. Chun, *Updating to Remain the Same*, 27.

Chapter 1

1. See Pasquale, *The Black Box Society*.
2. For more on "the role that human capital theory has played in the formulation of neoliberal subjects as 'never-human-enough,'" see J. Johnston, *Posthuman Capital and Biotechnology*, 20.
3. See Wallace, "E Unibus Pluram."

4. Charles, "Jennifer Egan's A Visit."
5. Waugh, *Metafiction*, 2.
6. Lovibond, "Feminism and Postmodernism," 395.
7. Who has the power to "clear" a person's internet history or data profile is itself an important conversation. Europe's General Data Protection Regulation, which "governs how personal data must be collected, processed, and erased" states, "The data subject shall have the right to obtain from the controller the erasure of personal data concerning him or her without undue delay and the controller shall have the obligation to erase personal data without undue delay" (Wolford, "Everything You Need to Know"). Currently, the United States has no such legal protections.
8. Hutcheon, *Narcissistic Narrative*, 51.
9. Dean, *Publicity's Secret*, 124.
10. Warner, *Publics and Counterpublics*, 70.
11. Egan, "Blackbox."
12. Egan, *A Visit from the Goon Squad*, 27. Further page citations appear parenthetically in the text.
13. Not only do Joe and Lulu appear in the novel's final chapter, they also reappear in Egan's Twitter story "Black Box." As Zara Dinnen writes in *Digital Banal*, "The way the future disturbs the present in *Goon Squad* is strange" (*Digital Banal*, 149).
14. Louise Matsakis clearly captures this gap in public understanding: "Consider what happens when someone sends a vial of saliva to 23andme. The person knows they're sharing their DNA with a genomics company, but they may not realize it will be resold to pharmaceutical firms. Many apps use your location to serve up custom advertisements, but they don't necessarily make it clear that a hedge fund may also buy that location data to analyze which retail stores you frequent. Anyone who has witnessed the same shoe advertisement follow them around the web knows they're being tracked, but fewer people likely understand that companies may be recording not just their clicks but also the exact movements of their mouse" (Matsakis, "The *Wired* Guide to Your Personal Data").
15. Fisher, *Capitalist Realism*, 22.
16. Terranova, *Network Culture*, provides a relevant and comprehensive discussion of free labor.
17. Klein, Browne, and Zuboff, "Surveillance in the Era."
18. Fisher, *Capitalist Realism*, 22.
19. Fisher, *Capitalist Realism*, 35.
20. Grosz, *Volatile Bodies*, 22.
21. Franzen, "Novelist Jonathan Franzen on Fresh Air."
22. Franzen's novel *Freedom* came out the same year as *Goon Squad* and was favored to win the Book Critics Circle Award, an assumption that the blog *Jezebel*

mocked with the headline, "Jonathan Franzen Loses Book Award to Some Lady" (North).

23. Helmuth, "Jonathan Franzen Is the World's Most Annoying Bird-Watcher."

24. Franzen ("My Bird Problem," 178) repeatedly refers to his ex-girlfriend as "the Californian" and states that he became "mystified and angered . . . when she took wing to Santa Cruz and refused to fly back."

25. Franzen, "My Bird Problem," 186.

26. Foucault, *Security, Territory, Population*, 11.

27. LaBelle, *Acoustic Territories*.

28. Foucault, *Security, Territory, Population*, 71.

29. Foucault, *Security, Territory, Population*, 48.

30. According to the NSA: "DROPOUT JEEP is a software implant for the Apple iPhone that utilizes modular mission applications to provide specific SIGINT functionality. This functionality includes the ability to remotely push/pull files from the device. . . . All communications with the implant will be covert and encrypted" (Kaine, "The NSA Reportedly Has Total Access").

31. Quoted in Levy, *The Perfect Thing*, 68.

32. Quoted in Levy, *The Perfect Thing*, 127.

33. Levy, *The Perfect Thing*, 131.

34. Levy, *The Perfect Thing*, 23.

35. Levy, *The Perfect Thing*, 210.

36. Goodreads, an Amazon subsidiary and social cataloging website for books, operates similarly, driving book sales and generating data to sell to third parties.

37. Mishra, "Modernity's Undoing."

38. Dinnen, *Digital Banal*, 147.

39. "The scene of Scotty's performance may at first appear to be a rejection of digital media, but this is just a temporary suspense of the narrative investment in a wholly mediational urban subject. Digital media is always already embedded in urban life; the affective novelty of this condition, which is effaced as the invisibility of media infrastructures, is displaced into the personal and cultural expression of the characters" (Dinnen, *Digital Banal*, 166).

40. Notably, Scotty shares a surname with Georges-Eugene Haussman, who was commissioned by Napoleon III to renovate Paris to be more easily surveilled by widening the city's boulevards, for example. This association undermines Scotty's supposed gestures toward authenticity and living "off the grid."

41. To this point, Allison Carruth clarifies, "The micropolitics of digital energy use—and of digital information—are, thus, not just a matter of how much power (and from what source) each stroke of the keyboard and swipe of the touch screen uses. They are also a matter of how one's desires to share experiences online and to access data from anywhere provide the foundation on which industries profit, including those industries like high-frequency trading

that are nearly invisible and so all the more difficult to hold to account for their ecological foot-print" (360).

42. Egan, "Conversation with Jennifer Egan."
43. Wallace, "E Unibus Pluram."
44. The word *creepy* captures a particular affect of surveillance. Eric Schmidt once explained that "Google policy is to get right up to the creepy line and not cross it" (Thompson, "Google's CEO").
45. Wallace, "E Unibus Pluram," 21.
46. Wallace, "E Unibus Pluram," 21.
47. Wallace, "E Unibus Pluram," 21.
48. Wallace, "E Unibus Pluram," 34.
49. Wallace, "E Unibus Pluram," 22, 23, 21.
50. Wallace, "E Unibus Pluram," 26.
51. Wallace, "E Unibus Pluram," 26.
52. Coover, "The End of Books."
53. Wallace, "E Unibus Pluram," 26.
54. Egan, "Conversation with Jennifer Egan."
55. Wallace, "E Unibus Pluram," 26.
56. Wallace, "E Unibus Pluram," 34.
57. Fitzpatrick, *Anxiety of Obsolescence*, 3.
58. DeLillo, *Mao II*, 43.
59. Berger, *Ways of Seeing*, 47.
60. Egan, "Conversation with Jennifer Egan."
61. Dean, *Publicity's Secret*, 129.
62. Dean, *Publicity's Secret*, 126.
63. Deleuze, "Postscript on the Societies of Control," 5.
64. D. A. Miller, *The Novel and the Police*, 16.
65. A. Smith, "Not-Seeing," 31.
66. Chun, *Updating to Remain the Same*, 160.

Chapter 2

1. Lyon, Introduction.
2. Goldberg, *Racial State*, 94.
3. Noble, "Algorithms of Oppression"; Browne, *Dark Matters*; Parenti, *The Soft Cage*; Lyon, *Surveillance Studies*; Robertson, *Passport in America*.
4. Parenti, *The Soft Cage*, 18.
5. Parenti, *The Soft Cage*, 20.
6. Parenti, *The Soft Cage*, 20.
7. Berlant, *Cruel Optimism*, 1.
8. Berlant, *Cruel Optimsim*; Ahmed, *Cultural Politics of Emotion*; Rankine, *Citizen*.
9. Lorde, "The Uses of Anger."

10. Berlant, *Cruel Optimism*, 27.
11. Berlant, *Cruel Optimism*, 64–65.
12. Chun, *Updating to Remain the Same*, 13.
13. Berlant, "Claudia Rankine."
14. Rothenberg, "Tennis's Top Women"; Clary, "It's Time to Appreciate."
15. Quoted in Clary, "It's Time"
16. Rankine, *Citizen*, 25. Further page citations appear parenthetically in the text.
17. Browne, "Race and Surveillance," 72.
18. Browne, "Race and Surveillance," 72.
19. Fiske, "Surveilling the City," 69.
20. Lorde, "The Uses of Anger," 124.
21. Quoted in Phillips, *The Right Set*, 156.
22. Ahmed, *Cultural Politics of Emotion*, 11.
23. Heilweil, "Members of Congress."
24. Between June 2014 and June 2015, however, Serena Williams made $10 million less in endorsements than white player Maria Sharapova (Badenhausen, "Serena Williams versus Maria Sharapova").
25. Lyon, *Surveillance Studies*, 197.
26. In 1955, Emmett Till, at fourteen years old, was brutalized and lynched after a white woman accused him of flirting with her in a grocery store. His murderers were acquitted. In September 2014, a twelve-year-old Black boy was suspended from school for "staring" at a white female student, a punishment upheld by the Ohio courts (Baldwin, "12-Year-Old Boy Suspended").
27. hooks, *Black Looks*, 168.
28. Browne, "Race and Surveillance," 77.
29. C. Anderson, "The End of Theory."
30. Behn, "The Data Don't Speak," 1.
31. Browne, *Dark Matters*, 115.
32. Berlant, "Epistemology of State Emotion," 46.
33. Berlant, "Claudia Rankine."
34. Berlant, "Claudia Rankine."
35. Chun, *Updating to Remain the Same*, 49.
36. Chun, *Updating to Remain the Same*, 49.
37. Berlant, *Cruel Optimism*, 243.
38. Sperry, "When the Profile."
39. Krauthammer, "Give Grandma a Pass."
40. Where I live, on Long Island, New York, a three-year investigation uncovered that local real estate agents treated Asian clients unfairly 19 percent of the time, Hispanic clients 39 percent of the time, and African American clients 49 percent of the time: "Along with steering minority testers to majority-minority areas, and white testers to mostly white areas, some agents required Black buyers to meet additional financial conditions that they didn't demand

of white buyers with the same profile. Sometimes, in exchanges recorded by undercover cameras, agents would deter white buyers from house hunting in minority areas." This racial discrimination clearly helps account for why Long Island is one of the most segregated suburbs in the country (Editorial Board, "The Jim Crow South?").

41. Berlant, "Claudia Rankine."
42. Chun, *Updating to Remain the Same*, 91.
43. While sold as more permanent, digital storage "perversely take[s] what is more lasting—what can remain and still be read for a long duration, such as paper—and make[s] it more volatile. This digital 'version' is more volatile not simply because magnetically stored data decay more quickly than paper, but also because software and hardware constantly change, manically upgrade" (Chun, *Updating to Remain the Same*, 78).
44. According to a study from Northwestern University, people who experienced racial discrimination during adolescence still had disrupted stress hormone levels twenty years later, even controlling for other factors that cause stress, such as socioeconomic status and depression (Adam et al., "Developmental Histories").
45. Ahmed, *Cultural Politics of Emotion*, 10.
46. Grosz, *Volatile Bodies*, 120.
47. Grosz, *Volatile Bodies*, 120.
48. Berlant, *Cruel Optimism*, 10.
49. Rankine, "In Citizen Poet."
50. Puar, "Regimes of Surveillance."
51. Puar, "Regimes of Surveillance."
52. Berlant, "Claudia Rankine."
53. Parenti, *The Soft Cage*, 20.
54. Berlant, *Cruel Optimism*, 12.
55. Berlant, "Claudia Rankine."
56. Berlant, "Claudia Rankine."
57. Parenti, *The Soft Cage*, 79.
58. Parenti, *The Soft Cage*, 89.
59. B. Anderson, *Imagined Communities*.
60. Chun, *Updating to Remain the Same*, 3.
61. Chun, *Updating to Remain the Same*, 16.

Chapter 3

1. Hayles, "Electronic Literature."
2. Pariser, *The Filter Bubble*, 19.
3. Bohé et al., "Data Monetization in the Age of Big Data," 3.
4. Bohé et al., "Data Monetization in the Age of Big Data," 1.

5. Bohé et al., "Data Monetization in the Age of Big Data," 4.
6. Deleuze, "Postscript on the Societies of Control," 5.
7. Tung, "Building Data Products as a Competitive Differentiator."
8. Fokkema, *Postmodern Characters*, 57.
9. Fokkema, *Postmodern Characters*, 64.
10. Latour, *We Have Never Been Modern*, 123.
11. Vadde, "Fiction as Streaming."
12. Hayles, "Electronic Literature."
13. Gibson, "I Never Imagined Facebook."
14. Gibson, *Pattern Recognition*, 2. Further page citations appear parenthetically in the text.
15. History Preservation Associates, "Buzz Rickson."
16. Pariser, *The Filter Bubble*, 18.
17. Marx, *Capital*, 279–80.
18. Murphet, "Behind the Scenes," 144.
19. Bittman, "Who Protects the Animals?"
20. D. A. Miller, *The Novel and the Police*, 16.
21. D. A. Miller, *The Novel and the Police*, 16.
22. Murphet, "Behind the Scenes," 161.
23. Murphet, "Behind the Scenes," 161.
24. Murphet, "Behind the Scenes," 161.
25. Murphet, "Behind the Scenes," 163.
26. Marx, *Capital*, 279.
27. Terranova, *Network Culture*, 78.
28. Terranova, *Network Culture*, 94.
29. G. Smith, "Surveillance Work(ers)," 108.
30. Sifferlen, "NFL Cheerleaders."
31. Terranova, *Network Culture*, 91.
32. Terranova, *Network Culture*, 79–80.
33. Cayce's job as a coolhunter professionalizes what Maurizio Lazzaroto calls "immaterial labor," "in other words, the kinds of activities involved in defining and fixing cultural and artistic standards, fashions, tastes, consumer norms, and, more strategically, public opinion" (Lazzaroto, "Immaterial Labor," 133).
34. Terranova, *Network Culture*, 91.
35. Terranova, *Network Culture*, 79–80.
36. Afaq and Shahid, "The Internet Is Becoming."
37. Heller, "The Claustrophobia."
38. Elon Musk (@elonmusk), "'Free speech is the bedrock of a functioning democracy, and Twitter is the digital town square where matters vital to the future of humanity are debated.'" Twitter, April 25, 2022. https://twitter.com/elonmusk/status/1518677066325053441.
39. Zeider, "Pattern Recognition."

40. Merchant, "Real Reason Facebook Changed Its Name."
41. Allyn, "Here Are Four Key Points."
42. David Foster Wallace wrote, "Metafiction is untrue, as a lover. It cannot betray. It can only reveal. Itself is the only object. It's the act of a lonely solipsist's self-love, a night-light on the black fifth wall of being a subject, a face in a crowd. It's lovers not being lovers" (*Girl with Curious Hair*, 332).
43. Describing the "destabilizing effects of reflexivity," Jodi Dean writes, "Bubbles, band-wagon effects, and boom-and-bust cycles result from investors' attempts to predict how others will perceive the future even as these very predictions bring a particular future into being" (Dean, *Blog Theory*, 11).
44. Balfour, "How Much Are You Worth."
45. Elon Musk, (@elonmusk), "So how do advertisers know what they're getting for their money?" Twitter, May 16, 2022. https://twitter.com/elonmusk/status/1526250477456965634.
46. Chun, *Updating to Remain the Same*, 42.
47. Quoted in Pariser, *The Filter Bubble*, 35.
48. Lury, *Brands*, 35.
49. Lury, *Brands*, 112.
50. Linden, Smith, and York, "Amazon.com Recommendations."
51. McAlone, "Why Netflix Thinks."
52. Dickson, "Can Alexa and Facebook Predict?"
53. As Jodi Dean poses in *Blog Theory*, "How could a blog ostensibly written by a logo or branded media image or even an actual person paid to blog by the company offer anything but spin?" (34).
54. Deleuze, "Postscript on the Societies of Control."
55. Harwell, "Cheating-Detection Companies."
56. See Peticca-Harris, deGama, and Ravishankar, "Postcapitalist Precarious Work."
57. T. Miller, *Routledge Companion to Global Popular Culture*, 59.
58. Egan, *A Visit from the Goon Squad*, 315.
59. N. Anderson, "Hillary Clinton Slams."
60. McLuhan and Lapham, *Understanding Media*, xi.
61. Terranova, *Network Culture*, 75.
62. Chun, *Updating to Remain the Same*, 17.
63. Preciado, "Pharmaco-Pornographic," 109.
64. Terranova, *Network Culture*, 90.
65. Hardt, "The Withering of Civil Society," 37.
66. Lury, *Brands*, 7.
67. G. Smith, "Surveillance Work(ers)," 111.
68. For a comprehensive discussion of this question, see Dinnen, *Digital Banal*.
69. G. Smith, "Surveillance Work(ers)," 111.
70. Lury, *Brands*, 112.

71. For more on Bigend's portrayal as vampiric, see Link, "Global War, Global Capital."
72. Zuboff, *The Age of Surveillance Capitalism*, 15.
73. Allison Carruth instructively writes, "Ursula K. Heise . . . observes that such metaphors of 'ecology' and 'environment' have served two opposing tendencies in media theory: on the one hand, to envision the internet as a 'unifying' system spanning the globe and, on the other, to stake out ground for a multiplicity of digital subcultures. She concludes that the digital world consequently eclipses 'natural environments' . . . Postman . . . himself suggested that the media ecology metaphor, in emphasizing the 'interaction between media and human beings,' has been an unabashedly anthropocentric lens within media studies that has short-circuited investigations of the 'interaction' between media technologies and ecosystems" (Carruth, "The Digital Cloud" 353).
74. As the CEO of Nike explains: "'we've come around to saying that Nike is a marketing company, and the product is our most important marketing tool. What I mean is that marketing knits the whole organization together. The design elements and functional characteristics of the product itself are just part of the overall marketing process'" (Lury, *Brands*, 49).
75. Terranova, *Network Culture*, 89.
76. Terranova, *Network Culture*, 89.
77. Foucault, *Discipline and Punish*, 30.
78. Deleuze, "Postscript on the Societies of Control," 5.
79. Deleuze, "Postscript on the Societies of Control," 6.
80. Apple, Amazon, Alphabet, Meta, and Microsoft.
81. Grosz, *Time Travels*, 158.
82. Musk, "Elon Musk Talks Twitter."
83. Musk, "Elon Musk Talks Twitter."
84. Preciado, "Pharmaco-Pornographic," 109.
85. Terranova, *Network Culture*, 90.
86. Terranova, *Network Culture*, 97.
87. Grosz, *Time Travels*, 116.
88. Amazon's joint obsessions with customer service and automation likewise indicates that "The ideal toward which it points is a world composed entirely of customers and no workers" (McGurl, "Everything and Less," 454).
89. Nietzsche, *Untimely Meditations*, 60.
90. Berlant, *Cruel Optimism*, 52.
91. Lury, *Brands*, 98.
92. History Preservation Associates, "About Us."
93. Link, "Global War, Global Capital," 216.
94. Link, "Global War, Global Capital," 217.
95. Bennett, *Vibrant Matter*.

96. Deleuze and Guattari, *Kafka*, 57.
97. Terranova, *Network Culture*, 75.
98. Vadde, "Amateur Creativity," 32.
99. Vadde, "Amateur Creativity," 32.
100. Terranova, *Network Culture*, 94; emphasis added.
101. Vadde, "Amateur Creativity," 32.
102. As David Lyon writes, "In database marketing the idea is to lull intended targets into thinking that they count when all it wants is to count them and, of course, to suck them into further purchases" (Bauman and Lyon, *Liquid Surveillance*, 54).
103. Braidotti, *Transpositions*, 276.

Chapter 4

1. For example, consider the following titles: *The Top 2%: How to Become the Highest-Paid, Highest-Profile Person in Your Industry* by Nightingale-Conant and the Staff of Entrepreneur Media, Inc.; *Profiles of Success* by Brian Mast; *Wire Yourself for Wealth: Discover Your Money Genius Profile to Effortlessly Create More Wealth* by Laura Leigh Clark; and *How to Brand Your Professional Profile? Define Your Brand, Reinvent Yourself* by Nick Brown.
2. Landrum, *Profiles*.
3. More examples: *E-Habits: What You Must Do to Optimize Your Professional Digital Presence* by Elizabeth Charnock; *Burn Your Résumé: You Need a Professional Profile* by Donald M. Burrows and Deborah Drake; *You Are a Brand!: In Person and Online, How Smart People Brand Themselves for Business Success* by Catherine Kaputa; and *Social Media Made Me Rich: Here's How It Can Do the Same for You* by Matthew Loop.
4. For instance, *Likable Social Media Revised and Expanded: How to Delight Your Customers, Create an Irresistible Brand, and Be Amazing on Facebook, Twitter, LinkedIn, Instagram, Pinterest, and More*, by Dave Kerpen et al.; and *How to Win Friends and Influence People in the Digital Age* by Dale Carnegie and Associates.
5. Gale, *Your Network Is Your Net Worth*.
6. Massey, "Neoliberalism Has Hijacked Our Vocabulary."
7. IMF Research Group, "Asia Rising."
8. Massey, "Neoliberalism Has Hijacked Our Vocabulary."
9. Hamid, *Filthy Rich*, 4. Further page citations appear parenthetically in the text.
10. Chun, *Updating to Remain the Same*, 84.
11. Elaine Scarry's work on *The Body in Pain* is particularly instructive here. Despite what the statistics suggest about "your" likelihood of survival, "for the person in pain, so incontestably and unnegotiably present is it that 'having pain' may come to be thought of as the most vibrant example of what it is to 'have certainty,' while for the other person it is so elusive that 'hearing about pain'

may exist as the primary model for what it is 'to have doubt.' Thus pain comes unsharably into our midst as at once that which cannot be denied and that which cannot be confirmed" (4).

12. Hamid, Interview, Chicago Humanities Festival.

13. Hamid, Interview, Chicago Humanities Festival.

14. Hamid, NPR Interview.

15. Chamayou, *The Theory of the Drone*, 41.

16. Chamayou, *The Theory of the Drone*, 41.

17. Hayden, Interview.

18. Quoted in Bauman and Lyon, *Liquid Surveillance*, 98.

19. Politically speaking, drones have been advantageous precisely because they reduced the political costs of losing American lives, the economic costs of armament, and the "ethical or reputational" costs of perceived destruction and harm (Chamayou, *The Theory of the Drone*, 9).

20. The speculative dimension of war that Hamid describes speaks to the distinctions between counterinsurgency and antiterrorism as outlined in *The Theory of the Drone*. According to the logic of antiterrorism, "the total body count and a list of hunting trophies take the place of a strategic evaluation of the political effects of armed violence. Successes become statistics. Their evaluation is totally disconnected from their real effects on the ground. . . . From this point of view, the objection that drone strikes are counterproductive because they allow the enemy, in a classic pattern of action and repression, to recruit more volunteers no longer applies. Never mind if the enemy ranks thicken, since it will always be possible to neutralize the new recruits as fast as they emerge. The cull will be repeated periodically, in a pattern of infinite eradication" (Chamayou, *The Theory of the Drone*, 69).

21. Clearly, the phrase "patronize the artists of war" is punning on the call for people to "patronize the arts," a means toward a decidedly different form of riches, but one that readers of this book are evidently pursuing.

22. They are also, unlike the panopticon, made deliberately invisible.

23. It is significant that Hamid refers to the "*world's* national security apparatuses" capturing the complicated cooperation and collusion between the US and Pakistani governments in what has been dubbed the "drone war" during the Bush and Obama presidencies. While the details are contested, it is incontrovertible that for at least some of the drone strikes, the United States operated with the approval of Pakistan's Inter-Services Intelligence. Former Pakistani President Pervez Mushaaraf told the *New Yorker* in 2014, for example, that he allowed the CIA to operate drone strikes in exchange for helicopters and night-vision gear (Coll, "The Unblinking Stare"). My references to government or military surveillance in this chapter are meant to include this mingling of military powers that Hamid portrays.

24. Poon, "Helping the Novel," 2.

25. To be sure, as the novel describes, the "artists of war" do produce in-depth profiles, through "what officials describes as 'pattern of life analysis,' using evidence collected by surveillance cameras on the unmanned aircraft and from other sources about individuals and locations . . . . As one Reaper drone operator explains, 'We can develop those patterns of life, determine who the bad guys are, and then get the clearance and go through the whole find, fix, track, target, attack cycle" (Chamayou, *The Theory of the Drone*, 47).
26. Chamayou, *The Theory of the Drone*, 42.
27. Again, Hamid might be referring to the Pakistani military here, but given the NSA's extensive surveillance abroad, the reference is appropriately ambiguous. For example, the NSA uses a plug-in called GUMFISH to seize control over laptop cameras and another called CAPTIVATEAUDIENCE to take over computer microphones (Gallagher and Greenwald, "How the NSA Plans to Infect 'Millions' of Computers"). Meanwhile, "using the NSA's XKEYSCORE software, analysts can see 'nearly everything a user does on the internet,' including emails, social media posts, websites you visit, addresses typed into Google Maps, files sent, and more" (Stray, "What You Need to Know").
28. Shelton, *Joint Vision 2020*, 22.
29. Bureau of Investigative Journalism, "Strikes in Pakistan."
30. Chamayou, *The Theory of the Drone*, 12.
31. Bureau of Investigative Journalism, "Strikes in Pakistan."
32. Quoted in Chamayou, *The Theory of the Drone*, 140.
33. Chamayou, *The Theory of the Drone*, 40.
34. Chamayou, *The Theory of the Drone*, 49.
35. Chamayou, *The Theory of the Drone*, 50.
36. Almasmari, "Yemen Says."
37. Chamayou, *The Theory of the Drone*, 23.
38. McClintock, "Slow Violence and the BP Oil Crisis."
39. Chamayou, *The Theory of the Drone*, 24.
40. As it is said, "Of course people would still die, but only on one side" (Chamayou, *The Theory of the Drone*, 24).
41. There are a host of blinking eyes behind each drone: "Among those invisible spectators are not only the pilot and sensor operators but also a mission intelligence coordinator, a safety observer, a team of video analysts, and a ground force commander, the last of whom will eventually give the go-ahead for an aerial strike. This network of eyes remains in constant communication with one another" (Chamayou, *The Theory of the Drone*, 2).
42. Chamayou, *The Theory of the Drone*, 20–21.
43. Chamayou, *The Theory of the Drone*, 22.

Conclusion

1. McGurl, "Everything and Less," 447.
2. McGurl, "Everything and Less," 453.
3. McGurl, "Everything and Less," 469.
4. McGurl, "Everything and Less," 469.
5. McGurl, "Everything and Less," 465.
6. McGurl, "Everything and Less," 463.
7. McGurl, "Everything and Less," 466.
8. McGurl, "Everything and Less," 453.
9. Stone, *The Everything Store*.
10. McGurl, "Everything and Less," 455.
11. Bezos, *Invent and Wander*, loc. 2392.
12. Williams, "5 Ways Amazon Monitors Its Employees."
13. Palmer, "Amazon Wins FAA Approval."
14. McGurl, "Everything and Less," 455.
15. Kantor, Weise, and Ashford, "Inside Amazon's Employment Machine."
16. Kantor, Weise, and Ashford, "Inside Amazon's Employment Machine."
17. Hayden, interview.
18. Isaacson, *Steve Jobs*, 494.
19. Vaidhyanathan, *Anti-Social Media*, 5.
20. Jodi Dean writes, "Even if geeks are 'about' justice and equality, the consequence of the widespread adoption and extension of their work is the most extreme economic inequality the world has ever known" (Dean, *Blog Theory*, 23).
21. Kantor, Weise, and Ashford, "Inside Amazon's Employment Machine."
22. Kantor, Weise, and Ashford, "Inside Amazon's Employment Machine."
23. Kantor, Weise, and Ashford, "Inside Amazon's Employment Machine."
24. Kantor, Weise, and Ashford, "Inside Amazon's Employment Machine."
25. Williams, "5 Ways Amazon Monitors Its Employees."
26. Joy Buolamwini delivered powerful oral and written testimony on the fallibility and harm of this technology before congress ("Facial Recognition Technology (Part One)").
27. Harwell, "Amazon Met with ICE Officials."
28. Bezos, *Invent and Wander*, loc. 3249.
29. McGurl, "Everything and Less," 447.
30. McGurl, "Everything and Less," 453.
31. According to Bezos, "The vision for Echo and Alexa was inspired by the *Star Trek* computer. The idea also had origins in two other arenas where we'd been building and wandering for years: machine learning and the cloud. From Amazon's early days, machine learning was an essential part of our product recommendations, and AWS gave us a front row seat to the capabilities of the

cloud. After many years of development, Echo debuted in 2014, powered by Alexa, who lives in the AWS cloud" (*Invent and Wander*, loc. 331). That Alexa was inspired by *Star Trek* should be unsurprising at this point, but Bezos's explanation that while the Echo may live on your countertop, Alexa "lives in the AWS cloud" is noteworthy. First, she is, of course, not alive. Nevertheless, this distinction between where the device and the software "live" is what allows for more than 150 different products to have Alexa built in with, as Bezos puts it, "much more to come!" (*Invent and Wander*, loc. 2649).

32. Schwartz, "Alexa Now Offers."
33. Stone, *The Everything Store*.
34. Stone, *The Everything Store*.
35. McGurl, "Everything and Less," 455.
36. Ezrachi and Stucke, "The Rise of Machines."
37. Ezrachi and Stucke, "The Rise of Machines."
38. Ezrachi and Stucke, "The Rise of Machines."
39. Ezrachi and Stucke, "The Rise of Machines."
40. Ishiguro, *The Remains of the Day*, 245.
41. One article boasts, "But in addition to being endlessly useful, [Alexa] also knows a roster of entertaining party tricks. Next time you have a group of people around (in-person or virtually), pass around the drinks and set your preferred Echo device center stage. This list of amusing Alexa voice commands will make your Alexa device the life of the party—her responses are hilarious" (Bizzaco and Coomes).
42. McGurl, "Everything and Less," 448.
43. Ishiguro, *Remains*, 16.
44. McGurl, "Everything and Less," 453.
45. McGurl, "Everything and Less," 450.
46. Dunbar, "Amazon KDP."
47. Voyles, "Amazon's Impact on Publishing."
48. Grossman, "2006 Person."
49. McGurl, "Everything and Less," 456.
50. McGurl, "Everything and Less," 456.
51. McGurl, "Everything and Less," 456.
52. Paul, "'They Know Us Better.'"
53. Quoted in McGurl, "Everything and Less," 454.
54. McGurl, "Everything and Less," 454.
55. McGurl, "Everything and Less," 464.
56. Fowler and Kelly, "Amazon's New Health Band."
57. Bezos, *Invent and Wander*, loc. 1306.
58. Companies including Pinterest, DropBox, Airbnb, Enel, Capital One, Intuit, Johnson & Johnson, Philips, Hess, Adobe, McDonald's, Time Inc., Netflix, GE, Major League Baseball, Tata Motors, Qantas, NTT DOCOMO, the

Financial Times, Condé Nast, Kellogg's, News Corp., and the Securities and Exchange Commission are either "using AWS to analyze and take action on vast amounts of data" or are "are migrating legacy critical applications and, in some cases, entire datacenters to AWS" (Bezos, *Invent and Wander*, loc. 1977–78).

59. Bezos, *Invent and Wander*, loc. 524.
60. McGurl, "Everything and Less," 460.
61. McGurl, "Everything and Less," 456.
62. McGurl, "Everything and Less," 460.
63. McGurl, "Everything and Less," 463.
64. McGurl, "Unspeakable Conventionality," 399.
65. McGurl, "Unspeakable Conventionality," 399.
66. McGurl, "Unspeakable Conventionality," 413.
67. McGurl, "Unspeakable Conventionality," 409.
68. Data for Black Lives, "Programs."
69. Onuoha, "About."
70. Onuoha, "On Missing Data Sets."
71. Onuoha, "On Missing Data Sets."
72. Buolamwini, "AI, Ain't I a Woman?"
73. Buolamwini, "Code4Rights."

BIBLIOGRAPHY

Adam, Emma K., Jennifer A. Heissel, Katharine H. Zeiders, Jennifer A. Richeson, Emily C. Ross, Katherine B. Ehrlich, Dorainne J. Levy, Margaret Kemeny, Amanda B. Brodish, Oksana Malanchuk, Stephen C. Peck, Thomas E. Fuller-Rowell, and Jacquelynne S. Accles. "Developmental Histories of Perceived Racial Discrimination and Diurnal Cortisol Profiles in Adulthood: A 20-Year Prospective Study." *Psychoneuroendocrinology* 62 (2016): 279–91.

Afaq, Sadaf, and Durraiz Shahid. "The Internet Is Becoming the Town Square for the Global Village of Tomorrow." *Cyber Insights Magazine*, July 27, 2021. https://www.cyber-insights.org/the-internet-is-becoming-the-town-square-for-the-global-village-of-tomorrow2/.

Ahmed, Sara. *The Cultural Politics of Emotion*. New York: Routledge, 2004.

Airwars. "Our Monitoring of Civilian Harm." *Airwars.org*, updated August 2021. https://airwars.org (accessed August 4, 2021).

Alexander, Michelle. *The New Jim Crow: Mass Incarceration in the Age of Colorblindness*. Rev. ed. New York: New Press, 2020.

Allyn, Bobby. "Here Are Four Key Points from the Facebook Whistleblower's Testimony on Capital Hill." NPR, October 5, 2021. https://www.npr.org/2021/10/05/1043377310/facebook-whistleblower-frances-haugen-congress.

Almasmari, Hakim. "Yemen Says U.S. Drone Struck a Wedding Convoy, Killed 14." CNN, December 13, 2013. http://www.cnn.com/2013/12/12/world/meast/yemen-u-s-drone-wedding/.

Altman, Howard, Jim Barry, Daniel Brook, Jenn Carbin, Daryl Gale, Mary F. Patel, Gwen Shaffer, Rick Valenzuela, and David Warner. "Nothing Will Ever Be the Same." *Philadelphia City Paper*, September 13–20, 2001. https://web.archive.org/web/20010918225504/http://www.citypaper.net:80/articles/091301/cov.wtc1.shtml.

Anderson, Benedict. *Imagined Communities: Reflections on the Origins and Spread of Nationalism*. Rev. ed. London: Verso, 2016.

Anderson, Chris. "The End of Theory: The Data Deluge Makes the Scientific Method Obsolete." *Wired*, June 23, 2008. http://www.wired.com/2008/06/pb-theory/.

Anderson, Nate. "Hillary Clinton Slams 'Information Curtain' of Censorship." *ArsTechnica*, January 21, 2010. https://arstechnica.com/tech-policy/2010/01/hillary-clinton-slams-information-curtain-of-censorship/.

Angwin, Julia, Ariana Tobin, and Madeleine Varner. "Facebook (Still) Letting Housing Advertisers Exclude Users by Race." *ProPublica*, November 21, 2017. https://www.propublica.org/article/facebook-advertising-discrimination-housing-race-sex-national-origin.

Bibliography

Angwin, Julia, Madeleine Varner, and Ariana Tobin. "Facebook Enabled Advertisers to Reach 'Jew Haters.'" *ProPublica*, September 14, 2017. https://www.propublica .org/article/facebook-enabled-advertisers-to-reach-jew-haters.

Apple, Max. *The Propheteers: A Novel*. New York: HarperCollins, 1987.

Arango, Tim. "How the AOL-Time Warner Merger Went so Wrong." *New York Times*, January 10, 2010. https://www.nytimes.com/2010/01/11/business/media/11merger .html.

Arrington, Michael. "Google's Eric Schmidt on Magical Potential of Mobile + Cloud." *TechCrunch*, October 29, 2009. https://techcrunch.com/2009/10/28/goo- gles-eric-schmidt-on-magical-potential-of-mobile-cloud/.

Auxier, Brook. "Five Things to Know about Americans and Their Smart Speakers." *Pew Research Center*, November 21, 2019. https://www.pewresearch.org/fact-tank /2019/11/21/5-things-to-know-about-americans-and-their-smart-speakers/.

Badenhausen, Kurt. "Serena Williams versus Maria Sharapova: By the Numbers." *Forbes*, July 9, 2015. https://www.forbes.com/sites/kurtbadenhausen/2015/07/09 /serena-williams-vs-maria-sharapova-by-the-numbers/.

Baldwin, Michael. "12-Year-Old Boy Suspended for Staring at Girl." *Fox19Now*, September 30, 2015. https://www.fox19.com/story/30158100/12-year-old-boy -suspended-for-staring-at-girl/.

Balfour, Lili. "How Much Are You Worth to Twitter?" *Huffington Business*, October 16, 2013. http://www.huffingtonpost.com/lili-balfour/how-much-are-you-worth-to -twitter_b_4099327.html.

Bauman, Zygmunt. *Liquid Modernity*. Malden, MA: Polity Press, 2000.

Bauman, Zygmunt, and David Lyon. *Liquid Surveillance: A Conversation*. Malden, MA: Polity Press, 2013.

Beckett, Lois. "Everything We Know about What Data Brokers Know about You." *ProPublica*, June 13, 2014. https://www.propublica.org/article/everything-we-know -about-what-data-brokers-know-about-you.

Behn, Robert. "The Data Don't Speak for Themselves." *Bob Behn's Public Management Report* 6, no. 7 (2009). http://www.hks.harvard.edu /publications/data-dont -speak-themselves.

Benjamin, Ruha. *Race after Technology: Abolitionist Tools for the New Jim Code*. Cambridge: Polity, 2019.

Bennett, Jane. *Vibrant Matter: A Political Ecology of Things*. Durham, NC: Duke University Press Books, 2009.

Berger, John. *Ways of Seeing*. London: Penguin Books, 1972.

Berlant, Lauren. "Claudia Rankine." Interview with Claudia Rankine. *Bomb Magazine* 129, October 1, 2014. https://bombmagazine.org/articles/claudia-rankine/.

Berlant, Lauren. *Cruel Optimism*. Durham, NC: Duke University Press, 2011.

Berlant, Lauren. "The Epistemology of State Emotion." In *Dissent in Dangerous Times*, edited by Austin Sarat, 46–78. Ann Arbor: University of Michigan Press, 2005.

Bibliography

Bezos, Jeffrey. *Invent and Wander: The Collected Writings of Jeff Bezos*. Cambridge, MA: Harvard Business Review Press and PublicAffairs, 2021. Kindle.

Biddle, Sam. "LexisNexis to Provide Giant Database of Personal Information to ICE." *The Intercept*, April 2, 2021. https://theintercept.com/2021/04/02/ice-database -surveillance-lexisnexis/.

Bittman, Mark. "Who Protects the Animals?" *New York Times*, April 26, 2011. https://opinionator.blogs.nytimes.com/2011/04/26/who-protects-the-animals/.

Bizzaco, Michael, and Kailla Coomes. "The Best Alexa Easter Eggs." *Digital Trends*, March 16, 2021. https://www.digitaltrends.com/home/best-alexa-easter-eggs/.

Bohé, Astrid, Montgomery Hong, Craig Macdonald, and Nigel Paice. "Data Monetization in the Age of Big Data." Accenture, 2013.

Booth, Wayne. *The Rhetoric of Fiction*. Chicago: University of Chicago Press, 1961.

Braidotti, Rosi. *Transpositions*. Cambridge: Polity Press, 2006.

Brown, Alleen, Will Parrish, and Alice Speri. "Leaked Documents Reveal Counter-terrorism Tactics Used at Standing Rock to 'Defeat Pipeline Insurgencies.'" *The Intercept*, May 27, 2017. https://theintercept.com/2017/05/27/leaked-documents -reveal-security-firms-counterterrorism-tactics-at-standing-rock-to-defeat -pipeline-insurgencies/.

Browne, Simone. *Dark Matters: On the Surveillance of Blackness*. Durham, NC: Duke University Press, 2015.

Browne, Simone. "Race and Surveillance." In *Routledge Handbook of Surveillance Studies*, edited by Kirstie Ball, Kevin Haggerty, and David Lyon, 72–79. New York: Routledge, 2012.

Buolamwini, Joy. "AI, Ain't I a Woman?" *YouTube*, June 28, 2018. https://www .youtube.com/watch?v=QxuyfWoVV98.

Buolamwini, Joy. "Code4Rights." *MIT Media Lab*, n.d. https://www.media.mit.edu /projects/code4rights/overview/.

Buolamwini, Joy. "Facial Recognition Technology (Part One): Its Impact on Our Civil Rights and Liberties." Congressional testimony, May 22, 2019. https://www.congress.gov/116/meeting/house/109521/witnesses/HHRG-116 -GO00-Wstate-BuolamwiniJ-20190522.pdf.

Buolamwini, Joy. "How I'm Fighting Bias in Algorithms." TedxBeaconStreet 2016, Brookline, MA. https://www.ted.com/talks/joy_buolamwini_how_i_m_fighting _bias_in_algorithms?language=en.

Bureau of Investigative Journalism. "Strikes in Pakistan." n.d. *Bureau of Investigative Journalism*, n.d. https://www.thebureauinvestigates.com/projects/drone-war /charts?show_casualties=1&show_injuries=1&show_strikes=1&location =pakistan&from=2004-1-1&to=now (accessed June 27, 2022).

Carruth, Allison. "The Digital Cloud and the Micropolitics of Energy." *Public Culture* 26, no. 2 (2014): 339–364. https://doi.org/10.1215/08992363-2392093.

Chamayou, Gregoire. *The Theory of the Drone*. Paris: New Press, 2015.

Bibliography

Chaffin, Joshua, and Aline van Duyn. "Disney's ABC to Offer TV Shows Free on Web." *Financial Times*, April 10, 2006. https://www.ft.com/content/341d65ba-c894 -11da-b642-0000779e2340.

Charles, Ron. "Jennifer Egan's *A Visit from the Goon Squad*." *Washington Post*, June 10, 2010. https://www.washingtonpost.com/wp-dyn/content/article/2010/06/15 /AR2010061504751.html.

Chun, Wendy Hui Kyong. *Updating to Remain the Same: Habitual New Media*. Cambridge, MA: MIT Press, 2016.

Clary, Christopher. "It's Time to Appreciate Serena Williams's Greatness." *New York Times*, July 28, 2015. http://www.nytimes.com/2015/07/14/sports/tennis/its-time-to -appreciate-serena-williamss-greatness.html.

Coll, Steve. "The Unblinking Stare." *New Yorker*, November 24, 2014. http://www .newyorker.com/magazine/2014/11/24/unblinking-stare.

Coover, Robert. "The End of Books." *New York Times*, June 21, 1992.

Coover, Robert. *The Public Burning*. New York: Grove Press, 1976.

Data for Black Lives (D4BL). "Programs." D4BL, n.d. https://d4bl.org/programs .html (accessed August 5, 2021).

Dean, Jodi. *Blog Theory: Feedback and Capture in the Circuits of Drive*. Malden, MA: Polity Press, 2013.

Dean, Jodi. *Publicity's Secret: How Technoculture Capitalizes on Democracy*. Ithaca, NY: Cornell University Press, 2002.

Deleuze, Gilles. "Postscript on the Societies of Control." *October* 59 (1992): 3–7. http://cidadeinseguranca.files.wordpress.com/2012/02/deleuze_control.pdf.

Deleuze, Gilles, and Félix Guattari. *Kafka: Toward a Minor Literature*. Minneapolis: University of Minnesota Press, 1986.

DeLillo, Don. *Mao II*. New York: Penguin Books, 1991.

Desjardins, Jeff. "How Much Data Is Generated Each Day?" *World Economic Forum*, April 17, 2019. https://www.weforum.org/agenda/2019/04/how-much-data-is -generated-each-day-cf4bddf29f/.

Dickson, E. J. "Can Alexa and Facebook Predict the End of Your Relationship?" *Vox*, January 2, 2019. https://www.vox.com/the-goods/2019/1/2/18159111/amazon -facebook-big-data-breakup-prediction.

Dinnen, Zara. *Digital Banal: New Media and American Literature and Culture*. New York: Columbia University Press, 2018.

Duarte, Marisa Elena. "Connected Activism: Indigenous Uses of Social Media for Shaping Political Change." *Australasian Journal of Information Systems* 21 (2017): 1–12. https://doi.org/10.3127/ajis.v21io.1525.

Duarte, Marisa Elena, Morgan Vigil-Hayes, Sandra Littletree, and Miranda Belarde-Lewis. "'Of Course, Data Can Never Fully Represent Reality': Assessing the Relationship between 'Indigenous Data' and 'Indigenous Knowledge,' 'Traditional Ecological Knowledge,' and 'Traditional Knowledge.'" *Human Biology* 91, no. 3 (2020): 163–78.

Bibliography

Dubrofsky, Rachel E., and Shoshana Amielle Magnet. Introduction to *Feminist Surveillance Studies*, edited by Rachel E. Dubrofsky and Amielle Magnet, 1–17. Durham, NC: Duke University Press, 2015.

Dunbar, Colin. "Amazon KDP: Your Seven Step Guide to Kindle Direct Publishing." *SelfPublishing.com*, April 29, 2022. https://selfpublishing.com/kdp/.

Dwoskin, Elizabeth. "Data Broker Removes Rape-Victims List after Inquiry." *Wall Street Journal*, updated December 19, 2013. https://www.wsj.com/articles/BL-DGB-31536.

Editorial Board. "The Jim Crow South? No, Long Island Today." *New York Times*, November 21, 2019. https://www.nytimes.com/2019/11/21/opinion/long-island-real-estate-discrimination.html.

Egan, Jennifer. "Black Box." *New Yorker*, June 4, 2012. http://www.newyorker.com/magazine/2012/06/04/black-box-2.

Egan, Jennifer. "Conversation with Jennifer Egan." *National Endowment for the Arts*, March 24, 2011. http://www.arts.gov/audio/jennifer-egan#transcript.

Egan, Jennifer. *A Visit from the Goon Squad*. New York: Anchor Books, 2010.

Ezrachi, Ariel, and Maurice Stucke. "The Rise of Machines—How Automated Digital Assistants Can Reduce Competition (and the Cash in Your Wallet)." *University of Oxford Faculty of Law*, October 5, 2016. https://www.law.ox.ac.uk/business-law-blog/blog/2016/10/rise-machines-how-automated-digital-assistants-can-reduce.

Fisher, Mark. *Capitalist Realism: Is There No Alternative?* Ropley, UK: O Books, 2009.

Fiske, John. "Surveilling the City: Whiteness, the Black Man, and Democratic Totalitarianism." *Theory, Culture, and Society* 15, no. 2 (1998): 67–88.

Fitzpatrick, Kathleen. *The Anxiety of Obsolescence: The American Novel in the Age of Television*. Nashville, TN: Vanderbilt University, 2006.

Fokkema, Aleid. *Postmodern Characters: A Study of Characterization in British and American Postmodern Fiction*. Amsterdam: Editions Rodopi, 1991.

Foucault, Michel. *Discipline and Punish*. Translated by A. Sheridan. New York: Vintage Books, 1995.

Foucault, Michel. *Security, Territory, Population*. Vol. 4 of Lectures at the Collège de France. Edited by Michel Senellart, translated by Graham Burchell. New York: Picador, 2009.

Foucault, Michel. *Society Must Be Defended: Lectures at the College de France 1975–1976*. Edited by M. Bertoni and A. Fontana. London: Penguin, 2003.

Fowler, Geoffrey A., and Heather Kelly. "Amazon's New Health Band Is the Most Invasive Tech We've Ever Tested." *Washington Post*, December 10, 2020. https://www.washingtonpost.com/technology/2020/12/10/amazon-halo-band-review/.

Franzen, Jonathan. "My Bird Problem." In *The Discomfort Zone*, 157–208. New York: Picador, 2006.

Franzen, Jonathan. 2001. "Novelist Jonathan Franzen on Fresh Air." NPR, October 15, 2001. http://www.npr.org/programs/fresh-air/2001/10/15/13008273/.

Bibliography

"Fusion Center Locations and Contact Information." Department of Homeland Security, n.d. https://www.dhs.gov/fusion-center-locations-and-contact-information (accessed August 4, 2021).

"Fusion Centers and Emergency Operations Centers." Department of Homeland Security, n.d. https://www.dhs.gov/fusion-centers-and-emergency-operations-centers (accessed August 4, 2021).

Gale, Porter. *Your Network Is Your Net Worth: Unlock the Hidden Power of Connections for Wealth, Success, and Happiness in the Digital Age.* New York: Atria Books, 2013.

Gallagher, Roy, and Glenn Greenwald. "How the NSA Plans to Infect 'Millions' of Computers with Malware." *The Intercept*, March 12, 2014. https://theintercept.com/2014/03/12/nsa-plans-infect-millions-computers-malware/.

Gandy, Oscar. "Statistical Surveillance: Remote Sensing in the Digital Age." In *Routledge Handbook of Surveillance Studies*, edited by Kirstie Ball, Kevin Haggerty, and David Lyon, 125–32. New York: Routledge, 2012.

Gates, Bill, Nathan Myhrvold, and Peter Rinearson. *The Road Ahead.* New York: Penguin Books, 1996.

Gibson, William. *Pattern Recognition.* New York: Berkley Books, 2005.

Gibson, William. "William Gibson: I Never Imagined Facebook." Interview by Michael Schulson. *Salon*, November 9, 2014. http://www.salon.com/2014/11/09/william_gibson_i_never_imagined_facebook/.

Glaser, Gabrielle. *The Nose: A Profile of Sex, Beauty, and Survival.* New York: Washington Square Press, 2002.

Goldberg, David Theo. *The Racial State.* Hoboken, NJ: Wiley-Blackwell, 2002.

Greenwald, Glen. "The Crux of the NSA Story in One Phrase: 'Collect it All.'" *The Guardian*, July 15, 2013. http://www.theguardian.com/commentisfree/2013/jul/15/crux-nsa-collect-it-all.

Greenwald, Glen. "NSA Collecting Phone Records of Millions of Verizon Customers Daily." *The Guardian*, June 6, 2013. http://www.theguardian.com/world/2013/jun/06/nsa-phone-records-verizon-court-order.

Grossman, Lev. "2006 Person of the Year." *Time Magazine*, December 25, 2006. http://content.time.com/time/magazine/article/0,9171,1570810,00.html.

Grossman, Lev. "Person of the Year 2010: Mark Zuckerberg." *Time Magazine*, December 15, 2010. http://content.time.com/time/specials/packages/article/0,28804,2036683_2037183_2037185,00.html.

Grosz, Elizabeth. *Time Travels: Feminism, Nature, Power.* Durham, NC : Duke University Press Books, 2005.

Grosz, Elizabeth. *Volatile Bodies: Toward a Corporeal Feminism.* Bloomington: Indiana University Press, 1994.

Hamid, Mohsin. *How to Get Filthy Rich in Rising Asia.* New York: Riverhead Books, 2013.

Hamid, Mohsin. Interview. Chicago Humanities Festival, YouTube, March 11, 2015. https://www.youtube.com/watch?v=oEaIkSNAsWU.

Bibliography

Hamid, Mohsin. Interview. "In Sly Self-Help Novel, Selling Clean Water Gets You 'Filthy Rich.' NPR Books, March 6, 2013. http://www.npr.org/2013/03/06/173532406/in-sly-self-help-novel-selling-clean-water-gets-you-filthy-rich.

Hardt, Michael. "The Withering of Civil Society." Social Text 45 (1995): 27–44.

Harwell, Drew. "Amazon Met with ICE Officials over Facial-Recognition System that Could Identify Immigrants." Washington Post, October 23, 2018. https://www.washingtonpost.com/technology/2018/10/23/amazon-met-with-ice-officials-over-facial-recognition-system-that-could-identify-immigrants/.

Harwell, Drew. "Cheating-Detection Companies Made Millions during the Pandemic. Now Students Are Fighting Back." Washington Post, November 12, 2020. https://www.washingtonpost.com/technology/2020/11/12/test-monitoring-student-revolt/.

Hayden, Michael. Interviewed by Glen Thrush. "Gen. Michael Hayden: Hillary Clinton Second Choice on National Security." Off Message podcast, March 28, 2016. https://overcast.fm/+EjPDsYclU/13:38.

Hayles, Katherine. "Electronic Literature and Future Books." Keynote address, Bartos Theater, Media Lab, May 4, 2012.

Heilweil, Rebecca. "Members of Congress Want to Know More about Law Enforcement's Surveillance of Protesters." Vox, updated June 10, 2020. https://www.vox.com/recode/2020/5/29/21274828/drone-minneapolis-protests-predator-surveillance-police.

Heller, Nathan, "The Claustrophobia of Facebook's New Private 'Living Room.'" New Yorker, March 8, 2019. https://www.newyorker.com/culture/cultural-comment/the-claustrophobia-of-facebooks-new-private-living-room.

Helmuth, Laura. "Jonathan Franzen Is the World's Most Annoying Bird-Watcher." Slate, July 16, 2012. http://www.slate.com/articles/arts/culturebox/2012/07/birders_the_central_park_effect_proves_that_jonathan_franzen_is_the_world_s_most_annoying_bird_watcher_.html.

Herman, David. Introduction. In Murial Spark: Twenty First Century Perspectives, edited by David Herman, 1–18. Baltimore: Johns Hopkins University Press, 2010.

Hill, Kashmir. "Wrongfully Accused by an Algorithm." New York Times, June 24, 2020. https://www.nytimes.com/2020/06/24/technology/facial-recognition-arrest.html.

History Preservation Associates. "About Us." History Preservation Associates, n.d. https://www.historypreservation.com/about-us/ (accessed August 6, 2021).

History Preservation Associates. "Buzz Rickson William Gibson MA-1 Flying Jacket." History Preservation Associates, n.d. https://www.historypreservation.com/products-page/brands/buzz-ricksons-william-gibson-collection-black-ma-1-intermediate-flying-jacket-modified-tailored-cut/ (accessed August 6, 2021).

hooks, bell. Black Looks: Race and Representation. New York: Routledge, 2015.

Hutcheon, Linda. Narcissistic Narrative: The Metafictional Paradox. Waterloo, ON: Wilfrid Laurier University Press, 2014.

Bibliography

International Monetary Fund (IMF) Research Group. "Asia Rising: Patterns of Economic Development and Growth." *World Economic Outlook, September 2006: Financial Systems and Economic Cycles.* Washington, DC: IMF, 2006.

Irigaray, Luce. *This Sex Which Is Not One.* Translated by Catherine Porter and Carolyn Burke. Ithaca, NY: Cornell University Press, 1985.

Isaacson, Walter. *Steve Jobs.* New York: Simon and Schuster, 2011.

Ishiguro, Kazuo. *The Remains of the Day.* New York: Vintage International, 1990.

Iyengar, Rishi. "Google Will Stop Letting Advertisers Target Housing Ads Based on Gender, Age and ZIP Code." CNN, updated June 11, 2020. https://www.cnn.com/2020/06/11/tech/google-housing-ads-policy/index.html.

Jay, Allan. "154 Impressive IoT Statistics: 2020/2021 Data Analytics and Market Share." *Finances Online,* n.d. https://financesonline.com/iot-statistics/ (accessed August 4, 2021).

Johnston, Justin. *Posthuman Capital and Biotechnology in Contemporary Novels.* Cham, Switzerland: Palgrave Macmillan, 2019.

Johnston, Katherine. "Metadata, Metafiction, and the Stakes of Surveillance in Jennifer Egan's *A Visit from the Goon Squad.*" *American Literature* 89, no. 1 (2017): 155–84.

Johnston, Katherine. "Profile Epistemologies, Racializing Surveillance, and Affective Counterstrategies in Claudia Rankine's *Citizen.*" *Twentieth Century Literature* 64, no. 4 (2019): 343–68.

Kaine, Erik. "The NSA Reportedly Has Total Access to the Apple iPhone." *Forbes,* December 30, 2013. http://www.forbes.com/sites/erikkain/2013/12/30/the-nsa-reportedly-has-total-access-to-your-iphone/#3ed993211604.

Kantor, Jodi, Karen Weise, and Grace Ashford. "Inside Amazon's Employment Machine." *New York Times,* June 15, 2021. https://www.nytimes.com/interactive/2021/06/15/us/amazon-workers.html.

Karsten, Jack, and Darrell M. West. "A Brief History of U.S. Encryption Policy." *Brookings,* April 19, 2016. https://www.brookings.edu/blog/techtank/2016/04/19/a-brief-history-of-u-s-encryption-policy/.

Kern, Eliza. "Facebook Is Collecting Your Data: 500 Terabytes a Day." *Gigaom,* August 22, 2012. https://gigaom.com/2012/08/22/facebook-is-collecting-your-data-500-terabytes-a-day/.

Kinder, Marsha. "Reorchestrating History: Transforming The Danube Exodus into a Database Documentary." In *Cinema's Alchemist: The Films of Peter Forgacs,* edited by Bill Nichols and Michael Renov, 235–55. Minneapolis: University of Minnesota Press, 2011.

Kindig, Beth. "Palantir IPO: Deep-Dive Analysis." *Forbes,* September 29, 2020. https://www.forbes.com/sites/bethkindig/2020/09/29/palantir-ipo-deep-dive-analysis/?sh=66903f4a1a14.

Klein, Naomi. *No Logo.* New York: Picador, 2009.

Klein, Naomi, Simone Browne, and Shoshana Zuboff. "Surveillance in the Era of

Bibliography

Pandemic and Protest." *The Intercept*, September 21, 2020. https://www.youtube
.com/watch?v=wJ_jvdAP-7U&t=1s.

Koepell, Harvey, and Randy Bean. "Big Data Analytics: The Currency of the 21st
Century Enterprise." *Information Management*, September 10, 2012. http://www
.information-management.com/news/news/big-data-analytics-the-currency-of
-the-21st-century-enterprise-10023139-1.html.

Kolodny, Lora. "Tesla Monitored Its Employees with Help of PR Firm during 2017
Union Push." *CNBC*, June 2, 2022. https://www.cnbc.com/2022/06/02/tesla-paid
-pr-firm-to-surveil-employees-on-facebook-in-2017-union-push.html.

Krauthammer, Charles. "Give Grandma a Pass." *Washington Post*, July 29, 2015.
http://www.washingtonpost.com/archive/opinions/2005/07/29/give-grandma
-a-pass/f31c88a5-e5d2-40ed-969c-de84ab99c5f3/.

LaBelle, Brandon. *Acoustic Territories: Sound Culture in Everyday Life*. New York:
Continuum, 2010.

Landrum, Gene N. *Profiles of Power and Success*. Buffalo, NY: Prometheus Books, 1996.

Lanier, Jaron. *You Are Not a Gadget*. New York: Vintage Books, 2010.

Latour, Bruno. *We Have Never Been Modern*. Trans. Catherine Porter. Cambridge, MA:
Harvard University Press, 1993.

Lazzarato, Maurizio. "Immaterial Labor." In *Radical Thought in Italy: A Potential
Politics*, edited by Paul Virno and Michael Hardt, 133–50. Minneapolis: University
of Minnesota Press, 1996.

Levy, Steven. *The Perfect Thing: How the iPod Shuffles Commerce, Culture, and Coolness*. New
York: Simon and Schuster, 2006.

LexisNexis. "Cast a Wider Net with Our Powerful Public Records Search." *LexisNexis*,
n.d. https://www.lexisnexis.com/en-us/products/public-records/powerful-public
-records-search.page (accessed August 4, 2021).

LexisNexis. "Streamline Criminal Investigations and Generate Actionable Leads."
LexisNexis Risk Solutions, n.d. https://risk.lexisnexis.com/law-enforcement-and
-public-safety/crime-and-criminal-investigations (accessed August 4, 2021).

Linden, Greg, Brent Smith, and Jeremy York. "Amazon.com Recommendations:
Item-to-Item Collaborative Filtering." *IEEE Internet Computing* (January–February
2003): 76–80. http://www.cs.umd.edu/~samir/498/Amazon-Recommendations
.pdf.

Link, Alex. "Global War, Global Capital, and the Work of Art in William Gibson's
Pattern Recognition." *Contemporary Literature* 49, no. 2 (2008): 209–31.

Lohr, Steve. "The Age of Big Data." *New York Times*, February 11, 2012. http://www
.nytimes.com/2012/02/12/sunday-review/big-datas-impact-in-the-world.html.

Lorde, Audre. "The Uses of Anger." In *Sister Outsider: Essays and Speeches*, 124–33.
New York: Ten Speed Press, 1984.

"'Lost,' 'SNL,' 'Grey's' Tops in Online Viewing, Nielsen Says." *TVWeek*, Febuary 12,
2009. https://web.archive.org/web/20160511075709/http://www.tvweek.com
/in-depth/2009/02/lost-snl-greys-tops-in-online/.

Bibliography

Lovibond, Sabina. "Feminism and Postmodernism." In *Postmodernism: A Reader*, edited by Thomas Docherty, 390–414. New York: Columbia University Press, 1993.

Lury, Celia. *Brands: The Logos of the Global Economy*. New York: Routledge, 2004.

Lyon, David. Introduction. In *Surveillance as Social Sorting: Privacy, Risk, and Digital Discrimination*, edited by David Lyon, 1–10. New York: Routledge, 2003.

Lyon, David. *Surveillance Studies: An Overview*. Cambridge: Polity, 2007.

Mac, Ryan, Caroline Haskins, Brianna Sacks, and Logan McDonald. "Your Local Police Department Might Have Used This Facial Recognition Tool to Surveil You. Find Out Here." *Buzzfeednews*, updated April 9, 2021. https://www.buzzfeednews .com/article/ryanmac/facial-recognition-local-police-clearview-ai-table.

MacLeod, Lewis. "Matters of Care and Control: Surveillance, Omniscience, and Narrative Power in *Abbess of Crewe* and *Loitering with Intent*." In *Muriel Spark: Twenty-First Century Perspectives*, edited by David Herman, 203–24. Baltimore: Johns Hopkins University Press, 2010.

Magnet, Shoshana Amielle. *When Biometrics Fail: Gender, Race, and the Technology of Identity*. Durham, NC: Duke University Press, 2011.

Magnet, Shoshana, and Tara Rogers. "Stripping for the State: Whole Body Imaging Technologies and the Surveillance of Othered Bodies." *Feminist Media Studies* 12, no. 1 (2012): 101–18.

Manovich, Lev. "From the Externalization of the Psyche to the Implantation of Technology." *Manovich.net*, 1995. http://manovich.net/content/04-projects/006 -from-the-externalization-of-the-psyche-to-the-implantation-of-technology/04 _article_1995.pdf.

Marks, Peter. "Imagining Surveillance: Utopian Visions and Surveillance Studies." *Surveillance and Society* 3, no. 2 (2005): 222–39.

Marx, Karl. *Capital*, Volume 1. Translated by Ben Fowkes. London: Penguin, 1990.

Massey, Doreen. "Neoliberalism Has Hijacked Our Vocabulary." *The Guardian*, June 11, 2013. http://www.theguardian.com/commentisfree/2013/jun/11 /neoliberalism-hijacked-vocabulary.

Matsakis, Louise. "The *Wired* Guide to Your Personal Data (and Who Is Using It)." *Wired*, February 15, 2019. https://www.wired.com/story/wired-guide-personal -data-collection/.

Maxwell, Richard, and Toby Miller. *Greening the Media*. New York: Oxford University Press, 2012.

McAlone, Nathan. "Why Netflix Thinks Its Personalized Recommendation Engine Is Worth $1 Billion per Year." *Business Insider Australia*, June 15, 2016. https://www.businessinsider.com/netflix-recommendation-engine-worth- 1-billion-per-year-2016-6.

McClintock, Anne. *Imperial Leather: Race, Gender, and Sexuality in the Colonial Contest*. New York: Routledge, 1995.

McClintock, Anne. "Slow Violence and the BP Oil Crisis in the Gulf of Mexico: Militarizing Environmental Catastrophe." *Hemispheric Institute E-Misferica* 9,

nos. 1–2 (Summer 2012). https://hemisphericinstitute.org/en/emisferica-91/9-1
-dossier/slow-violence-and-the-bp-oil-crisis-in-the-gulf-of-mexico-militarizing
-environmental-catastrophe.html.

McGurl, Mark. "Everything and Less: Fiction in the Age of Amazon." *Modern Language Quarterly* 77, no. 3 (2016): 447–71.

McGurl, Mark. "Unspeakable Conventionality: The Perversity of the Kindle." *American Literary History* 33, no. 2 (2021): 394–415.

McLuhan, Marshall, and Lewis H. Lapham. *Understanding Media: The Extensions of Man.* Cambridge, MA: MIT Press, 1994.

Merchant, Brian. "The Real Reason Facebook Changed Its Name." *The Atlantic*, October 28, 2021. https://www.theatlantic.com/ideas/archive/2021/10/facebook
-metaverse-mark-zuckerberg/620538/.

Mijente. "Stop the Tech-Talent Pipe-Line: A Toolkit for Organizing Your Campus against ICE." *NoTechForICE*, n.d. https://notechforice.com/wp-content/uploads
/2019/08/V10_StudentToolkit_8.5-x-11-template-with-bleed-trim.pdf (accessed August 4, 2021).

Miller, D. A. *The Novel and the Police.* Berkeley: University of California Press, 1989.

Miller, Toby. *The Routledge Companion to Global Popular Culture.* New York: Routledge, 2015.

Mishra, Pankaj. "Modernity's Undoing." *London Review of Books* 33, no. 7 (2011): 27–30.

Monahan, Torin. *Surveillance in the Time of Insecurity.* New Brunswick, NJ: Rutgers University Press, 2010.

Murphet, Julian. "Behind the Scenes: Production, Animation, and Postmodern Value." *Sydney Studies in English* 32 (2006): 143–65.

Musk, Elon. "Elon Musk talks Twitter, Tesla and how his brain works at TED2022." April 14, 2022, https://www.youtube.com/watch?v=cdZZpaB2kDM.

Nakashima, Ellen. "Obama Administration Had Restrictions on NSA Reversed in 2011." *Washington Post*, September 7, 2013. https://www.washingtonpost.com
/world/national-security/obama-administration-had-restrictions-on-nsa-reversed
-in-2011/2013/09/07/c26ef658-0fe5-11e3-85b6-d27422650fd5_print.html.

Nietzsche, Friedrich. *Untimely Meditations.* Edited by Daniel Breazeale, translated by R. J. Hollingdale. Cambridge: Cambridge University Press, 1997.

Nixon, Rob. *Slow Violence and the Environmentalism of the Poor.* Cambridge, MA: Harvard University Press, 2011.

Noble, Safiya Umoja. *Algorithms of Oppression: How Search Engines Reinforce Racism.* New York: New York University Press, 2018.

North, Anna. "Jonathan Franzen Loses Book Award to Some Lady." *Jezebel*, March 14, 2011. http://www.jezebel.com/5781688/jonathan-franzen-loses-book
-award-to-some-lady.

Nowak, Mark, "Documentary Poetics." *Poetry Foundation*, April 17, 2010. https://www
.poetryfoundation.org/harriet-books/2010/04/documentary-poetics.

Bibliography

O'Brien, Luke. "The Far-Right Helped Create the World's Most Powerful Facial Recognition Technology." *Huffington Post*, updated April 9, 2020. https://www.huffpost.com/entry/clearview-ai-facial-recognition-alt-right _n_5e7d028bc5b6cb08a92a5c48.

Onuoha, Mimi. "About." *Mimionuoha*, n.d. https://mimionuoha.com/about (accessed August 5, 2021).

Onuoha, Mimi. "Notes on Algorithmic Violence." *GitHub*, February 22, 2018. https://github.com/MimiOnuoha/On-Algorithmic-Violence.

Onuoha, Mimi. "On Missing Data Sets." *GitHub*, updated January 24, 2018. https://github.com/MimiOnuoha/missing-datasets.

Palmer, Annie. "Amazon Wins FAA Approval for Prime Air Drone Delivery Fleet." *CNBC*, August 31, 2020. https://www.cnbc.com/2020/08/31/amazon-prime-now -drone-delivery-fleet-gets-faa-approval.html.

Parenti, Christian. *The Soft Cage: Surveillance in America from Slavery to the War on Terror.* New York: Basic Books, 2003.

Pariser, Eli. *The Filter Bubble: What the Internet Is Hiding from You.* Old Saybrook, CT: Tantor Media, 2011.

Pasqual, Frank. *The Black Box Society: The Secret Algorithms That Control Money and Information.* Cambridge, MA: Harvard University Press, 2015.

Paul, Kari. "'They Know Us Better Than We Know Ourselves': How Amazon Tracked My Last Two Years of Reading." *The Guardian*, February 3, 2020. https://www.theguardian.com/technology/2020/feb/03/amazon-kindle-data -reading-tracking-privacy.

Perez, Evan. "Secret Court's Oversight Gets Scrutiny." *Wall Street Journal*, June 9, 2013. http://www.wsj.com/articles/SB10001424127887324904004578535670310514616.

Perlroth, Nicole, Jeff Larson, and Scott Shane. "NSA Able to Foil Basic Safeguards of Privacy on Web." *New York Times*, September 5, 2013. http://www.nytimes .com/2013/09/06/us/nsa-foils-much-internet-encryption.html?_r=0.

Peticca-Harris, Amanda, Nadia deGama, and M. N. Ravishankar. "Postcapitalist Precarious Work and Those in the 'Drivers' Seat: Exploring the Motivations and Lived Experiences of Uber Drivers in Canada." *Organization* 27, no. 1 (2020): 36–59.

Phillips, Caryl. *The Right Set: A Tennis Anthology.* New York: Vintage, 1999.

Poon, Angelia. "Helping the Novel: Neoliberalism, Self-help, and the Narrating of the Self in Mohsin Hamid's *How to Get Filthy Rich in Rising Asia*." *Journal of Commonwealth Literature* 52, no. 1 (2015): 139–50.

Preciado, Paul. "Pharmaco-Pornographic Politics: Towards a New Gender Ecology." *Parallax* 14, no. 1 (2008): 105–17.

Puar, Jasbir. "Regimes of Surveillance." *Cosmologics*, December 4, 2014. https://web .archive.org/web/20160306084248/http://cosmologicsmagazine.com/jasbir-puar -regimes-of-surveillance/.

Rankine, Claudia. *Citizen: An American Lyric.* Minneapolis: Graywolf, 2014.

Rankine, Claudia. "In *Citizen* Poet Strips Bare the Realities of Everyday Racism."

Bibliography

NPR, January 3, 2015. https://www.npr.org/2015/01/03/374574142/in-citizen-poet
-strips-bare-the-realities-of-everyday-racism.

Ricker, Thomas. "The US, Like China, Has About One Surveillance Camera
for Every Four People, Says Report." *The Verge*, December 9, 2019. https://www
.theverge.com/2019/12/9/21002515/surveillance-cameras-globally-us-china
-amount-citizens.

Robertson, Craig. *The Passport in America: The History of the Document.* Oxford: Oxford
University Press, 2010.

Rodrigo, Chris Mills. "Pressure Mounts on DHS to Stop Using Clearview AI Facial
Recognition." *The Hill*, April 19, 2021. https://thehill.com/policy/technology
/548932-pressure-mounts-on-dhs-to-stop-using-clearview-ai-facial-recognition.

Rossi, Ben. "Data Revolution: The Gold Rush of the Twenty-First Century."
Information Age, August 21, 2015. http://www.information-age.com/technology
/information-management/123460039/data-revolution-gold-rush-21st-century.

Rothenberg, Ben. "Tennis's Top Women Balance Body Image with Ambition."
New York Times, July 11, 2015. https://www.nytimes.com/2015/07/11/sports/tennis
/tenniss-top-women-balance-body-image-with-quest-for-success.html.

Sabharwal, Anil. "Google Photos: One Year, 200 Million Users, and a Whole Lot of
Selfies." *Google Photos*, May 27, 2016. https://blog.google/products/photos/google
-photos-one-year-200-million/.

Said, Edward. "The Public Role of Writers and Intellectuals." In *Nation, Language,
and the Ethics of Translation*, edited by Sandra Bermann and Michael Wood, 15–29.
Princeton, NJ: Princeton University Press, 2005.

Scarry, Elaine. *The Body in Pain: The Making and the Unmaking of the World.* Oxford:
Oxford University Press, 1987.

Schmidt, Eric. Foreword. In Rob Austin and Lee Devin, *Artful Making: What Managers
Need to Know about How Artists Work.* Upper Saddle River, NJ: Pearson Education,
2003.

Schmidt, Eric. "Google CEO Eric Schmidt on Privacy." *YouTube*, December 8, 2009.
https://www.youtube.com/watch?v=A6e7wfDHzew.

Schneier, Bruce. *Data and Goliath: The Hidden Battles to Collect Your Data and Control Your
World.* New York: Norton, 2015.

Schwartz, Eric Hall. "Alexa Now Offers Personalized Reading Recommendations."
Voicebot.ai. October 20, 2020. https://voicebot.ai/2020/10/20/alexa-now-offers
-personalized-reading-recommendations/.

Selinger, David. "Big Data: Getting Ready for the 2013 Big Bang." *Forbes*, January 15,
2015. http://www.forbes.com/sites/ciocentral/2013/01/15/big-data-get-ready-for
-the-2013-big-bang/#21fb24741678.

Seltzer, Mark. *Henry James and the Art of Power.* Ithaca, NY: Cornell University Press,
1984.

Shelton, General Henry H. *Joint Vision 2020: America's Military Preparing for Tomorrow.*
Washington, DC: US Government Printing Office, 2000.

Siegler, M. G. "Eric Schmidt: Every 2 Days We Create as Much Data as We Did Up to 2003." *TechCrunch*, August 4, 2010. http://techcrunch.com/2010/08/04/schmidt -data/.

Sifferlen, Alexandra. "NFL Cheerleads File Suit Saying They Make as Little as $2.85 per Hour." *Time*, February 14, 2014. http://time.com/44069/cheerleaders-rebel -over-low-wages/.

Singer, Natasha, and Cade Metz. "Many Facial-Recognition Systems Are Biased, Says U.S. Study." *New York Times*, December 19, 2019. https://www.nytimes .com/2019/12/19/technology/facial-recognition-bias.html.

Smith, Andrea. "Not-Seeing: State Surveillance, Settler Colonialism, and Gender Violence." In *Feminist Surveillance Studies*, edited by Rachel E. Dubrofsky and Shoshana Amielle Magnet, 21–38. Durham, NC: Duke University Press, 2015.

Smith, Gavin J. D. "Surveillance Work(ers)." In *Routledge Handbook of Surveillance Studies*, edited by Kirstie Ball, Kevin Haggerty, and David Lyon, 107–16. New York: Routledge, 2012.

Sperry, Paul. "When the Profile Fits the Crime." *New York Times*, July 28, 2005. http:// www.nytimes.com/2005/07/28/opinion/when-the-profile-fits-the-crime.html.

Stone, Brad. *The Everything Store: Jeff Bezos and the Age of Amazon*. New York: Little Brown, 2013.

Stray, Jonathan. "What You Need to Know about the NSA's Surveillance Programs." *ProPublica*, August 5, 2013. https://www.propublica.org/article/nsa-data-collection -faq.

Terranova, Tiziana. *Network Culture: Politics for the Information Age*. London: Pluto Press, 2004.

Thompson, Derek. "Google's CEOs: 'The Laws Are Written by Lobbyists.'" *Atlantic Monthly*, October 1, 2010. http://www.theatlantic.com/technology/archive/2010 /10/googles-ceo-the-laws-are-written-by-lobbyists/63908/.

Tkachenko, Yegor, and Kamel Jedidi. "What Personal Information Can a Consumer Facial Image Reveal? Implications for Marketing ROI and Consumer Privacy." June 1, 2020. Available at SSRN: https://ssrn.com/abstract=3616470.

Tung, Teresa. "Building Data Products as a Competitive Differentiator." Accenture, February 8, 2022. https://www.accenture.com/us-en/insights/technology/data -products.

Vadde, Aarthi. "Amateur Creativity: Contemporary Literature and the Digital Publishing Scene." *New Literary History* 48, no. 1 (2017): 27–51.

Vadde, Aarthi. "Fiction as Streaming, Genre as Portal: Jennifer Egan and Ivan Kreilkamp." *Novel Dialogue* podcast, September 16, 2021. https://noveldialogue .org/2021/09/16/2-1-fiction-as-streaming-genre-as-portal-jennifer-egan-and-ivan -kreilkamp-jp/.

Vaidhyanathan, Siva. *Anti-Social Media: How Facebook Disconnects Us and Undermines Democracy*. New York: Oxford University Press, 2018.

Bibliography

Voyles, Bennett. "Amazon's Impact on Publishing Transforms the Book Industry."
    TechTarget, January 13, 2021. https://searchaws.techtarget.com/feature/Amazons
    -impact-on-publishing-transforms-the-book-industry.
Wallace, David Foster. "E Unibus Pluram: Television and U.S. Fiction." In *A
    Supposedly Fun Thing I'll Never Do Again*, 21–82. New York: Back Bay Books, 1998.
Wallace, David Foster. *The Girl with Curious Hair*. New York: Norton, 1996.
Warner, Michael. *Publics and Counterpublics*. New York: Zone Books, 2005.
Watson, Amy. "Streaming in the U.S.—Statistics and Facts." *Statista*, August 25,
    2020. https://www.statista.com/topics/1594/streaming/.
Waugh, Patricia. *Metafiction: The Theory and Practice of Self-Conscious Fiction*. New York:
    Routledge, 1984.
Wiener, Janet, and Nathan Bronson. "Facebook's Top Open Data Problems."
    Facebook Research, October 22, 2014. https://research.fb.com/blog/2014/10/facebook
    -s-top-open-data-problems/.
Williams, Annabelle. "5 Ways Amazon Monitors Its Employees, from AI Cameras to
    Hiring a Spy Agency." *Business Insider*, April 5, 2021. https://www.businessinsider
    .com/how-amazon-monitors-employees-ai-cameras-union-surveillance-spy
    -agency-2021-4.
Wolford, Ben. "Everything You Need to Know about the 'Right to Be Forgotten,'"
    GDPR.EU, n.d. https://gdpr.eu/right-to-be-forgotten/ (accessed August 5, 2021).
Woodman, Spencer. "Palantir Provides the Engine for Donald Trump's Deportation
    Machine." *The Intercept*, March 2, 2017. https://theintercept.com/2017/03/02
    /palantir-provides-the-engine-for-donald-trumps-deportation-machine/.
Zeidner, Lisa. "Netscape: Pattern Recognition: The Coolhunter." *New York Times
    Book Review*, January 19, 2003. http://www.nytimes.com/2003/01/19/books/review
    /19ZEIDNET.html.
Zuboff, Shoshana. *The Age of Surveillance Capitalism: The Fight for a Human Future at the
    New Frontier of Power*. New York: Public Affairs, 2019.
Zuckerberg, Mark. "F8 2011 Keynote." *YouTube*, September 24, 2011. https://www
    .youtube.com/watch?v=9r46UeXCzoU.

INDEX

Accenture, 89–90

Acker, Kathy, 27

Acxiom, 89

affect (and affective epistemology), 31, 76–81, 86

Agrawal, Parag, 100

Ahmed, Sara, 64, 81

Alexa, 146, 151–55, 157–58, 184n41; origin of, 183n31

Alves, Mariana, 67–69

Amazon Web Services (AWS), 16, 158, 183n31, 185n58

Amazon.com, 8, 16, 33, 101, 145–61, 162; CIA ties with, 150; customer service at, 33, 151, 152–53, 156–57, 159, 179n88; genre fiction at, 151, 159–61, 162; publishing programs at, 155–56, 159–61; subsidiaries of, 158. *See also* Alexa; Kindle

Anderson, Benedict, 7

anti-Semitism, xiii, 14

Apple, 15, 46, 94, 148; Apple Safari, 43; Apple TV, 12

Apple, Max, 28

artificial intelligence (AI), 146, 153–54, 163

Ashe, Arthur, 70–71

Atwood, Margaret, 159

Baldwin, James, 86

Barth, John, 27, 57

Barthelme, Donald, 57

Bauman, Zygmunt, 19, 63

Behn, Robert, 76

Benjamin, Ruja, 4

Bennett, Jane, 117

Bergson, Henri, 116

Berlant, Lauren, 64–65, 76–77, 85, 116, 170n91

Bezos, Jeff, 33, 146–53, 156–57, 158, 183n31

Bhabha, Homi, 85, 86

Big Data, 11–13, 22, 24–26, 29–30, 118, 163–64

biological determinism, xiv, 74

biometrics, 74, 84, 150

Black Lives Matter movement, 72, 81

Booth, Wayne, xv

Braidotti, Rosi, 25, 120

Brontë, Charlotte, xi

Browne, Simone, xiv–xv, 4, 11, 14, 63, 67

Brynjolfsson, Erik, 21–22

Bull, Michael, 46

Buolamwini, Joy, 4, 163

Burroughs, William S., 57

Bush, George W., 76, 117

Butler, Judith, 74, 79

capitalism, 10, 37, 41–43, 58; communicative, 27; "friction-free," 18; in Gibson, 95–98, 110, 119; Marx on, 112; 9/11 response of, 117; racial, 81, 83; surveillance, 7, 11, 33, 46, 82, 88, 95–96, 103, 110, 146, 147, 155

Capriati, Jennifer, 68

Carruth, Allison, 6, 173n41, 179n73

celebrity culture, 10, 17, 31, 37–38, 51, 53–55, 58–60

Central Park jogger case, 60, 69

Chabon, Michael, 159

Chamayou, Gregoire, 126, 132–33

characters (in fiction), 26–28, 90

Charles, Ron, 36

Chun, Wendy Hui Kyong, 16, 21, 25, 61,

Index

Index

THE NEW AMERICAN CANON